Barbara Schönig (ed.)

Variations of Suburbanism

Approaching a Global Phenomenon

STÄDTEBAU – ARCHITEKTUR – GESELLSCHAFT

Herausgeber: Prof. Dr. Harald Bodenschatz, Prof. Dr. Barbara Schönig
ISSN 2191-0472

1 *Juliane Lorenz*
  More Urban to Suburbia
  Städtebauliche Strategien zur Bekämpfung von *Sprawl*
  in der Metropolenregion Toronto
  ISBN 978-3-8382-0141-2

2 *Clara Franziska Maria Weber*
  Unité d'habitation Typ Berlin
  Anspruch und Wirklichkeit einer Wohnmaschine
  ISBN 978-3-8382-0285-3

3 *Jana Richter*
  Die Wechselwirkungen zwischen Tourismus und urbanem Raum
  Funktionsprinzipien am Beispiel der räumlichen Entwicklung und der gegenwärtigen
  Ausprägung der Touristenmetropole Berlin
  ISBN 978-3-8382-0327-0

4 *Aline Delatte*
  Urban Development on a Participatory Democracy Basis
  How to Actively Involve Citizens as Local Experts and Partners in Urban Governance
  The Urban Renewal Program *Aktives Stadtzentrum Turmstraße*, Berlin
  ISBN 978-3-8382-0464-2

5 *Barbara Schönig (ed.)*
  Variations of Suburbanism
  Approaching a Global Phenomenon
  ISBN 978-3-8382-0619-6

Barbara Schönig (ed.)

VARIATIONS OF SUBURBANISM

Approaching a Global Phenomenon

ibidem-Verlag
Stuttgart

Bibliografische Information der Deutschen Nationalbibliothek
Die Deutsche Nationalbibliothek verzeichnet diese Publikation in der Deutschen Nationalbibliografie; detaillierte bibliografische Daten sind im Internet über http://dnb.d-nb.de abrufbar.

Bibliographic information published by the Deutsche Nationalbibliothek
Die Deutsche Nationalbibliothek lists this publication in the Deutsche Nationalbibliografie; detailed bibliographic data are available in the Internet at http://dnb.d-nb.de.

Dieses Vorhaben wird aus Mitteln des Bundesministeriums für Bildung und Forschung gefördert. Die Verantwortung für den Inhalt dieser Veröffentlichung liegt beim Autor.

∞

Gedruckt auf alterungsbeständigem, säurefreien Papier
Printed on acid-free paper

ISSN: 2191-0472

ISBN-13: 978-3-8382-0619-6

© *ibidem*-Verlag
Stuttgart 2015

Alle Rechte vorbehalten

Das Werk einschließlich aller seiner Teile ist urheberrechtlich geschützt. Jede Verwertung außerhalb der engen Grenzen des Urheberrechtsgesetzes ist ohne Zustimmung des Verlages unzulässig und strafbar. Dies gilt insbesondere für Vervielfältigungen, Übersetzungen, Mikroverfilmungen und elektronische Speicherformen sowie die Einspeicherung und Verarbeitung in elektronischen Systemen.

All rights reserved. No part of this publication may be reproduced, stored in or introduced into a retrieval system, or transmitted, in any form, or by any means (electronic, mechanical, photocopying, recording or otherwise) without the prior written permission of the publisher. Any person who does any unauthorized act in relation to this publication may be liable to criminal prosecution and civil claims for damages.

Printed in the EU

Content

Introduction: Variations of Suburbanism 7
Barbara Schönig

Part I: (Re-)developing Suburban Spaces

Mapping Urban Landscapes - Between understanding, interpreting and negotiating 17
Sigrun Langner

Challenge of maturation - Life cycles and patterns of change in suburban settlement space 41
Jan Polívka

Designing suburban infrastructure: The A 40/ B1 Bochum 75
Stefanie Bremer

Airport (Sub)Urbia - Transforming Berlin Brandenburg's periphery 83
Johanna Schlaack

Part II: Suburban Spaces - Global Variations

Unfinished suburbanization - Leipzig between Suburbia, Creative City and Shrinking 99
Arvid Krüger

A Big Gamble for "Greater Paris" 129
Elodie Vittu

Don't trust the idyll. Meritorious objectives and arguable substance in Dutch suburbia 157
Holger Gladys

The dynamics of the Eastern European suburbs. Kazan, Kyiv and Bucharest 181
Iana Korolova, Ion Alexandru Retegan and Iana Samakaeva

Suburban development in Argentina: a historical overview and the current trends. The case of Cordoba 215
Carlos Grezzi, Monica Ramé, Christian Terreno and Regina Vidosa

Geographies of suburban transformation: the case of Amman, Jordan 239
Mazen Alazazmeh

Changing Face of Suburbia: A Narrative of Indian Cities 257
Priyambada Das and Vaishali Anavatti Satyamurthy

Authors 282

Introduction: Variations of Suburbanism

Barbara Schönig

Planners and urban designers alike tend to dislike what is commonly referred to as "Suburbia" or "Post-Suburbia" and even more the spatial pattern that is the result of intensive suburbanization, known as sprawl (Bodenschatz/Schönig 2004: 59). Appreciated instead is what is conceptually understood as the material-spatial antithesis of sprawl, the ideal "European city": compactness, density, mixed use, walkability - altogether: a model of sustainable urbanism. But flying over the globe and looking out of the plane, we can easily recognize that this ideal form of the city can rarely be found, even in Europe. The traditional "European cities" that still roughly match these criteria are usually part of large urban agglomerations. Those densely populated and built out areas integrate smaller cities, villages, and far stretched monofunctional parcels of single family homes, service clusters, malls or industrial sites, linked by networks of highways, transportation and technical infrastructures such as waterways and energy lines. From birds eye view we can recognize a patchwork of urban structures, industrialized agriculture, and natural reserves. Beyond the borders of traditional cities, we see an urbanized landscape that some time ago already ceased to be "sub-urban", in the sense of being "subordinated" to a core city in a functional or economic way.

This, in a truly literal sense of the word, "post-sub-urban" landscape, this "In-Between-City" (Sieverts 1997), may not be well liked by planners and urban designers. But we need to admit that it is simply there and will be of a growing importance in the decades to come in terms of population and economic activity located there, but also with regard to challenges for urban society and urban development (see Keil 2014; Phelps 2010; Modarres/Kirby 2010). This holds true not only for urban areas in Europe or Northern America, but also for those in other parts of the world. Urbanization in the global south to a large part takes place not within cities but at their fringe (McGee 2013: 20) where large housing developments, informal housing settlements, economic and service clusters, government or university campuses, entertainment and shopping districts are stretching out into the hinterland of city centers. Noone thinking about the sheer numbers of people moving to urban areas and the scarcity and cost of land in central cities could be surprised that the growth of cities actually takes place as an extension of urban areas into city surroundings where land is still available and mostly also cheaper than in inner areas of cities. It is beyond city limits, in suburbanized areas where "a majority of Americans, many Europeans, and a growing number of Asians, Afrians, and Latin Americans live" (Kirby 2010: 66). Therefore, the start of the "urban millenium" that was pronounced by the UN in 2007 when the majority of people on the globe lived in cities for the first time (UNFPA 2007: 1), actually could be understood as the start of a "sub-urban millennium".

However, "sub-urban" could hardly be understood in the sense of its original meaning that derived from the model of the North American (and also European) city (McGee 2013: 20). "Suburban" in the original sense points to a dichotomy of center and periphery, indicating differences concerning the area's role and function within the metropolitan region, its building and population density, its land uses, its socio-economic structure and also the way of life dominating there. Even at a first glance at the morphological, social and functional diversity as well as the heterogeneity of the emerging respectively already existing urbanized areas beyond city borders hints to the fact that this dichotomy might not be claimed. Instead, it seems convincing to follow the hypothesis that talking about "suburbanization" here indicates nothing more than an "increase in non-central city population and economic activity, as well as urban spatial expansion" (Keil 2013: 9).

Studying suburbanization and suburban areas in that sense in different parts of the world as done in this book not only reveals that there are major differences to be found with regard to urban morphologies, socio-spatial structures, infrastructure and governance. It also shows that suburban areas will face major challenges in their future urban development. However, the challenges to be confronted in the context of suburbanization are just as manifold as suburban areas themselves, even within same national contexts. Looking at Europe or the United States, e.g., these challenges range from the renewal and adaption of existing areas to demographic shrinkage, aging or poverty in shrinking areas to the securing of green spaces or agricultural land, the provision of low cost housing within suburban spaces or the development of more sustainable urban structures and metropolitan planning in areas facing urban growth (Modarres/Kirby 201: 114; Schönig 2014: 105-110; Münter 2015: 21-22). Urban research until now has little knowledge and answers to the questions that lie at hand here: How can monofunctional single family home areas be adapted to the needs of an aging population? How can the decline of suburban neighborhoods be avoided when building structures lie idle due to economic restructuring or the loss of population. How can auto-oriented urban structures be transformed into more sustainable urban patterns? Postsuburbia in the developped countries is in need of a new kind of "urban regeneration", the regeneration and adaption of suburban structures. But confronting governmental fragmentation, social polarization and the strength of market forces predominant in suburban development, it won't be easy to implement strategies of sustainable urban regeneration and regional development on a metropolitan scale.

Despite the divergences of production, form, sociospatial structures and governance of suburban spaces all over the world it is obvious that any urbanist or urban researcher needs to have in mind that the main challenge of the "urban millennium" will be to understand, design and develop what is usually not at the forefront of our attention: the urbanized areas beyond city cores and city boundaries. This however will necessitate conceiving suburban spaces as research topics of "their own right" (Kirby 2010: 65) that can not be defined solely by being different to the city. Instead it implies to approach suburbanized areas as complex urban spaces that are connected to but not completely and inherently dependent on the adjoining core cities (1), that are "place[s] of mixed, economic activity, mixed densities, mixed housing tenure and, by no means least, mixed demographics" (Modarres/Kirby 2010: 120) (2) and can show distinct and different local and regional characteristics and logics (3). Understanding suburban areas in that sense as being complex and heterogeneous urban spaces shaped by local and regional contexts can be understood as a prerequisite to develop adequate design and planning strategies for these parts of urban agglomerations. It will also enable us to disclose suburban areas from a perspective of international comparative urban research.

As shown up to here, thinking about suburban landscapes and suburbanization in Europe and on a global scale raises many questions to urban planning and urban studies. This book gives an insight into the complexity of suburbanization processes, their dependence on specific parameters of urban development in different settings and also the heterogeneity and diversity of suburban landscapes all over the globe. Rather than answering all questions, it compiles different disciplinary perspectives on postsuburban areas in different parts of the world thereby adding to the discourse on and knowledge about postsuburban spaces as an area of urban studies of its own right. It documents parts of a lecture series and a research seminar at Bauhaus-Universität Weimar, Germany, in which postsuburbanization as a global phenomenon was disussed from different disciplinary perspectives. It integrated theoretical papers on specific aspects, such as terminology, sociological aspects, building morphology or infrastructure in postsuburbia, as well as case studies on different metropolitan areas in Europe and beyond.

This book is divided into two parts: The first part contains articles that show different approaches to understand, redevelop and design suburban areas applied to or examined by looking at suburban sites in Germany. *Sigrun Langner* as a landscape architect focusses on the question how the complexity of fragmented metropolitan landscapes that poses a major obstacle to receive attention and (public or political) support for metropolitan planning and design can be addressed by strategies of mapping. The urban planner *Jan Polívka* discusses whether and to what extent the model of urban life cycles can be used to explain the development and maturation of suburban settlements and what challenges suburbs face when approaching the state of maturation. Stefanie Bremer and Johanna Schlaack, both from the perspective of an architect, address different aspects of the role infrastructural development and design plays within suburban areas. *Stefanie Bremer* suggests to understand suburban highways, the roads taken by thousands of commuters day by day as a part of the city that is worth receiving the attention of urban designers. She explains her concept by presenting a Masterplan for the A40, the main highway passing through the metropolitan Ruhr area in Germany. *Johanna Schlaack* on the other hand discusses the way in which airport cities and major airports must be understood as important nodes of metropolitan areas, as places that need to be carefully designed in the context of their immediate surrounding and metropolitan area and that need to be thoughtfully planned using participative strategies that integrate not only key players but also the general public.

The second part of the book includes a number of case studies: According to the issues of the respective case studies presented, the authors focus on different aspects of postsuburban developments in the metropolitan areas discussed. Compiled are articles on Western European cases, namely Leipzig (Germany), Paris (France) and the "Randstad" (Netherlands) (*Arvid Krüger, Elodie Vittu and Holger Gladys*), Eastern Europe, namely Kazan (Russia), Bukarest (Romania) and Kiev (Ukraine) (*Iana Samakaeva, Ion Alexander Retegu, and Iana Korolova*). These articles are followed by perspectives on suburbanization in the Arabic world (Amman in Jordan by *Mazen Alazazmeh*), in South Asia (Bangalore and Kolkata in India, written by *Vaishali Satyamurthi and Pryiambada Das*) and in the Latin American context (Córdoba in Argentina, written by *Carlos Grezzi, Monica Rame, Cristian Terreno and Regina Vidosa*). These cases impressively show that indeed "Variations of Suburbanism" are to be found globally. But they also point to the fact that metropolitan areas despite of different characteristics, governance structures and drivers of suburbanization face similar problems when confronted with rapid and extensive suburbanization: weak planning, social fragmentation, low quality of urban and architectural design as well as a lack of infrastructure in suburban spaces, and ecological damages. While it might be false to claim these problems in any context as being caused by a specifically suburban development in the notion of "suburbia" as something "different" or "other" to development within the city, it nevertheless seems to be necessary to consciously turn the attention of urban researchers and planners towards the suburban areas. This book is an attempt to move forward in that sense.

I would like to thank all authors who contributed to this book, Britta Weisser, Frederike Rode, and Matti Drechsel who assisted with the editing and layout. Also, I would like to thank the Zentrum für Universitätsentwicklung at the Bauhaus-Universität Weimar which supported the lecture series and the seminar through a "Lehrfond"-grant, financed through money from the Federal Ministry of Education and Research ("Professional.Bauhaus" and "Studium.Bauhaus").

References

Bodenschatz, Harald/ Schönig, Barbara (2004), Smart Growth - New Urbanism - Liveable Communities. Programm und Praxis der Anti-Sprawl-Bewegung in den USA, Wuppertal: Müller + Busmann.

Keil, Robert (2013), "Welcome to the suburban revolution", in: Keil, Robert (ed.): Suburban Constellations, Berlin: Jovis Verlag, 8-17.

Kirby, Andrew/ Modarres, Ali (2010), "The suburban question. An Introduction", Cities, 27(1), 65-67.

McGee, Terry (2013), "Suburbanization in the Twenty-First-Century World", in: Keil, Robert (ed.): Suburban Constellations, Berlin: Jovis Verlag, 18-25.

Modarres, Ali/ Kirby, Andrew (2010), "The suburban question. Notes for a research program", Cities, 27(1), 114-121.

Münter, Angelika (2014), „Suburbia im demographischen Wandel", in: Roost, Frank et al. (eds.): Jahrbuch StadtRegion 2013/14, Schwerpunkt Urbane Peripherie, Berlin, Toronto: Opladen, 19-42.

Phelps, Nicholas A. (2010), "Suburbs for Nations? Some interdisciplinary connections on the suburban economy", Cities, 27(1), 68-76.

Schönig, Barbara (2014), „Umbauen, reparieren, umdenken - Suburban Retrofitting in der Krise", in: Roost, Frank et al. (eds.): Jahrbuch StadtRegion 2013/14, Schwerpunkt Urbane Peripherie, Berlin, Toronto: Opladen, 96-114.

Sieverts, Thomas (1997), Zwischenstadt, zwischen Ort und Welt, Raum und Zeit, Stadt und Land, Braunschweig, Wiesbaden: Vieweg.

United Nations Population Fund (2007), State of World Population 2007. Unleashing the Potential of Urban Growth. New York.

Part I
(Re-)developing Suburban Spaces

Mapping Urban Landscapes - Between understanding, interpreting and negotiating

Sigrun Langner

Introduction

In the context of global urbanization in the era of late capitalism, an urbanized landscape is emerging whose dynamics and origins we need to understand more comprehensively. Urban landscapes are shaped by the complex interplay of socio-economic and ecological processes that we need to become more familiar with, if we are to influence them productively or to enhance the quality of urban landscapes. The complexity of today's urban landscapes requires instruments that can help us to read and reveal the processes that shape the landscape, and the spatial impacts these processes have.

The increasing availability of atlases and other cartographic representations of the diverse interrelationships in urban landscapes seem to suggest that maps are eminently suitable for this purpose. Various designers have described the use of mapping as an active practice of the creative interpretation and reinterpretation of an existing situation (Corner/MacLean 1996; Corner 1999; Berger 2002; Beelen 2010). This practice has arisen in the context of a growing general awareness of the need to address urban development issues at a regional scale. The use of cartography as a creative practice of producing ideas and knowledge, especially for large-scale planning purposes, has gained increasing attraction within planning and design disciplines in recent years.[1]

---

[1] In particular in large-scale design projects, maps are presented as an integral part of the design project. Examples can be seen in the work of Studio 09 - Bernardo Secchi / Paola Vigano on the "Le Grand Paris" competition (Stadtbauwelt 182 I 2009 on the topic of "Le Grand Paris"), the work of Chora, e.g. the Taiwan Strait Incubator (Bunschoten 2010), the work of Comhrá (Bunschoten/Doherty 2004) or the Water Atlas Studio Urbane Landschaften (IBA Hamburg 2008).

Taking a large-scale landscape and design-oriented perspective on current urbanization processes, this article examines the potential of design-oriented cartography as a practice of generating knowledge and ideas for the design of large-scale landscapes in the context of the pressures of global urbanization processes.

Using examples from selected design projects, this article discusses mapping as a practice of understanding, interpreting and negotiating of urban landscapes.

1. A large-scale landscape perspective on urbanization processes

Many of the pressing issues concerning the future of urban space, such as the effects of climate change, of demographic change in shrinking regions, or issues such as the quality of daily life in large spatial agglomerations, can only be studied seriously within large-scale regional contexts (Meijsmann 2010: 5).

The consideration of complex socio-economic and ecological interrelationships goes beyond our perception of urban space in the usual spatial categories of city and country. This relational notion of urban space allows us to think of it as a continuous "urban fabric" that extends across the land - sometimes woven more densely and sometimes more loosely (Lefèbvre 1970).

Taking a look around, it can be seen that a new urban reality is emerging: town and city centers, estates of detached houses, farmland, industrial and commercial areas, urban open spaces and nature preservation areas are all becoming interwoven into a single urban region. Various spatial constructs have been proposed to describe this phenomenon, such as "Zwischenstadt" (Sieverts 1997), "Netzstadt" / "Urban System" (Baccini/Oswald 1998) or "urban landscapes" (Seggern 2010). All of these concepts merely go beyond describing visually perceptible spatial attributes: The complex system of socio-economic and ecological factors that shapes modern environments results in a web of relationships that does not stop at a designated spatial boundary. Urban space is increasingly being used, and perceived, on a day-to-day basis at a broader, regional scale. This "urban fabric" can only be grasped intellectually through its relationships.

Maps can be a helpful instrument for visualizing and understanding such spatial interrelationships and in turn empower the wider community to participate in a more nuanced way in decision-making processes that concern their urbanized environment. Maps have the capacity to depict simultaneity in space (Schlögel 2007: 97). They are representations of coexistence, and thus can draw what is physically separated into a spatial system of relatedness (Löw et al. 2007: 68). In the context of a relational notion of space this makes them an important means of expression.

In the current discourse on regionalization, the concept of the "city" is being increasingly eroded: The city is no longer understood as a physical unit defined by its settlement structure but as a fluid space that is also defined by the flow of people, information and goods (Castells 2001). This system of relationships within a global network is constantly in flux. Global urbanization processes stimulate regionalization: In order to remain competitive, regions restructure themselves and establish collaborative networks between their various institutions and enterprises (Castells 2001: 436ff.). These efforts aim to create coherent, effective regions and cooperative city networks that are better prepared to respond to fierce international competition than individual cities are able to on their own. In the context of this increasing competition between regions, and the sometimes extreme disparities between them, the protagonists of region-building need to ask themselves: What is the specific quality of the region? What are its inimitable features? Where does its potential lie? And, above all, how can all this be communicated and developed?

These issues are exacerbated when funds are scarce and resources are limited. The pressure of competition and the antithetic constitution of regions demand that we address the varying economic, social and cultural foundations of each region on its own merits if we are to develop it sustainably out of its "Eigenlogik" as Berking and Löw (2008) have called it. Consequently, an increase in urban research into the structures that describe a city's intrinsic logic can be noticed. How will the specific spatial qualities of a region as a habitat and economic unit look like in the future? What are the specific (landscape) resources, spatial use patterns and development strands of a region? How does one trace and define its intrinsic logic?

These questions play a key role in the search for the respective particularities of places and their different "features, aptitudes and qualities" within the wider urban fabric (Sieverts 2004: 23). This focus on a locality's endogenous potential becomes even more important in times of limited municipal financial resources; not so much with respect to inter-municipal competition but rather as a way of working towards a mutually beneficial functioning urban system based on inter-municipal collaboration and communication.

> "The development of complementary local features, 'aptitudes' and qualities within the wider differentiated urban landscape offers considerable potential for improving productivity and quality of life." (Sieverts 2004: 23)

The development of cooperative systems of relationships requires different spatial design approaches: Approaches are needed which consider urban space at a regional level and which can mediate between global and local conditions, but also approaches which can reveal the potential for complementary inter-municipal collaboration, and which can promote their respective local "aptitudes" (Sieverts 2004: 23). Therefore, the large-scale regional level of urban spaces has become an important subject and field of action for spatial design and planning disciplines.

By searching for the particular characteristics and "intrinsic logic" (Berking/Löw 2008) of a region and the development of its specific features - aptitudes and qualities - a landscape perspective needs to be adopted in order to improve the quality of life, perception and accessibility of a region and to promote its sustainable urban development. A landscape perspective helps to understand the connections between closed and monofunctional systems that follow global patterns of development and the specific conditions of a locality. Even within the concept of a "space of flows", actual places still exist. The significance of local conditions for an urban system becomes especially apparent when catastrophes such as flooding occur, which reveal the vulnerability of urban systems. At a more general level, the way in which we experience and access landscapes on a daily basis is also an important measure of the quality of life in a region, and a locational factor that can no longer be ignored. A landscape perspective therefore searches for regional development perspectives that emerge from the intrinsic logic of the landscape.

By looking at the ecological, social, economic and also aesthetic aspects of space from an integrative viewpoint, urban landscape can be perceived as a multi-dimensional performative process, which Hille von Seggern defines "Raumgeschehen" (Seggern 2012: 194). Here the term "urban landscape" denotes not a spatially enclosed territory, such as a city region, but rather the social reality as shaped by global urbanization processes (Seggern 2009: 275). In this sense, it is a defining cultural category for almost complete urbanization. Adjacent spatial units may be quite different, however, whenever they can be seen as related parts of a larger system they are interpreted as a landscape. This "placing within a relationship" happens at both the perceptive and experiential level as well as at the structural level. What belongs functionally together and constitutes a system? Which dynamic socio-economic and ecological processes shape the spatial relationships?

By taking the landscape perspective it becomes possible to see the interrelationships between the global and the local, between systems of relationships and spatial units, between natural processes, human action, and economic patterns.

> "In the future, urban landscapes will need to be stronger mediators between the local place and the global level than they are now [...] They will have to accommodate both global elements that follow global rules and local elements that serve the small living and working worlds of the local area." (Sieverts 2008: 263)

2. A design-oriented perspective of large-scale urbanization processes

In the light of stronger interregional competition for limited resources, the sustainable development and design of regions as livable everyday environments is of great importance. In this context, the inclusion of perception and design need to be included as dimensions of planning. These must be considered as part of the development of possible future scenarios for sustainable living and working in regions shaped by the interaction of global forces and local conditions. A design-oriented perspective creates the conditions for new ideas and approaches in order to deal with and shaping such relationships and interactions.

Within spatial design disciplines, renewed interest in these large-scale relationships and the design issues that arise in connection with them can be noticed. Until recently, such large-scale areas were the domain of regional planning. The method of spatial design is gradually being used and discussed within large-scale urbanization processes as a possible means of developing new approaches to familiar problem as well as for revealing new research questions and for investigating sustainable development (Koch/Schröder 2006; Meijsmann 2010; Seggern 2012). In the context of large-scale design projects a shift in the way design is applied can be observed: it is less typological and more situational, less product-oriented and more process-oriented. Likewise, the role of the architect has shifted away from the image of the creative genius or distinguished expert towards the image of the mediator or curator. Thomas Sieverts (2008) sees great potential in a more comprehensive understanding of design at a regional scale: design can be used as a means of coming up with new knowledge and ideas within complex, large-scale problems (as a method of cognition). It serves as a means of promoting understanding within difficult and protracted negotiation processes at a regional level (as a means of communication). Additionally it can be used to shape and improve relationships and connections within the urban landscape (as an instrument of design). (Sieverts 2008: 262)

In recent years, numerous creative-productive approaches to the design of large-scale areas have been developed in teaching, research and practice. The studys "ZwischenStadtEntwerfen" (Bormann et al. 2005), which deals with improving qualities of the Zwischenstadt, "Creating Knowledge" (Seggern et al. 2008), which is concerned with the design of urban landscapes, and "Designing for a Region" (Meijsman 2010), which focuses on spatial design at a regional scale, provide a good overview of the current design approaches and methods for tackling large-scale design problems. Many of these methods involve an intensive and creative investigation of the existing situation and the corresponding processes that contribute to producing the landscape.

André Corboz (2001) describes a shift in regional planning thinking away from the "tabula rasa formulae" that view space as an abstract field of activity towards a conception of space as a long-term accumulation of successive layers. In this "palimpsest", the various territorial processes of the past, the geological traces and traces of former uses can all be read - and taken into consideration before intervening in this stratification (Corboz 2001: 163f.).

Therefore instruments are required which make it possible to read and reveal these relationships and their spatial impacts. The proliferation of cartographic representations and atlases (especially for large-scale projects) indicates that cartography has been discovered as a helpful tool being capable of revealing the intrinsic logic of an urban landscape. This becomes especially relevant when searching for the specific resources of a region.

In spatial design disciplines, working with maps is a familiar and fundamental activity. Mostly, however, maps serve as a neutral analytical tool for preparing the subsequent creative design work as well as an objective basis for making decisions, and as a means of defining fixed parameters within which the design and planning process operates. This way of using maps remains rooted in the cartographic notion of maps that sees maps as a neutral representation of a given spatial reality. Cosgrove (1999) has described how the understanding of maps has shifted away from the objective, scientific representation of the earth's surface to a broader view that takes into account the cultural dimension and influence of maps within particular contexts and processes (Cosgrove 1999: 3ff.). Maps can be seen as an expression of the performative practice of understanding spatial relationships (Kitchin/Dodge 2007; Crampton 2010). This notion of maps considers them in the context of their situational use, and this in turn points to their use in design. From a design-oriented perspective, maps are a means - and mapping the practice - of generating knowledge and ideas within the design process. As it will be demonstrated in the following examples maps have the capacity to serve as a medium for the practice of orientation, of construction and of negotiation. Additionally they are capable to facilitate the design and development of large-scale landscapes.

3. Mapping as a practice of orientation: reading and understanding urban landscapes

Throughout the ages and different cultures around the world, maps have served and continue to serve as a means of orientation in space and time. The wish to find one's way in the world and understand the structure of space was and is closely linked with the development of cartography and the visualization of spatial information in the form of maps. Mapping can be understood as the ancient cultural practice of wishing to understand (cf. Harley/ Woodward 1987; Crampton 2010). Urs Primas (2008) has discussed the increasing role of maps in urban design as a need to understand what happens around us:

> "The use of maps in urban design is becoming ever more important and indicates above all that we want to understand what is actually happening." (Primas 2008: 66)

Cartography is seen as a suitable way of tracing the logic of urban landscape and understanding its complex developmental interrelationships. With the help of maps the complex spatial dependencies and systems of relationships within an urban landscape can be read, revealed, presented and understood.

An understanding of urban landscapes and the processes that produce the landscape is vital in order to develop new ideas for it. It is through the process of understanding that the idea emerges. This is a transformative process in which there is a "fusion of horizons" between the past, the present and the connection to the future (Seggern 2008: 228ff.). While the process of understanding cannot be operationalized into a method, it can be supported by different practices. An intensive and creative investigation of the existing situation can facilitate the process of understanding. Additionally the mapping of urban landscapes is a possible means of undertaking this dynamic investigation.

From a landscape-oriented view of urban development, it is initially of interest to observe and comprehend the reciprocities between the natural spatial conditions of a landscape and its urban development. The aim is, with the help of cartographic representations, to uncover the internal mechanisms of urban landscapes, to read its underlying structures, and to reveal and understand its importance and historical origins. How did landscapes come to be what they are today (genesis of the landscape)? Which natural spatial and socio-economic processes form urban landscapes? How is landscape produced? What are the links and dependencies between landscape and urban development?

A well-known example of research into natural regional conditions and urban structural development through cartographic depiction is Ian L. McHarg's (1969) study "Designing with nature". In a series of different layers, maps show how the spatial structure of the development of Washington was influenced by natural spatial conditions, e.g. the underlying geological conditions.

Examples of how topological relationships and structures can be expressed through maps can also be seen in James Corner's cartographic representations of the American landscape. In the book "Taking Measures Across the American Landscape", American landscapes and their particular qualities are described through a combination of photographs (by Alex S. MacLean) and cartographic representations by the landscape architect James Corner (Corner/MacLean 1996). In his maps of the American landscape, Corner reveals the diverse relationships between the forms and techniques which are being used when working with landscape and the existing features of the natural landscapes and the respective unique images of the landscape that they give rise to. Corner sees mapping as a means not only of exploring what exists but also of reformulating and interpreting what is there.

> "The capacity to reformulate what already exists is the important step. And what already exists is more than just the physical attributes of terrain (topog-

raphy, rivers, roads, buildings) but includes also the various hidden forces that underlie the workings of a given place." (Corner 1999: 214)

In "Drosscape", Alan Berger (2002) uses cartographic depictions to visualize how "waste landscape" is produced through processes of suburbanization and deindustrialization (Berger 2002). Berger's maps portray the American West as a landscape in transition, which is produced by mining and engineering work which when seen in these dimensions has an aesthetic quality of its own, that does not run the risk of negating the landscape.

Another example for visualizing landscape producing processes is the book "Schichten einer Region" (Layers of a Region, own translation), an annotated set of maps that intends to show new approaches to the future development of the structure and characteristic urban features of the Ruhr metropolitan region. The "Landscape Machine" is part of this project (Langner 2011). The metaphor of the landscape machine offers a new view of the "landscape producing forces" and the historical genesis of the landscape structures in the Ruhr conurbation. The focus of the project lies in revealing the reciprocal effects between interventions in the orographical situation (terrain machine), the management of the water resources (water machine) and urban development. The transformation of the topography of the Ruhr and its impact on the water resources are made clear by comparing maps of the situation in 1840 with the present day. The "terrain machine" has sculpted the hills and valleys of the landscape. The most effective shaping forces are water and mining. The "water machine" keeps the water system of the Rivers Emscher and Ruhr functional and usable by pumping, diverting, channeling, branching and damming the water. Individual maps show the different mechanisms of the complex water machinery. The combination of terrain and water machines leads to the formation of three "Ruhr lands" each with their own characteristics: the Polderland, Hellwegland and Bergland.

The final map in the chapter emphasizes on the one hand the specific characteristic features of each of these Ruhr lands, and on the other hand links them as a coherent Ruhr landscape. Each of these "lands" is

Figure 1: Ruhr Lands: the Polderland, Hellwegland and Bergland (Langner)

crossed by a line in the landscape (the River Emscher, the Ruhrschnellweg roadway, and the River Ruhr) that has the capacity to be an identifying characteristic at a regional level as well as to be a green infrastructure that offers great potential for the development of attractive and diverse Ruhr landscapes.

These few examples illustrate how mapping reveals the underlying logic of a landscape and how their landscape producing processes, coherences and relationships concealed in the status quo can be unveiled and visualized. Such maps contain analytical information while simultaneously permitting interpretative readings. Deciphering particular spatial and process nexuses from conventional maps can be an inducement to see new landscapes. Also, new ideas emerge through making hitherto unseen nexuses visible (Corner 1999: 249).

The use of maps in these examples goes beyond representing the existing spatial attributes. The intention here is not to present available knowledge in different, more legible ways but to use the maps to reveal previously unseen relationships, in turn generating new knowledge about urban landscapes that can serve as a basis for future actions. This approach of uncovering the existing logics of landscapes as a basis from which to reformulate reality is described by Kelly Shannon as "descriptive landscape urbanism":

"A descriptive landscape urbanism could evolve from the careful reading of layered contested territories and the designerly investigation of their potential." (Shannon/Manawadu 2007: 17)

4. Mapping as a practice of construction: interpreting and constructing urban landscapes

Maps are more than visualizations of simple relationships in urban landscapes. The way in which these relationships are presented influences our idea of the space. As such, maps are not a neutral representation of a given reality but present a concept - or a construct - of space (Löw et al. 2007: 68).

The way in which a map portrays the specific features and characteristics of a landscape, and in which it highlights certain structures, spatial relationships and themes, tells a story about the landscape and communicates a way of looking at the landscape. It shows a constructed view of the landscape. With the help of maps, a designer interprets and (re)configures the systems of relationships within urban landscapes. Thus, the map can tpresent new perspectives and projections of the urban landscape that serve as a basis for discovering new possibilities for its development.

That does not mean that maps are works of fiction. They are rather always an interpretation of an existing situation. A map simultaneously describes an existing situation and influences its perception. With the help of maps new realities can be explored and shaped (Corner 1999: 250). It is an analytical and descriptive tool that also has the capacity to imagine and construct space. The way in which the existing features are shown and (re)configured when describing and visualizing existing structures and processes reveals new ways of looking at it. In this sense, maps can serve as a window onto the future. The cartographic reconfiguration of an existing situation presents an imagined projection of its future condition. The landscape is not just shown and described but becomes a space of possibilities. And from the description of this space of possibilities actions can follow. This kind of design mapping shifts back and forth between describing the existing situation and designing and encompasses

Mapping Urban Landscapes 29

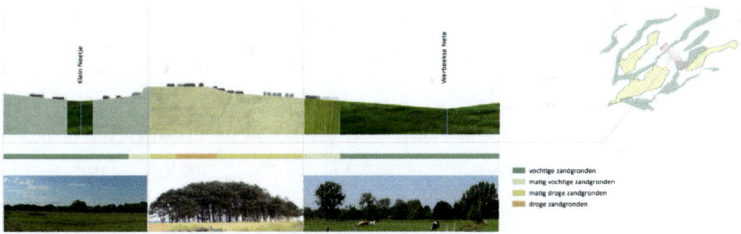

Figure 2: Landscape of Dry- and Wetland (Station C23 + OSA)

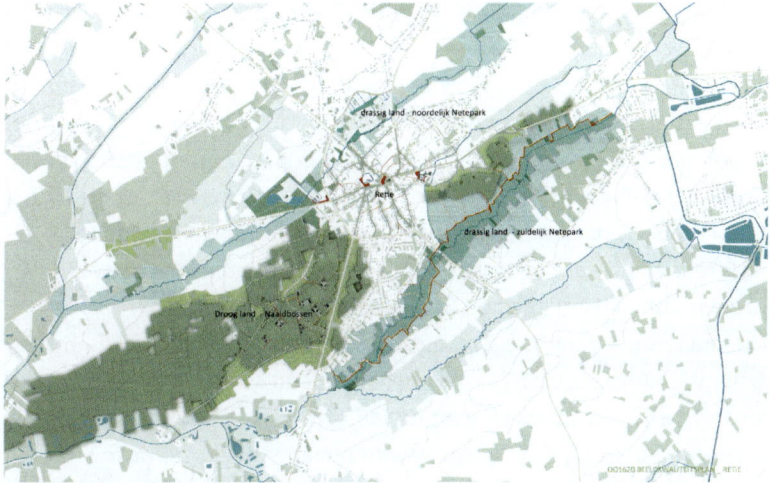

Figure 3: (Re)interpretation and (Re)configuration of the landscape into Dry- and Wetland (Station C23 + OSA)

both the descriptive, analytical character of a map as well as the suggestive and projective character of a plan. Design mapping uses the power and mechanisms of maps not just to (re)interpret and re(present) a landscape but also to transform and (re)configure it. The following example of an image quality plan for the municipality of Retie in Belgium shows how this works in practice.[2]

---

[2] The masterplan from the image quality plan for the municipality of Retie, by OSA, KU Leuven (Prof. Dr. Kelly Shannon) together with Station C23, was part of the "Open Oproep" competition in 2009.

Firstly, the existing characteristics of the landscape were recorded and their qualities identified as a basis for further development. The aim was to draw up a long-term development concept for the future urban development of the region. At the scale of the Region of Groot Retie, the image quality plan has a dual aim: to make the logic of the landscape legible and to restore natural ecologies, and to show possibilities for the future urban development of the region that take into account the specific qualities of the landscape.

After an intensive cartographic investigation of the particular qualities of the landscape, specifically the shift from the higher dry dune areas and the elongated stretches of the wet lowloads of the seven Neetjen, the "wetland-dryland" polarity was identified as a theme for the future development of the landscape. This "wetland-dryland" interpretation of the landscape helps to make its future development potential legible. Using cartographic representations, a specific image of the landscape for Retie was (re)configured: the town of Retie sits on the duneland between two stretches of wetland, the north and south Neetje.

The maps show how the wetlands can be differentiated based on their existing characteristics. The northern wetland will be designed as the North Neetjepark in which existing industrial and commercial areas are incorporated along with the rainwater management infrastructure to create a public water park. The wetlands along the south arm of the Neetje already encompass stretches of green meadows that are designated as a bird sanctuary. By converting some of the agricultural land into meadowland, a contiguous Neetjepark can be created with corresponding sustainable leisure concepts. In the dry areas between the wetlands, the pine woodland will be extended and developed into a woodland park with settlements located in clearings in the wood.

The central map of the image quality plan interprets the existing situation and the structures of the landscape and highlights potential aspects for future development. The production of the map results in a cartographic reconfiguration of the landscape: the map constructs new perspectives and projections of the urban landscape, and makes new development possibilities imaginable. Design mapping is therefore always also the search for possible options in what already exists. The map simultaneously describes what exists and reveals design possibilities.

> "[...] the unfolding agency of mapping may allow designers and planners not only to see certain possibilities in the complexity and contradiction of what already exists but also to actualize that potential." (Corner 1999: 214, emphasis in the original)

5. Mapping as a practice of negotiation: communicating and negotiating urban landscapes

Maps present a concept of space and represent a particular way of looking at space. The capacity of maps to serve as a basis for imagining the future can reveal possible courses of action and make them communicable. In this case the map is not regarded as an objective representation of real space but as a possible interpretation of a system of spatial relationships and its accompanying development possibilities. By visualizing a particular viewpoint, it becomes an argument within a process of negotiation.

> "The map is not a picture. It is an argument." (Wood/ Fels 2008: xvi)

Wood and Fels (2008: vii) see maps less as images than as cartographic conversations. What interests them is the performative character of maps in such conversations and how meaning is constructed and ultimately leads to action (Wood and Fels: xvi). Therefore, maps cannot claim to be absolutist, precise representations of reality. Rather they are a hypothesis or a proposition of how space can be perceived and interpreted which is open to negotiation.

How a cartographic image can facilitate the negotiation and communication of an urban development process can be seen in the project "Rheinliebe" (Rhinelove).[3] The project is part of the IBA Basel 2020 international

---

[3] The study and spatial image for the joint development of the Rhine landscape is part of the IBA Basel 2020 and was developed by Station C23 and sabine rabe landschaften with consultation from Prof. Dr. Hille von Seggern and Henrik Schultz.

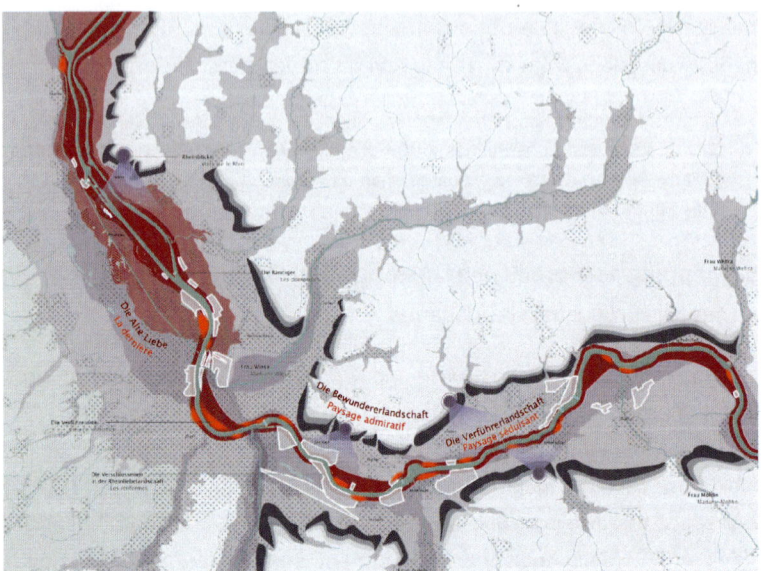

Figure 4: Cartographic interpretation of the Rhine landscape around Basel according to the notion of "Rheinliebe" (Station C23 + Sabine Rabe Landschaften)

building exhibition. The main goal of the IBA Basel is to build up a new cross-border planning culture and community of responsibility. The slogan of the IBA is: "growing together" and "together growing" in the tri-national district. The IBA program focusses on the question of how growth and growing together can be created sustainably in city regions in the 21st century. The Rhine as the backbone of the region plays a politically and economically important role for the region and its identity.

The aim was to design a holistic cartographic image of the region that allows the specific qualities of the urban agglomeration around Basel to come to the fore. It raises questions about how the Rhine can be conceived as a common area of responsibility for the three countries. The image serves as a framework within which to embed and to qualify the IBA projects, and as a communication platform for the long-term development of the tri-national border landscape(s).

The project elaborates a cartographic image that re-interprets the specific and special character of the Rhine landscape around Basel based

Figure 5: Landscape of Seduction (Sabine Rabe Landschaften + Station C23)

on four landscape typologies. The intention is to highlight the different spatial qualities of the Rhine-Landscape and to re-interpret them according to the notion of "Rheinliebe". For each landscape typology, future questions were developed to help qualifying existing IBA projects and reveal new project ideas.

The "landscape of seduction" (river bank) characterizes the contact zone between water and land. The intention here is to develop different ways in which the Rhine can be experienced directly. Key questions include: How can the landscape of seduction become a common good? How accessible is the river bank? Is the Rhine seductive? Other aspects, such as water quality and collaborative flood protection, are also addressed. The "old love landscape" (former wetland) denotes the areas of the former wetlands of the River Rhine. In the nature reserves one still has a sense of this old love, and these wetlands are being artificially reconstructed. At the same time, there need to be new ways of relating to water in this area, for example through developing gravel pit lakes as new recreational areas. Key questions include: What kind of sustainable water management concepts are suitable? How can the ground water table be raised?

Figure 6: New Love (Sabine Rabe Landschaften + Station C23)

What role can new ways of relating to water ("new love") play? What role does agriculture play?

The "landscape of admiration" is the old and attractive cultural landscape with its vineyard-clad slopes along the alluvial plains overlooking the Rhine from a respectful distance. Key questions include: How can we enhance the views and highlight the existing landscape qualities? What maintenance and development measures are necessary for this? What course might a tri-national upland trail take?

The "no-go landscapes" are the isolated industrial areas and infrastructural strips along the river. How can they be integrated into the river landscape? How can they be opened up for better accessibility to the river? How can they become part of the Rhinelove landscape? The unusual language of "Rheinliebe" stimulates the imagination and helps to reveal possible projects. The narrative image is open to interpretation and further elaboration. The intention is on the one hand to highlight the existing spatial conditions of the Rhine landscape and on the other to establish a communication tool for finding a common language among different planning cultures in the adjacent countries. In this sense, the map

Figure 7: Landscape of Admiration (Sabine Rabe Landschaften + Station C23)

functions as a communication tool (that works in three different countries and cultures: a threesome language). Within the framework of inter-municipal discussions, the notion of "Rheinliebe" offers an emotional way to relate to the region as a whole. It provides an opportunity to think outside entrenched ways of thinking and the formal vocabulary of regional planning.

"Rheinliebe" represents a first step on the path to developing a cross-border planning culture and is used as a communication tool in the professional planning discourse between the planning departments of the municipalities, the IBA and the Rhine working group. The image of "Rheinliebe" is used in planning workshops and in public as a way of discussing existing projects and new project ideas, and how they contribute to this sense of common identity. By connecting the levels of spatial discourse with everyday language, it makes it much easier to communicate with the public. For example, a column was started in a local newspaper, the Badische Zeitung, entitled "Rheinliebe" in which residents were interviewed about their relationship to the Rhine (Kistner 2013).

Figure 8: No-Go-Landscape (Sabine Rabe Landschaften + Station C23)

The basis for communication that maps can provide is helpful not only for talking about common aims and interests in spatial planning processes. Maps can also set social processes of negotiation in motion by presenting provocative viewpoints or by revealing contradictory and conflicting aspects. As a means of presenting an argument, maps are generally taken seriously because we know that they are not totally
fictional. They relate existing processes and structures to one another and present an interpretative perspective of a real situation.
As such, maps represent a spatial design embedded within a communicative process of negotiation on how a space can be perceived and envisaged.

Conclusion

In the design of large-scale urban landscapes, there is a need for instruments and methods that can reveal the existing logics of urban landscapes with a view to developing the specific qualities of an urban region.

The above project examples show the potential of using mapping strategies in large-scale design processes and how these can be a helpful design practice for:
- reading and understanding the intrinsic logic of a landscape;
- interpreting this logic, (re)formulating the existing and opening up perspectives;
- negotiating possible future of urban landscapes.

Explorative mapping helps to reveal systems of relationships in urban landscapes that are not usually noticed. And because maps are able to represent simultaneity in spaces (Schlögel 2007: 97), they are well suited for describing spatial-topological aspects. Relationships and dependencies can be seen at a glance. Unusual presentation methods can help to uncover previously unseen relationships and make it possible to find new potential within an existing situation. In the process, the boundary between the descriptive and visionary capacity of maps blurs. We can look back (How and why has an urban landscape become what it is?) and forward (What possibilities does this present for its future development?). It links the given conditions of an urban landscape with its possible future images, combining the "re/source material" of a region with feasible images of its future. Finally, maps are used to design and to communicate concepts for spaces that through their incorporation in social negotiation processes are changed, transformed and developed further.

> "Mapping is a fantastic cultural project, creating and building the world as much as measuring and describing it." (Corner 1999: 213)

References

Baccini, Peter/ Oswald, Franz (1998), *Netzstadt: Transdiziplinäre Methoden zum Umbau urbaner Systeme*, Zürich: VDF Hochschulverlag.
Beelen, Karl (2010), "Imag(in)ing the Real. The 'Region' as a Project of Cartographic Re-Configuration", in: Meijsmans, Nancy (ed.), *Designing for a Region*, Amsterdam: SUN Academia, 24-37.
Berking, Helmut/ Löw, Martina (2008) (eds.), *Die Eigenlogik der Städte. Neue Wege für die Stadtforschung*, Frankfurt/New York: Campus.
Berger, Alan (2002), *Reclaiming the American West*, New York: Princeton Architectural Press.
Bormann, Oliver/ Koch, Michael/ Schmeing, Astrid/ Schröder, Martin/ Wall, Alex (2005) (eds.), *Zwischen Stadt Entwerfen*, Wuppertal: Müller + Busmann.
Bunschoten, Raul/ Doherty, Gary (2004), "Comhrá Karten, Clonmany, Ireland", *Topos 47*, 70-78.
Bunschoten, Raul (2010), "Urban Prototypes", in: Mostafavi, Mohsen/ Doherty, Gareth (ed.), *Ecological Urbanism*, Baden, 616-621.
Castells, Manuel (2001), *Der Aufstieg der Netzwerkgesellschaft: Teil 1 Das Informationszeitalter*, Opladen: Leske + Budrich.
Corboz, André (2001), *Die Kunst, Stadt und Land zum Sprechen zu bringen*, Basel: Birkhäuser Verlag.
Corner, James/ MacLean, Alex (1996), *Taking Measures Across the American Landscape*, New Haven/London: Yale University Press.
Corner, James (1999), "The Agency of Mapping: Speculation, Critique, Invention", in: Cosgrove, Denis (ed.), *Mappings*, London, 213-252.
Cosgrove, Denis (1999), "Introduction. Mapping Meaning", in: Cosgrove, Denis (ed.), *Mappings*, London, 1-23.
Crampton, Jeremy W. (2010), *Mapping. A Critical Introduction to Cartography and GIS*, Chichester: John Wiley & Sons.
Harley, J.B./ Woodward, David (1987) (eds.), *The History of Cartography-Volume One. Cartography in Prehistoric, Ancient, and Medieval Europe and the Mediterranean*, Chicago: University Press.

IBA Hamburg /Studio Urbane Landschaften (2008) (eds.), *Wasseratlas. WasserLand-Topologien für die Hamburger Elbinsel*, Berlin.

Kistner, Roland (2013), "RHEINLIEBE: Meine Heimat ist am Rhein", in: *BadischeZeitung*,02.August2013,http://www.badischeitung.de/rheinfelden/rheinliebe-meine-heimat-ist-am-rhein74107344.html (Accessed February 26, 2015).

Kitchin, Rob/ Dodge, Martin (2007), "Rethinking maps", in: *Progress in Human Geography*, 31(3), 331–344.

Koch, Michael/ Schröder, Martin (2006), "ZwischenStadtEntwerfen. Plädoyer für konzeptionelle Strategien im regionalen Maßstab oder: Für ein raumplanerisches Entwerfen", *Deutsches Architektenblatt (DAB)*, 9/2006, 18-21.

Langner, Sigrun (2011), "Landschaftsmaschine. Landschaftsproduzierende Kräfte im Ruhrgebiet", in: Reicher, Christa/ Kunzmann, Klaus R. / Polívka, Jan/ Roost, Frank/ Utku, Yasemin/ Wegener, Michael (eds.), *Schichten einer Region - Kartenstücke zur räumlichen Struktur des Ruhrgebiets*, Berlin: Jovis Verlag GmbH, 132-157.

Lefèbvre, Henri (2003), *Die Revolution der Städte (Originalausgabe 1970)*, Dresden: Postplatz Verlag.

Löw, Martina/ Steets, Silke /Stoetzer, Sergej (2007), *Einführung in die Stadt- und Raumsoziologie*. Opladen: Leske + Budrich.

McHarg, Ian L. 1992 (1969), *Design with Nature*, New York: Wiley.

Meijsmans, Nancy (2010) (ed.), *Designing for a Region*, Amsterdam: SUN Architecture.

Primas, Urs (2008), "Die Wirklichkeit des Kartografen", *StadtBauwelt*, 24/2008, 58-66.

Schlögel, Karl (2007), *Im Raum lesen wir die Zeit*, Frankfurt /M: Fischer Taschenbuch Verlag.

Seggern, Hille von/ Werner, Julia/ Grosse-Bächle, Lucia (2008), *Creating Knowledge. Innovationsstrategien im Entwerfen urbaner Landschaften*, Berlin: Jovis Verlag GmbH.

Seggern, Hille von (2008), "Ohne Verstehen keine Entwurfsidee", in: Seggern, Hille von/ Werner, Julia/ Grosse-Bächle, Lucia (2008) (eds.),

- *Creating Knowledge. Innovationsstrategien im Entwerfen urbaner Landschaften*, Berlin: Jovis Verlag GmbH, 212-251.
- (2009), "Raum + Landschaft + Entwerfen", in: Eisel, Ulrich/ Körner, Stefan (eds.), *Befreite Landschaft. Moderne Landschaftsarchitektur ohne arkadischen Ballast? Beiträge zur Kulturgeschichte der Natur*, Bd. 18, Freising, 265-286.
- (2010), "Der soziologische Beitrag zum Entwerfen urbaner Landschaften", in: Hardt, Annette/ Scheller, Gitta (eds.), *Soziologie in der Stadt- und Freiraumplanung. Analysen, Bedeutung und Perspektiven*, Wiesbaden: VS Verlag für Sozialwissenschaften, 215-232.
- (2012), "Design as a crossover of research and practice", in: Diedrich, Lisa/ Moll, Claudia/ Kandiee, Thierry (eds.), *In touch: landscape architecture in Europe*, Wageningen: Academic Publishers, 193-200.

Shannon, Kelly/ Manawadu, Samitha (2007), "Indigenous landscape urbanism: Sri Lanka's reservoir & tank system", *JoLA*, autumn, 6-17.

Sieverts, Thomas (1997), *Zwischenstadt: zwischen Ort und Welt, Raum und Zeit, Stadt und Land*, Braunschweig/Wiesbaden: Vieweg.
- (2004), "Die Gestaltung der Stadtlandschaften - eine europäische Aufgabe!", in: Bölling, Lars/ Sieverts, Thomas (eds.), *Mitten am Rand. Auf dem Weg von der Vorstadt über die Zwischenstadt zur regionalen Stadtlandschaft*, Wuppertal: Müller + Busmann, 12-23.
- (2008), "Die Qualifizierung fragmentierter urbaner Landschaften - eine weltweite Aufgabe", in: Seggern, Hille von/ Werner, Julia/ Grosse-Bächle, Lucia (eds.), *Creating Knowledge. Innovationsstrategien im Entwerfen urbaner Landschaften*, Berlin: Jovis Verlag GmbH, 252-265.

Wood, Denis/ Fels, John (2008), *The Natures of Maps. Cartographic Constructions of the Natural World*, Chicago/London: University Press.

Challenge of maturation - Life cycles and patterns of change in suburban settlement space

Jan Polívka

Introduction

German suburban residential areas established during the second half of the 20th century are currently witnessing a significant maturation process. The existing suburban housing stock now offered on the real estate market is - despite regional differences - gradually overtaking the portion of newly constructed suburban housing in quantity (Dransfeld et al. 2010). An increasing portion of the current suburban discourse conceptualizes suburbia in various contexts outside of canonical urban-to-suburban trajectories. These are traditionally based on the monofaceted expansion of the settlement space. As a consequence, the definition of suburbia alongside a narrative of sprawling successive novelty outside the core or compact city is losing its dominant position. Instead, the maturation of suburbia is becoming significant. Besides its changing dynamics in growth, suburbia is increasingly diversifying in several ways. Along with the ethnical, social and functional variety of both suburban and urban reality, the evidence of absorbing urban functions beyond residence and production and becoming multifunctionally clustered post-suburbia is beginning to promote diversity on functional and spatial levels (Zimmer 1975 in: Choldin et al. 1980; Teaford 1997; cf. Hayden 2004; Phelps 2010). Within the metropolitan context (Knieling 2009) taken, among others, as a merging alternative for urban and suburban distinction, physical and functional typologies of suburban settlement, interactions among these and towards the urban core are used as a basis for describing entities within the blurrily defined suburban settlement space.
It is this development which has changed the canonical understanding of the concept of suburbia. The "classic" definition of suburbia, understood and analyzed as a particular non-urban settlement type, is therefore shifting towards a dynamic understanding of an ongoing suburban development path as a transition process in time, where the perspectives of the post-suburban diversifica-

tion of suburban space increasingly become a central issue of the discourse.[1] On behalf of a "longitudal development", its examination in metropolitan context opened a broad discursive field for development-oriented research and strategic planning approaches (cf. McManus/Ethington 2007: 318ff.). However, the evidence from vast areas of mature suburbia and its divergent development patterns also raises questions regarding the suburban development process and its maturation and resilience as a whole.

This article is divided into five parts. It first deals with the impact of the traditional urbanization models on the anticipation of suburban growth. The second and third parts define suburban settlement areas as social-ecological systems, arguing that they underlie the rules of resilience that make them adjust to changing situations, such as development changes within the metropolitan context. The fourth part examines three case studies on how strategies of resilient development path are generated under the circumstance of an otherwise stagnating or shrinking mature suburban area. The last two sections draw conclusions on the main conditions of resilient change within local mature suburban settlement areas.

1. Suburbia's Maturation in the Context of Regional Urbanization Models

The maturation process of suburbia has an impact on the interpretation of urbanization cycle theories, which are interpreted regionally but implemented also locally. In most of these, the period of concentric urbanization alternates with a period of centrifugal expansion, showing that the rise of the one comes along with the decline of the other. Impressed by the post-war suburbanization wave, Hall (2001) presented four phases of urban development. These began with centralization at the core, followed by two decentralization periods (relative & absolute) and, finally, the absolute decline of the urbanized region due to the fatal inhabitant lost at the urban core. During the 1980s and 1990s, the

---

[1] They may arise e.g. as technoburbs (Fishman 1987), outtowns (Goldberger 1987) or edge cities (Garreau 1991), superburbs (Bourne 1996), etnoburbs (Li 1998), Zwischenstadt (Sieverts 1997), exopolis (Soja 2000), edgeless cities (Lang 2003), zoomburbs (Hayden 2004), boomburbs (Lang/LeFurgy 2007) or in-between spaces (Keil/Young 2010), or also beyond this as a phenomena of a rural-urban fringe (Scott 2013). Others are gradually maturing as generational settlement typologies to be physically and functionally re-qualified (Sieverts 1997; Dunham-Jones/Williamson 2011; Kadono 2010; Aring 2012 and others).

cycle-based urbanization theories were strongly influenced by the net inhabitant reconcentration in the core cities after a long phase of post-war deconcentration. In 1981, Klaasen et al. introduced a "recurring" cycle of reconcentration. One of the first phase-based deep analyses of the urbanization process was undertaken by Fielding (1982), who analyzed the phases of urbanization and counterurbanization on the basis of net migration and settlement size (Champion 2001).

Van den Berg et al. (1982) used a circular urbanization pattern by defining urban development in the four phases of urbanization, suburbanization, counter- or desurbanization and reurbanization based on population change in the urban core and at the periphery.[2] During the urbanization phase, large cities emerged and the population of the region grew, concentrating on the urban cores.[3] In a second phase, the centripetal population development was replaced by suburbanization. It redistributed the highly concentrated population from urban cores to adjacent space, causing spatial expansion of the settlement area by means of a declining density. This phase is again supported by many factors, among which the spatio-functional conflicts in the core pushes, and individual wealth pulls a significant part of the inner-city population to move out towards adjacent suburban areas. This phase was then replaced by counterurbanization, which drew the population from the agglomeration core area further to its outskirts and to the adjacent rural areas beyond. It was reliant, among others, on ubiquitous infrastructure (Siedentop 2008), functional spread and diversification as well as a lack of favourable spatial alternatives closer to the agglomeration's already urbanized and suburbanized core (Kadono 2010). In this phase, both the core city and suburbia may have lost population. Finally, within reurbanization, the urbanized area begins to gain inhabitants at its core(s) and again in the adjacent suburbia via a parallel decline in growth in external areas.

The universal urbanization model developed by van den Berg's team had been widely influential in interpreting the dynamics of metropolitan area development, as it enabled scholars to principally describe spatial attributes of the pro

---

[2] which includes suburban areas of the metropolitan settlement area.
[3] Tisdale (1942) defines urbanization as a process of population concentration in two ways: the multiplication of points of concentration and the increase in their sizes (cf. Champion 2001). In the modern age, such concentration - especially in the European context - was evoked by the urban industrialization era (Ourednicek 2008).

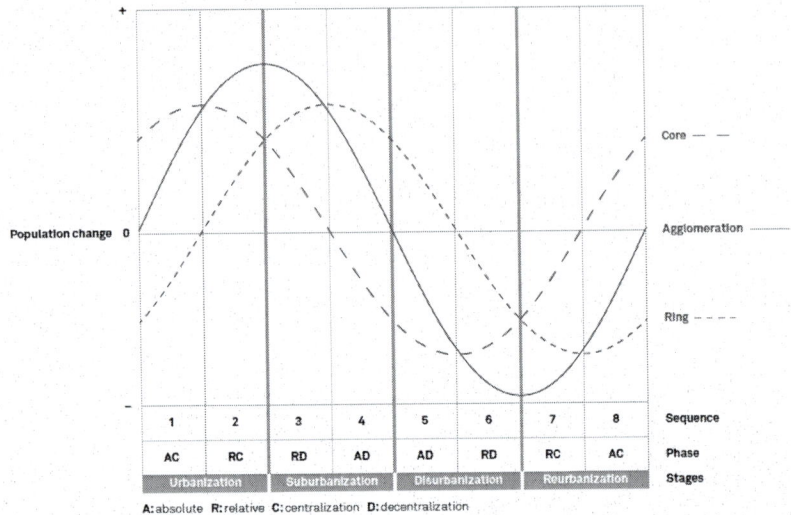

Figure 1: van den Berg Urbanization Model (Champion 2001: 147)

cess of metropolitan growth and density change, and included the post-industrial regrowth of the cores after counterurbanization. However, the basic model of urbanization has been subject to several alterations, mainly due to its rigidity. Geyer/Kontuly (1993) proposed a model of "differential urbanization" based on the relation of migration and settlement size also to accommodate dynamics.[4]

The analysis by Herfert/Osterhage (2012) further shows that regions may skip certain phases of the cycle and switch into others, and that different phases may run simultaneously.[5]

---

[4] Ourednicek (2004) remarks that the ideas of the models might be effective in principle. But in addition to the fact that these merely apply to cities that experienced a rapid industrial expansion, they have not yet been empirically proven - at least for Europe. He quotes, among others, Cheshire and Hay (Cheshire/Hay 1989; Cheshire 1995), who in studies on metropolitan areas found that none of 200 cases went through all phases and only 18% went through at least the half of the cycle. Furthermore, he points out that even in the research made by van den Berg et al. (1982), empirical affirmation could not been delivered.

[5] Herfert/Osterhage (2012: 107ff.) point out that reurbanization is a prevailing - though not the only - trend among German cities and metropolitan areas regardless of their actual population trend. At the same time, reurbanization might overlap with further centrifugal development, even though a clear desurbanization (conterurbanization) phase is not evident.

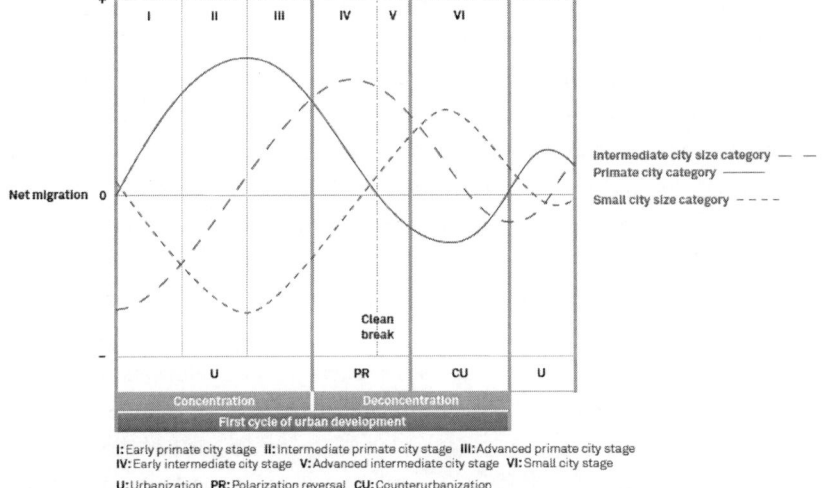

Figure 2: Geyer & Kontuly Differential Urbanization Model (Champion 2001: 146)

Based on the concepts of urban development cycles, some scholars have emphasized the correlation between a shrinking core and growing outskirts and vice versa. Accordingly, since a steady reurbanisation trend has been observed in German cities, since the turn of the millenium (Herfert/Osterhage 2012), significant challenges caused by shrinkage were also expected within suburban areas. These were expected to affect especially its most prevalent function of housing - including both apartment buildings and detached family housing (Häußermann 2007; cf. Aring 2012).

Theories on the basic life cycle process of settlement development have also influenced the conceptualization of suburban development. After a growth phase, suburbia was to a certain extent expected to decline during the reurbanization phase. Scenarios of decline were fed by many different contexts, including the painful 20th-century experience of urban decline (Jacobs 1961), peak oil[6] and discussions regarding transport and land use (Becker et al. 2011) as well as

---

[6] Sieverts (2007) assumes that every historical revolution in an energy medium also had a fundamental impact on the settlement structure. Still there is no evidence that this necessarily affected the previous structures; it rather modified the existing and added a new one by increasing the mobility of the individuals and goods among them fundamentally.

changes in lifestyle preferences (2012)[7]. Although they pick up on a certain important shift in societal history, empirical data shows that such approach is unable to provide a general explanation of urban-suburban development trends. Similar to what has been mentioned above, rather than "pure" phases of reurbanisation, a "complex restructuring process in the context of the urban regions" (Jessen/Siedentop 2010 in: Aring 2012: 72) is taking place, in which many outcomes are possible, including both growth and decline, but also adaption and transition.[8]

This short overview already shows that the diversifying development within metropolitan areas refutes to a cetrain extent the regional urbanization model. Therefore, even though on the general regional level tendencies of urbanization phases and their succession may be statistically identified, these may suspend contradictory parallel developments within certain parts of the region and their quarters or neighborhoods. Similarly, there seems to be a limited space for predictions of general cyclic development within suburbia. This especially regards the general growth, maturity, decline and regression of a whole existing settlement type - in this case, the decline of suburbia - during a reurbanization cycle exclusively on behalf of exogenously defined conditions[9] of location, demography and economy.

Summarizing this, one can conclude that maturity may shift urban systems to an even more diversified development. The maturation process in time is accompanied by divergent influences on the macro-, meso- and micro-levels[10]. As exogenous conditions, these influences define individual development paths at all levels as well as at the micro-level "sub-systems", which can be broken down to particular households.[11] As such, the diversified developments on the micro-

---

[7] Brake argues that a.o. due to interdependencies to structural changes resulting from changed societal and economic backgrounds; many individuals tend to live in urbanized rather than suburbanized contexts.

[8] Here, partly similar to basic resiliency theories, "adaption" stands for change of a system without its fundamental restructuring, and "transition" stands forfundamental changes which switch a system into a nother one (cf. Holling 1986; Walker 2006; Martin 2010).

[9] "Exogenous" and "endogenous conditions" refer to characteristics based on facts such as statistical data, stakeholder constellations as well as physical shapes and functional interrelations outside and inside the area.

[10] Here: macro = region, meso = city/municipality, micro = (sub)urban quarter.

[11] Vice versa, Beilein (2013; October 9th, 2014) points out that especially family home ownership puts families into a decisive role as "sub-systems" on the micro-level. House owners de-

level become important in relation to the general models of regional and urban development. Indeed, even though the methods of life cycle phase analysis are mostly concerned with the macro view on intraregional shifts, some authors indicate that the phases of the life cycles also need to be tackled on the neighborhood level (Siedentop 2008; Aring 2012; Hesse et al. 2013; Schnur 2014). The development of particular parts of suburbia in different societal concepts and spatial as well as economic contexts follows neither a pre-determined pattern nor is it necessarily stable and remains the same throughout its development trajectory. Instead, one can identify a differentiated range of development perspectives for particular parts of suburban areas.

Therefore, in order to understand the development in suburbia as a differentiation in time, it is necessary to ask in which way the life cycle model can accommodate diversification within particular suburban residential spaces. The suggestion followed here advocates for a deeper insight into the particular development paths of different suburban areas and its sub-systems. This needs to be based not only on quantitative data, but try to reach a certain level of qualitative comprehensive insight into the path dependencies that shape individual diversification patterns. According to such an approach, it might be necessary to divide the regional demographic and/or economic growth and decline discussion from the subject of the local suburban quarters or neighborhoods. In terms of individual life cycle development, the functional, demographic, economic and political situation as well as the resulting societal situation in suburbia also develops along specific development paths. These may not only make particular suburban areas develop within completely diversified external and internal contexts and exogenous and endogenous conditions[12] (and a resulting complexity after some decades of existence). They may also give them a different scope of further development options along differentiated path dependencies (cf. Martin/Sunley 2010; Martin 2010; Martin 2012). Such views offer the

---

termine the fate of their family house regarding its pattern and intensity of use, investment or disposal. In this way they co-shape the endogenous conditions at the micro-level.

[12] Here, "external context" signifies the characteristic of a particular settlement area defined on behalf of externally ascribed attributes. It often has to do with the role of the particular area in both urban (meso-) and regional (macro-) contexts, - regardless of whether it is defined mentally, spatially or functionally (cf. Schnur 2014). The "internal context" stands for the sum of characteristics defined by the inhabitants and internal stakeholders of a particular settlement area. Both external and internal contexts stand separately from "exogenous" and "endogenous conditions" (see footnote nr. 11).

opportunity for a more dynamic understanding of suburban change, taking into account the dynamics of the process within the suburban development trajectories instead of solely focusing on evidence offered through general theoretical frameworks and statistically approved local data, as well as visual signs of physical decline.

2. Using the Life Cycle Concept to Understand the Dynamics of Suburban Change

The resilience and system theories deliver a meaningful approach to understand the suburban diversification. According to Swanstrom et al. (2009: 8),[13]

> "Resilience is the ability to respond to a challenge by 1) redeploying assets or expanding organizational repertoires; 2) collaborating across governments and across the public, private, and non-profit sectors; 3) mobilizing or capturing resources from external sources."

Even though the definition of ecological adaptive cycles as established by Holling (1986) could be related to demographic life cycles or those of physical buildings, there is a portion of yet uncategorized strategic patterns to encounter transitions within social-ecological systems. Holling's system is based on the characteristics of two basic development loops, both consisting of two phases. Together, they make up the lifecycle system: the "Fore loop", consisting of a "Growth phase", where the system is under construction and retains a high level of flexibility to adapt to changing conditions, and of a "Conservation phase", where the system strengthens the form which it achieved during the growth phase, changing it into a more stable (but less flexible) one.

The "Back loop" consists of a "Release phase", where the resources are used not to stabilize, but rather to retain the system in its shape, thus preventing changes and adaptations. Its second part is the "Adaption" or "Transformation phase", where the stable system is no longer able to retain in its previous shape due to thresholds and adapts according to the changed situation, using available internal and/or external resources, or instead collapses and transforms into

---

[13] Even though his text refers to social phenomena, it has been also interpreted as a general definition for resiliency within social-ecological systems (cf. Walker et al. 2006) that human settlement, including suburbia, account for.

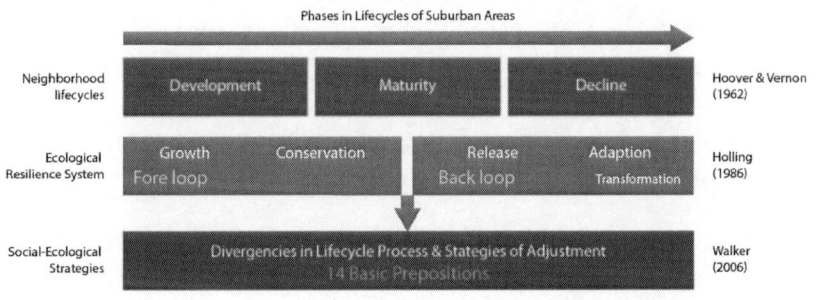

Figure 3: Approaches on Phases in Life Cycles of Suburban Areas as Social-Ecological Systems (Polívka 2014)

a completely different system. According to the heuristics of adaption and transformation by Walker et al. (2006), compared to ecological systems, human actors in social-ecologic systems account for 14 different resiliency propositions. Any system, once established, uses the capacity of self-regeneration by individual management responding with resilient adaptions using strategies of social-ecological systems as far as the particular path dependence allows. The crucial point is that

> "... social-ecological systems may have very different dynamics when compared to the ecological component, because the social domain contains the element of human intent. Management actions can deliberately avoid or engineer the crossing of actual and perceived thresholds." (Walker et al. 2006: 7)

This illustrates the complex dependency between physical layers and stakeholders within a social-ecological system of particular interests and both institutional and functional interconnections that condition each other. On behalf of its endogenous dynamics, such as anticipatory intent manifested in inner conflicts, agreements, rationalities or specific milieu, common values or socialization cultures, or simply by endogenous functional changes caused by the aging of the system's social (human) or ecological (physical) parts, the process of reaction might become quite individual and complex.

A question therefore remains whether patterns can be identified that are followed within the suburban transition by social-ecologic systems in terms of space, place and society. Or: to what extent do the social-ecologic systems generate a complex dynamic of transition based on situational determined principles; simply put - do general suburban differentiation trajectories exist, and if yes, what types could be identified?

3. Resilience and Path Dependence: a Stability Phenomenon in Mature Suburbia

According to canonical path dependence concept, systems[14] are switching into the "Adaption phase" or remain static in their development path and collapse after a shock (cf. Martin 2010). However, in social-ecological systems, changes in external conditions such as the economic situation, the regional planning framework and the supply and demand of housing or workforce usually develops unsteadily, with many ups and downs.

As a consequence, the internal development of a system undergoes a continuous change in constellations, together with the external influences, in a continuous process. Thus, processes of systemic change can be understood as a constant adjustment to every currently relevant situation. Changes are not necessarily a direct response to concrete destabilizing "shocks" to a particular system that make the system "stand" or "switch" away from an imaginary passive equilibrium[15] into a phase of immediate reaction of adaption or transition, or fast or slow decline.[16] Most often, changes appear as continuous adaptions (Martin 2010).

According to Walker et al. (2006), social-ecological systems encounter exogenous changes with an intentional individual and thus endogenous adjustment. Inner constellations shaping the development path may widen or narrow the scope of possible action of a system within time. Beilein (2013) adds that en-

---

[14] Social-ecological "systems" are defined here as particular suburban areas or neighborhoods with stakeholder constellations affecting the micro level (particular suburban settlement areas) and also including a panarchic constellation of stakeholders across the levels.

[15] For further theoretical background on the context of urban settlement, see also Simmonds et al. 2013.

[16] As Martin (2010; 2012) states, there is no particular reason to take for granted that exogenous conditions along the development trajectory would influence social-ecological systems only at certain points of their existence. Instead, it is possible that adjustment happens steadily when a need is recognized as sufficiently strong. This happens when it is stimulated by different triggers that intensify it at one place and at the same time. Accordingly, the decline or collapse of a system could rather be seen as the disfunction of a continuous adjustment within a system.

dogenous adjustments are mostly based on a subjective rationality, which cannot be necessarily directly explained or steered by objective planning measures. Finally, Dransfeld (cf. August 25, 2014) sees the reason here for why changes within settlement structures (especially if individually owned) are much more long-lasting and unpredictable than the basic life cycles would lead us to believe.[17] Seeing individual households as sub-systems, all of their different physical, demographic, societal and economic measures and subjective intents come together to create an individual path dependence. Even areas built at the same time and with the same architectural morphology are likely to fade out into individual paths, and possibly with completely different results. Within such individual paths, social-ecological systems have the chance (and time) to create their own adjustment strategies.

In the next chapter, three study cases are presented. They have been chosen to help answer the basic question surrounding the subsequent systemic ones formulated below: How do some local suburban settlement areas manage to resist demographic and economic decline on the meso and macro levels and thus remain stable at their local level, while others do not? Having settled the lifecycle concept and accommodated basic suburban development patterns into the basics of their evolutionary perspective, the following questions regarding suburban residential systems arise:

- When and why do suburban residential systems enter the "Adaption phase", or remain steady to collapse after a shock?
- How does adaption function and by which measures it can it be defined?
- Can we identify certain development patterns for suburban areas as of social-ecological systems in terms of space, place and society? Or do they generate a complex dynamic of transition based on merely random, situational determined principles?

---

[17] Such belief is being merely assumed on behalf of homogeneity assumptions (cf. Schnur/Drilling 2011; de Temple 2005; Nierhoff 2008).

4. German Metropolitan Area Case Studies

In our empirical study on the maturation of suburban micro-areas (Hesse et al. 2013),[18] we discussed the assumptions of individual path-dependent lifecycles on the background of an empirical study presenting twelve German micro case studies (suburban quarters) in four cities (meso-level) of four macro (= regional) areas (metropolitan regions). The studies were conducted between 2010 and 2012 in differentially prospering, stable or shrinking regions. We started using heuristic assumptions regarding the basic life cycle pattern of particular suburban quarters, defined by their urban morphological, historical and functional coherence. We defined basic phases of growth, maturity and decline[19], marked by the urbanization process (y = number of housing units and number of inhabitants) in time (x) (see Fig. 4). On behalf of definitions in internal conditions based on physical construction and demographic development, current lifecycle phase for a particular micro-level has been identified (cf. Bizer et al. 2008; Hesse et al. 2013).

The growth period was marked by the physical construction of structures and thus the remarkable increase in housing units as well as a significant growth in the number of inhabitants. Seeing the "quarter" as a micro-level system, if compared to the meso-level (usually the city) and the macro-level (mostly the region), a relatively lower-than-average age of the inhabitants and buildings can be observed. There is also a marginal portion of single households.

---

[18] The aim of the study was to find basic types of suburban change within German metropolitan areas according to their growth, stagnation or decline in terms of economy, population and enlargment of the settlement space. We then looked into particular areas in order to find out how they deal with the regional trends under their specific circumstances. Given by the case study's framework, the approach was merely heuristic, and has not yet been further theoretically deepened and interpreted, as I am attempting to do in this article.

[19] The concept of life cycles taken here as a base is the industry life cycle model, with its three basic stages of growth, maturity and decline as defined by Keppler (1997) and others. Understanding the micro-level as a unit of the social-ecological system (Walker 2006), here the resilience approach by Band/Jax (2007) is followed and looked at it through the prism of economic geography by Ron Martin (2010), who discusses the change factors within the life cycles of companies. The reason for not sticking with the van den Berg et al. (1987) "urban life cycle" model when looking at the life cycles on the micro-level ist the fact that the model is rather targeting the development on the macro and meso levels. It allows one to assume growth or shrinkage in certain areas according to its cycles (urbanization, suburbanization, desurbanisation, reurbanization), but it does not explain any abberation from this model.

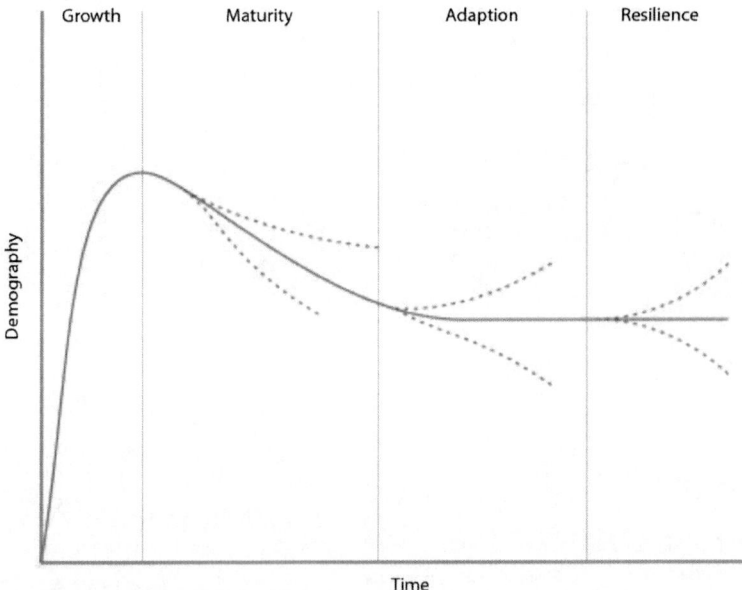

Figure 4: Basic life cycle concept (adapted from Hesse et al. 2013)

The maturity phase is characterized by the end of physical growth, which merely means that a large portion of physical construction has been already finished. There are four different sub-phases within the maturity phase:

1. Pre-maturity phase: The number of inhabitants only increases in cohorts under the age of 18 and the average population age increases. There is a marginal portion of single and twin households. The inhabitant structure is quite homogeneous, mostly based on the pattern of the modern nuclear family.
2. Mid-maturity phase: Marginal growth of the age cohorts under 18, beginning of marginal physical adjustments, and an average age of inhabitants if compared to the meso and macro levels.
3. Late maturity: Physical decline and structural adjustment, repair and densification. Some uses are replaced by alternative ones. As cohorts of children move out, there is a significant increase in residential space per capita, while at the same time the number of inhabitants within a household is shrinking.

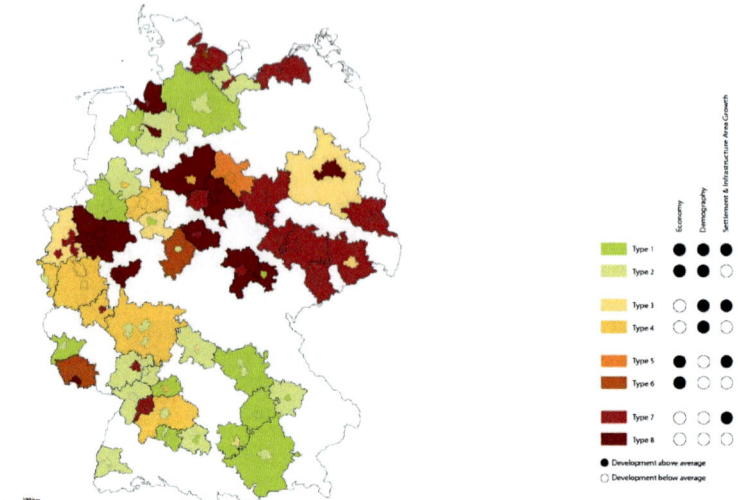

Figure 5: Typology of suburban areas and urban cores within the designated German metropolitan areas (adapted from Hesse et al. 2013: 39)

4a. Stable maturity: After household sizes shrink and begin to decrease in absolute numbers, stabilization begins by the selective settlement of younger inhabitants. A gradual but significant adjustment of the physical structures takes place. Due to the mixture of old and young inhabitants, the average age and density comes close to that of the meso and macro levels.

4b. Decline phase: In contrast to stable maturity, a demographic decline phase may occur when the demography is marked by highly above-average age and a decrease in total population as well as a declining number of households. Physically, vacancy and dilapidation may occur. It is usually seen as the beginning of a downgrading development of a neighborhood (Choldin 1980; Schnur 2010; Zakrzewski 2011).

This is the cannonical view on development phases within the basic life cycle. However, by means of the endogenous influences already mentioned, phases such as these are probably only seldom ideal, and mostly irregular and differentiated from case to case. Irregularity develops as a consequence of the dynamics on the meso and/or macro-levels. Furthermore, this is determined by local strategies for dealing with changed circumstances in order to persist. These strategies may lead to partial or complete change within each of the actual phases (see Fig. 4). In order to understand the change, it is more efficient to look beyond the regular cycle model towards the real development paths of suburban areas.

For the basic analysis, this study uses the National Spatial Survey[20] macro-level data set for the years 1997 to 2009 to indicate types of suburban areas within particular metropolitan contexts as a macro-level distinction. We used:
- Socio-demographic development 1997 - 2009 (population, percentage of seniors (65 and older), migration rate, natural migration rate)
- Economic development 1997 - 2009 (percentage of people entitled to social insurance contributions, percentage of employees in the tertiary sector, unemployment rate)
- Structural development 1996 - 2008 (percentage of built-up land and land used for transportation)

To learn more about trajectories, we then conducted twelve micro-studies. The micro-studies were selected according to their different locations within the suburban area: one on the immediate urban-suburban fringe, one within the suburban commuter zone and one outside of the suburban commuter zone. The four regions were chosen according to differences in their economic, demographic and spatial dynamics, defined according to the generated typology. As a further step in the case study analysis and the typology of adjustment and transition patterns, a search for adequate strategies to steer the development in the context of future policy and planning was conducted. Three selected examples from the twelve case studies, detailed in further qualitative surveys and reinterpreted here, should illustrate the main transition strategies found within different development cycles and trajectory contexts.

Case 1: Adaption within growth phase – a housing site stuck in the build-up phase which adapted using a flexible growth strategy, Borsdorf[21]

The Leipzig metropolitan area is located around 200 kilometers south of the German capital Berlin and has a population of around 700,000 of which about

---

[20] In German: "Laufende Raumbeobachtung", a standardized data survey carried out by the Federal Institute for Research on Building, Urban Affairs and Spatial Development (BBSR).
[21] For more details on case studies and quotes refer to Hesse et al. 2013.

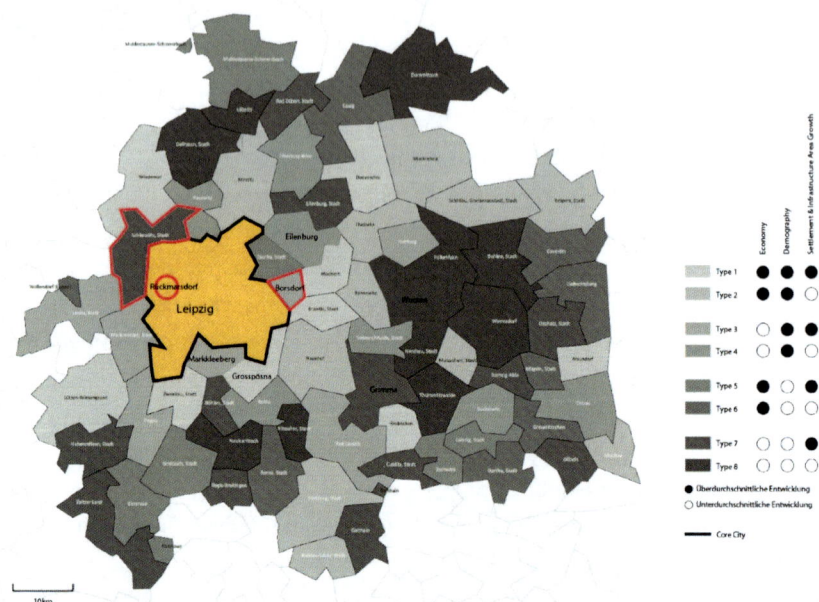

Figure 6: Typology of suburban areas and urban cores in the Leipzig metropolitan area (adapted from Hesse et al. 2013: 73). Marked are three areas of investigation, one of which is the Borsdorf case presented here

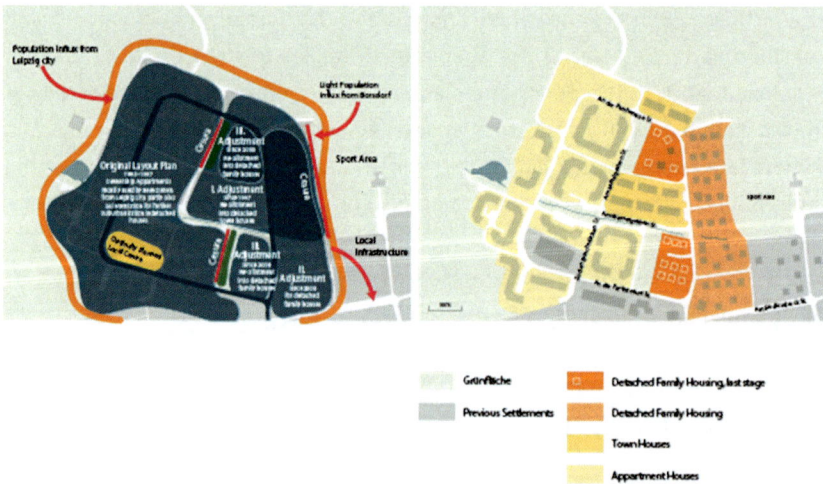

Figure 7: Situational mapping of the life cycle change in Parthenaue, Borsdorf: Adjustment within the build-up/growth phase (adapted from Hesse et al. 2013: 75/77)

530,000 live within the borders of the city of Leipzig. Due to years of neglect of historical buildings in many inner-city neighborhoods and a parallel general lack of housing, the city's outskirts and the neighboring counties experienced a housing and service construction boom after the end of the socialist era and reunification in 1990 (see also Krüger in this volume).

Due to high demand, standardized, detached housing areas as well as dense apartment housing projects mushroomed in the city's outskirts mainly between 1991 and 1994, when the real estate bubble burst (Braun/Komm July 7th, 2012; Planert July 5th, 2012).

One of the products of the post-unification real estate bubble was the Parthenaue settlement (see Fig. 7) planned in a municipality adjacent to Leipzig, the city of Borsdorf with 8,000 inhabitants that is located some twelve kilometres west of the center of Leipzig. Due to a direct train and highway connection to Leipzig, this area has traditionally been a favorable location for suburban development. On a 16-hectar greenfield-site, 1,200 apartments in three-to-four storey buildings were planned, and two thirds of these were built between 1992 and 1994. After the growth bubble burst in 1994, around a third of the area remained unused, though the infrastructure had already been built. The collapse of the housing market, however, did not mean a complete stop to construction. As land prices sank, the original plan was adapted to a new one comprising sixty lots of semi-detached homes. Later, the plan of the remaining lots was changed again to accommodate detached homes with larger plots and a higher-quality environment (Planert July 5th, 2012).

Plans were changed several times between 1997 and 2007 at the cost of the municipality of Borsdorf, which had to act as the main driver of the development after the Munich-based developer group IGB went bankrupt in 1994. The still ongoing process of transition enabled the investors together with the city to continuously sell lots, even though the real estate market was changing dramatically. The changing tool was based on a repeatedly adjusted land development plan in cooperation between the investors, the city and the regional government (ATKIS-DLM 2012; Planert July 5th, 2012).

Summarized in terms of life cycle adaption: As the first growth phase was stopped by a housing crisis in 1994, an adjustment by means of adaption started in order to maintain growth and finish the planned project in an alternative manner. The adjustments were initiated by private investors and approved by the city government by means of a legally binding land development plan. After the bubble burst, adaption was pursued by the local municipality (meso-level), which repeatedly (in the years 1997 and 2000) alternated the legally binding land development plan according to the changing demand by fulfilling this demand and attracting investment. Through the adjustment of land use, a diversified area in terms of both urban morphology and the social status of inhabitants evolved.

The regional ward Leipzig Ost (macro-level), by which binding plans for Borsdorf had to be approved, followed a policy of channeling suburban development into already developed land by forbidding the further designation of residential areas. Approving the alternations of existing plans was seen as a tool to canalize the shrinking and changing demand into existant development areas and thus to consolidate regional sprawl. Such an adaption through macro-level action during the growth phase combined with strong management at the macro-level led to the pursual of growth even under the conditions of a very relaxed suburban housing market. It created the possibility to finish the development and reach a relatively stable maturity phase on the micro-level, especially regarding semi-detached and detached housing. However, forced adjustment is still necessary through the maturity phase. Due to the relaxed housing market, a high turnover rate remained in apartment housing. Those who purchased their apartments during the real estate bubble between 1991 and 1994 are now facing a collapse of real estate value by between 30% and 40%. High mortgages force some owners to sell below the price of purchase, so that ownership often ends in bank repossessions. Seen from the perspective of the households that rent the apartments, these are often used as transitional residences for those who first move into apartment housing in the suburbs before moving into their own detached houses[22] (Planert July 7th, 2012; Sommer August 11th, 2013).

---

[22] It is one of the examples showing that focussing solely on semi-detached or detached family housing issue when talking about residential neighborhoods in maturity conceals the complex view on the issue. Housing remains strongly interrelated not only to the macro and meso levels, but also to different typologies, between which inhabitants choose. Low bank interest rates caused by monetary policy of the central banks in Germany and the EU in reaction of the Lehman-Brother crisis from 2008/2009 e.g. remarkably increased demand also for suburban family houses even under circumstances of stagnation or shrinking, by lowering demand on rental appartments at the same time, and vice versa, in the subsequent years (Vetterlein August 11th, 2014). Thus, demography and morphology should in any case be seen as the exclusive drivers of residential development pattern.

In sum, in this residential area once planned to be developed beween 1991 and 1996 (growth phase), one of the last lots was sold in late 2013, so that the growth phase ended up taking 23 years to be completed. By that time, the settlement had already vastly differentiated itself morphologically, demographically and socially due to different types of ownership and housing. It is therefore very unlikely that the maturation of the neighborhood during its life cycle's "Back loop" will lead to a sudden demographic or other shock: first, every part of the settlement will reach the state of maturity at a different speed. Second, referring to the development to date, it is likely that further adjustments or partial developments not merely of a physical, but rather of a functional or societal nature, will follow.

Case 2: Adaption in maturity phase – stagnating maturity and a consolidation strategy by the local community, Resser Mark

The second case examines a suburban neighborhood in the city of Gelsenkirchen, situated in the Ruhr region, a metropolitan agglomeration of 13 large and 40 smaller cities in the western part of Germany known for its coal mining and industrial heritage. With a loss of a sixth of its inhabitants since 1960, the Ruhr region (macro) had around 5.1 Million inhabitants in 2013. The city of Gelsenkirchen, one of the eight largest cities in the Ruhr region, shrank between 1960 and 2013 from nearly 400,000 inhabitants to less than 260,000. Even though the city is now stagnating, a further decline of eight percent is expected between 2006 and 2025. The regional population prognosis for the Ruhr region is also negative. Despite these macro and meso-level figures, there is a spatial evidence of selective decline and shrinkage in particular urban and suburban areas. Some areas retain social stability and low vacancy rates even though they stand out from the average in terms of income, inhabitant influx or aging.[23]

The micro-study area of Resser Mark is an older, detached residential suburb on the urban-suburban fringe, with 3,800 inhabitants. Even though several areas are marked by homogenous family houses extending over a significant portion of the case study area, the neighborhood also includes different types of apartment, semi-detached and detached housing of different ages. Spatially it

---

[23] Statistical data used in this case have been kindly provided by the Statistical Office of Gelsenkirchen. Survey data including the age of built structures have been kindly provided by the courtesy of Alfred Richau from the Gelsenkirchen Planning Department.

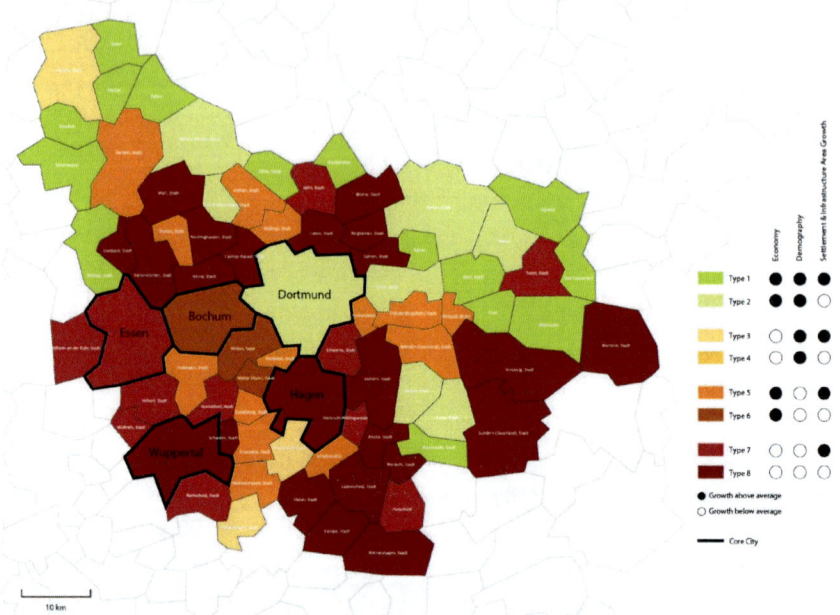

Figure 8: Typology of suburban areas and urban cores in the Ruhr metropolitan area (adapted from Hesse et al. 2013: 86)

reveals a pattern of the onion-like addition of new layers, where suburban structures as well as small developments have been continuously added to the edges of the existing structure. The place is known for its active community, concentrated around a small local center and adjacent middle class family houses. The neighborhood contains a kindergarten, a school and a church as well as youth and senior community centers. A senior residence was established in the 1980s, and 47% of the clients today originate from the local community. Most of the buildings were constructed between 1940 and 1960. The challenge for Resser Mark is demographic change and physical maturity. It displays old buildings with partly outdated housing standards, a declining population density and a growing average age. The area as a whole accounts for one statistical district, which includes different types of housing and has never been completely homogenous. But still most of the inhabitants worked in the coal mines in the surrounding areas. Since the 1960s, due to mine closures and the

Challenge of Maturation – Life Cycles and Patterns of Change in Suburban Settlement Space 61

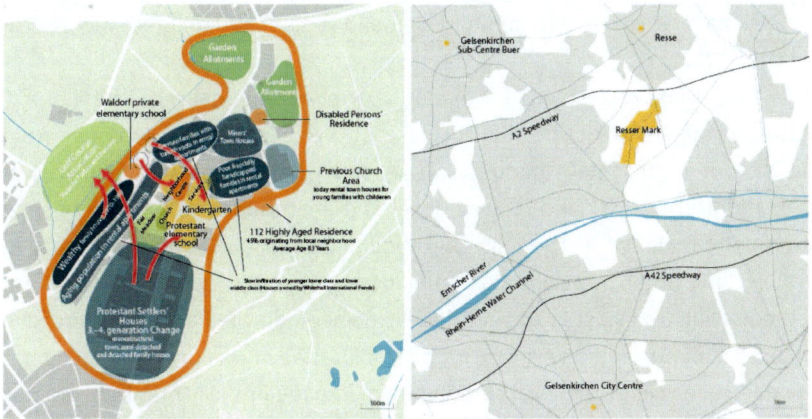

Figure 9: Situational mapping of the life cycle change in Resser Mark, Gelsenkirchen, within the build-up phase (adapted from SUR 2013: 82/85)

negative demographic trends in the region, social differences have risen. Inhabitants of the apartments have changed from miners to other groups, including low-income residents, but also middle-class ethnic groups. As the strong local Christian communities had to give up one of their two churches, the Catholic and Protestant community share one building. The site of the other church was redeveloped into 34 additional semi-detached housing units for rent in 2006, which have been rented to young families with at least three children. These houses were the first new development in the area in 25 years. The church did not sell, but rather lent the units in order to create a sustainable income opportunity to finance its own social activities within the neighborhood. The apartments generated a local demand for the community's educational infrastructure and stabilized the local kindergarten and school.

Therefore, the whole area has attracted additional young families. On the micro-level, the attractivity of the service infrastructure also managed to stabilize real estate values despite a shrinking meso and macro context. The local church community hopes that some of the families that rent houses will later buy older houses in the quarter when seeking new real estate. Furthermore, the possibility for senior citizens to move into a serviced senior residence within the area and remain in the community and among friends and family offers the possibility to motivate the individual decision-makers to sell or at least to lease housing while remaining in the community (Feldmann June 6th, 2014; Biermann February 14th, 2012).

The Resser Mark case stands for one of a variety of internal regeneration processes in stagnating mature suburban areas. The following can be drawn from the case: it represents a maturity phase of an aging suburb combined with stagnation on the city and regional level and a city-supported, local Christian community initiative as the main stakeholder and leader of local advocacy in strategic investments to consolidate the local community. Additionally, the limited possibility to invest in the individually owned detached housing stock gave the local community a crucial role in the stabilization of the local environment.

The adjusting role of the local community marks the intrinsic maturing process of the suburbia parallel to decline and shrinkage. In the case of Resser Mark, these can easily be traced by quantitative data analyses on macro-, meso- and micro-levels. As growth underlies the basics of the lifecycle theory, this kind of transition process aims at system consolidation rather than at its adaption or transformation. What is transforming, however, is the local community and its action in the neighborhood; it is becoming more strongly financed by means of the community. This is a rather subtle strategy, which does not primarily target any structural adaption or transformation of the local regime, as growth and adaption would. What seems important here is that physical decline and aging as such, representing the visible proof of the cyclic period, is not the leading trigger for change. Consolidation rather gives evidence of stabilizing continuity within the mature phase for the existing operative system itself represented by the local community. This kind of "consolidation" is a gateway to something as ideal as "stable maturity". It places the normative idea of sustainable development into a changing context, not only emphasizing issues such as vulnerability and adaptation, but relating problems and strategies to different phases within the spatial development trajectory.

Case 3: Adaption in transition phase (decline): stopped adaption of an "overmatured" suburban development, Rückmarsdorf

The third example, again from the Leipzig metropolitan area, once again shows the importance of the interrelation between the macro-, meso-, and micro-layers of action. In this case a local community just outside the boundaries of

Leipzig that had acted relatively freely until it was amalgamated, has since been decisively influenced by strategic targets on the macro-level.

After German reunification, as the compact urban area was still busy with ownership restitutions and dealing with the highly dilapidated housing after the breakdown of the communist system, the city outskirts became a playground for greenfield development.[24] The collapse of the socialist regime left a planning vacuum, which enabled an un-conceptional but relatively free choice of development space to accommodate the demand for housing and retail - both scarce goods during the socialist era. According to the financial influx from the western part of Germany within the now reunified state, eastern Germany disposed with a sufficient amount of resources to immediately answer such demands - a situation far different to other post-communist regions (Schwarzlose June 5th, 2012).

On the highway B181 to the freeway A9 in the direction of Halle (pop.: 180,000), the second largest city in the metropolitan region, the new retail and housing strip profited from its strategically convenient position. In Eastern Germany the boom in residential and retail functions outside the city cores begun immediately after the state unification in 1990. A 40,000 square-meter shopping center was established, with adjacent shopping units, car dealerships, a gas station and a hotel. Next to these, housing in apartment buildings and detached family housing was developed. In 2002, the autonomous village of Rückmarsdorf was amalgamated with the city of Leipzig, thus underlying a completely new meso and macro-level residential development policy with the strategic target of a compact city and the enforcement of reurbanization (Freydank November 6th, 2012).

---

[24] The unification of the East and West Germany in 1990 ended more than forty years of two German states and re-established a unified German federal state for the first time after WWII. The change was a consequence of the fall of the so-called Iron Curtain, which divided Europe into the influence areas of the socialist-based eastern and the capitalist western part. The border between the two blocks also divided Germany into western and eastern parts. By the time of the re-unification, the economic system of East Germany was significantly weaker than that of West Germany. This situation led to massive investment of West German capital into the former East Germany. A significant part of the accumulated needs in East Germany was the lack of housing and the accordantly urgent demand for more and better dwellings. Being faster in planning and realization, greenfield developments outpaced the renovation of housing stock within integrated urban areas, which led to rapid sprawl around East German cities during the 1990s.

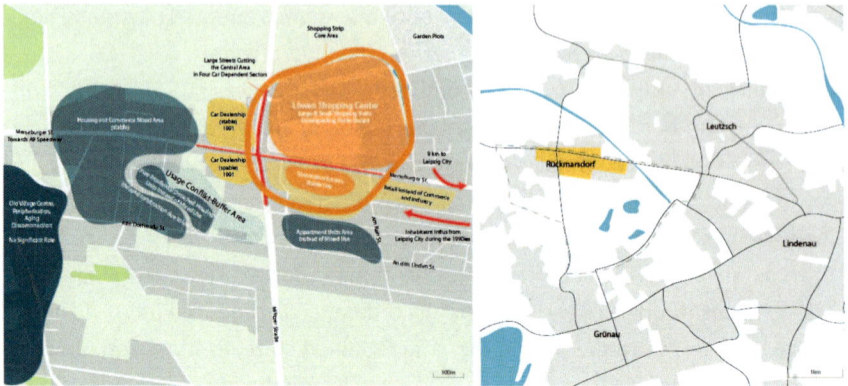

Figure 10: Situational mapping of the life cycle change in Rückmarsdorf, Leipzig, within the maturation phase (adapted from SUR 2013: 87/89)

By that time, the retail area was already more than ten years old, and found itself in a late mature phase, while the housing built during the boom of the 1990s had just entered the maturity phase. Until lately, significant areas zoned for residential use had for long not been developed and thus still remained in a prolonged growth phase.[25] Within the retail areas, the competition among peripheral shopping centers grew steadily. A number of retail areas just outside Leipzig city limits have been established, some of them being further enlarged during the last years, seeking competitive advantage in scale. Furthermore, the attractivity of Leipzig's city center as an urban retail and service area was improved significantly by means of the city's strong "compact city" policy[26]. In order to pursue this policy, the City of Leipzig managed to incorporate some of the adjacent communes by a state law issued in 2000. Since then, the city has blocked any endeavors by the Rückmarsdorf retail actors to adjust both the existing retail buildings and the assortment of goods sold in them through a number of planning measures. These included creating a new retail masterplan in favor of an integrated inner-city area, a new legally binding land development plan[27] that fixed the status quo and prevented the site from further

---

[25] Cf. footnote nr. 24.
[26] The "compact city" policy of the City of Leipzig may be seen as a reaction to the strong sprawl development during the 1990s, a declining population and the consequently growing amount of dilapidated buildings within the inner city (SSDI 2010; Braun/Komm July 6th, 2012).
[27] Bebauungsplan

(re)development. Additionally, the city cancelled a previous plan to improve the car-oriented tangential connection between the city center and Rückmarsdorf in order to motivate city inhabitants to use inner-city shopping venues (Braun/Komm July 6th, 2012; Freydank November 6th, 2012).

In terms of life cycle adaption, the transition has been stopped at the end of the maturity phase by higher-level stakeholders. The local development by the incorporation of the Rückmarsdorf village into the City of Leipzig has been subordinated under the path-dependent development strategy of the city. For the retail and service strip in Rückmarsdorf, this means that before continuous adjustment to changing demand and competition in size, retail and the mixture of service or architecture could have been started, it was stopped by the conservation of the status quo by the City of Leipzig. These regulations further caused a kind of "precarious maturity", similar to what Walker et al. (2006: 3) define as "very resilient but undesirable regimes", in this case added externaly in order to initiate an intentional decline. In such cases, the owners who have been quite isolated in their endeavors no longer see any prospects for the location and mostly decide to refrain from investment. As a consequence, the site loses its value. Currently, particular buildings together with the lots are changing owners quickly, becoming "poor dogs" of stock market real estate packages (Braun/Komm July 6th, 2012).

5. General Findings

The three case studies show a variety of situations and development paths for settlements within suburban space. They prove that suburban areas are significantly characterized not only by differing socio-demographic, economic and structural conditions, but also by individually steered potentials and challenges. The life cycles in the case studies illustrated specific development paths. These on one hand were caused by different sudden exogenous disruptions, such as the consequences of the unification of the German state, the housing real estate crisis, or sudden changes in strategic policies. On the other hand, slow changes such as demographic aging, social differentiation or long planning lasting strategies have also been accomodated by the adjustment strategies of local stakeholders and their partners[28]. The case studies revealed highly differentiated micro-level plans of action by politics, planning institutions and private companies or other stakeholders in order to actively adjust the development path. With the exception of the Rückmarsdorf case, stakeholders acted in a rather panarchic than a hierarchic manner. The adjustments lie within the range of the particular development path dependency, but not necessarily within a canonical life cycle represented by the basic life cycle model of growth, maturity and decline. These phases proved to be temporarily flexible and differentiated. In Borsdorf, the layout plan has been adjusted several times to fit to the changing demand of the housing market. This has been the only possibility to generate enough investment activity at the site within a stagnating real estate market and thus to accomplish the growth phase on all lots available at the site of development. In Resser Mark, the local church took strategic measures to counteract the aging of the community and to create income opportunities for further social work on site by providing rental housing to families. On the other hand, the Rückmarsdorf case shows that the external strategy of an "intentional decline" at higher levels may intentionally narrow resilience at the micro-level by institutionally limiting the scope of local stakeholder action in preventing legal frames of external collaboration and thus keeping stakeholders from mobilizing external resources to invest in necessary physical and functional adjustments. In summary, the cases showed that:

1. Adjustment strategies do not only occur during the late maturity or release phase. Specific strategies of adaption are pursued within the growth phase as well as the maturity and decline phases. System collapse is only probable when the options within the development path are (being) limited and the adaption potential within the system is too low or not used. Such weakness means a lack of resiliency tools, which account for a lack of ability to respond to a challenge, especially when local stakeholders are not able to fulfill the conditions for a resilient development path defined by Swanstrom et al. (2009: 8).
2. Adaption is a response of the social-ecological system to exogenous and endogenous changes. Both slow and fast changes can be responded to. The de-

---

[28] These included communes and regional administration, but also financial investors, such as banks that credited the investments. With the exception of the Rückmarsdorf case, they all acted in a rather panarchic then a hierarchic manner.

velopment paths are created by external and internal influences. In summary, parallel to the basic ideal life cycles of growth, maturity and decline, three conceptual models for adaption strategies on the micro-level in which the path dependent development occurs could be defined: growth, consolidation and adaption. The formation process of action as well as the creation and use of underlying policies differed from case to case within the three observed levels. At the same time, the adaption strategies remain multileveled and therefore linked between the local area, the municipality or the region, interacting between policies and socio-economic frameworks at each level.

Adjustment strategies further do not necessarily serve to stabilize the actual phase, but to move from an inacceptable situation to a state more convenient to the system and its stakeholders. A full cycle (including decline) occurs when resilient adaption is not possible. However, within the twelve case studies conducted, only the Rückmarsdorf case developed along the whole basic lifecycle.

6. Conclusion

What seems to be conceptionally meaningful for understanding suburban micro-areas - functional areas, quarters or neighborhoods - and their change and maturation development in time is therefore not necessarily the "meta-model" of the urbanization or the life cycle concept as such, but the focus on aberrations from this model. The temporal and functional diversification of suburban areas within their developmental paths is the most typical effect of such aberrations. To develop in time, not only one but several individual ways of adaption along the individual development path at the micro-level may apply. They are marked by the ability of a resilient respond to challenges, guided by internal organizational resetting, collaboration outside the micro-areas on different levels in a panarchic network of stakeholders, and to generate resources from outside (cf. Swanstrom et al. 2009: 8). This not only explains why shock changes are so rare. These most likely occur only when there are no other options, such as in fatal market failures due to extraordinary change in the demography and economy of a place. More often, decline is a consequence of a long-lasting lack of the ability or possibility to build a stakeholder structure that would control the adjustment process. Therefore, rather than just to concentrate on the quantitative indicators of maturity, also in suburbia endogenous potentials for stakeholder constellations should stand at the forefront of conceptual strategic interest when considering change processes. Undoubtedly, diversification as a resilience strategy of a locally based stakeholder panarchic systems across the macro, meso and micro-levels is a sign of an intrinsic potential for resilience and vitality in suburban areas.

References

ATKIS_DLM (2013), *Flächennutzungsplan und Bodenrichtwertkarte Borsdorf,* http://www.borsdorf.eu/bodenrichtwerte.html (Accessed November 17, 2013).

Aring, Jürgen (2012), "Einfamilienhäuser der 1950er bis 1970er Jahre in Westdeutschland: Eine neue Herausforderung für die Stadtentwicklung", in: Eichenlaub, Alexander/ Pristl, Thomas (eds.), *Umbau Mit Bestand,* Berlin: Reimer-Verlag, 68-85.

Band, Fridolin S./ Jax, Kurt (2007), "Focusing the meaning(s) of resilience: Resilience as a descriptive concept and a boundary object", *Ecology and Society,* 12, 1, 23.

Becker, Udo/ Beckmann, Klaus J./ Würdemann, Gerd/ Köller, Mareike/ Wegener, Michael (2011), "Postfossile Mobilität und Raumentwicklung 89 der Akademie für Raumforschung und Landesplanung (ARL)", *ARL Positionspapier.* Hannover: ARL, 22.

Beilein, Andreas (2013), "Process of Transition on single owned Family Houses as Framework for Local Interventions - case of the Ruhr Region", in: Blotevogel, Hans H./ Frank, Susanne/ Holz-Rau, Christian/ Scheiner, Joachim/ Schuster, Nina (eds.), *Mobilitäten und Immobilitäten. Menschen - Ideen - Dinge - Kulturen - Kapital, Dortmunder Beiträge zur Raumplanung,* Dortmund, Frankfurt/M.: Springer, 295-309.

Bernt, Matthias/ Liebmann, Heike (2013), *Peripherisierung, Stigmatisierung, Abhängigkeit? Deutsche Mittelstädte im Umgang mit Peripherisierungsprozessen,* Berlin: Springer, 225.

Bizer, Kilian/ Dappen, Claudia/ Deffner, Jutta/ Heilmann, Sven/ Knieling, Jörg/ Stieß, Immanuel (2008), "Nutzungszyklus von Wohnquartieren in Stadtregionanen. Modellentwicklung", *Neopolis working papers,* No.3, Hamburg.

Bourne, Larry (1996), "Reinventing the suburbs: Old myths and new realities", *Progress in Planning,* 46, 163-184.

Brake, Klaus (2012), "Reurbanisierung - Interdependenzen zum Strukturwandel", in: Brake, Klaus/ Herfert, Günter (eds.), *Reurbanisierung: Materialität Und Diskurs in Deutschland.* Wiesbaden: VS Verlag für Sozialwissenschaften, 22-33.

Brake, Klaus/ Herfert, Günter (2012), *Reurbanisierung: Materialität und Diskurs in Deutschland*, Wiesbaden: VS Verlag für Sozialwissenschaften, 422.

Champion, Tonny (2001), "Urbanization, Suburbanization, Counterurbanization and Reurbanization", in: Paddison, Ronan (ed.): *Handbook of Urban Studies*, London, Thousand Oaks, New Dehli: Sage Publications, 143-161.

Cheshire, Paul (1995), "A New Phase of Urban Development in Western Europe? The Evidence for the 1980s", *Urban Studies*, 32, 7 , 1045-1063.

Cheshire, Paul/ Hay, Dennis (1989), *Urban Problems in Western Europe: An Economic Analysis*, London: Unwil Hyman, 291.

Choldin, Harvey M./ Hanson, Claudine/ Bohrer, Robert (1980), "Suburban Status Instability", *American Sociological Review*, 45, 972–983.

De Temple, N. (2005), *Einfamilienhaussiedlung im Wandel: Eine Untersuchung zum Generationswechsel vor dem Hintergrund des soziodemographischen Wandels am Beispiel der Stadt Dortmund*, Diplomarbeit, Berlin: TU Berlin, 196.

Dransfeld, Egbert/ Pfeiffer, Petra/ Platzek, Carola (2010), *Boden 2030. Anforderungen an die kommunale Bodenpolitik und den Umgang mit Einfamilienhausgebieten der 1950er, 1960er und 1970er Jahre*, Dortmund: Forum Baulandmanagement, 64.

Dunham-Jones, Ellen/ Williamson, June (2011), *Retrofitting Suburbia. Urban Design Solutions for Redesigning Suburbs*, NJ: Wiley, Hoboken, 304.

Fielding, Anthony (1982),"Counterurbanisation in Western Europe", *Progress in Planning*, 17, 1-52.

Fishman, Robert (1987), *Bourgeois Utopias: The Rise and Fall of Suburbia*, New York: Basic Books, 272.

Garreau, Joel (1991), *Edge City: Life on the New Frontier*, New York: Doubleday, 548.

Geyer, Hermanus S./ Kontuly, Thomas (1993), "A Theoretical Foundation for the Concept of Differential Urbanization", *International Regional Science Review*, 12, 157-177.

Goldberger, Paul (1987), "When suburban sprawl meets upward mobility", *New York Times*, 14.

Hall, Peter (2001), "Global city-regions in the twenty-first century", in: Allen J. Scott (ed.), *Global City-Regions. Trends, Theory, Policy*, Oxford: Oxford University Press, 59-77.

Häußermann, Hartmut (2007), "Suburbia im Umbruch", *archithese* 37, 3, 28-31.

Hayden, Dolores (2004), *Building Suburbia: Green Fields and Urban Growth*, New York: Vintage Books, 336.

Hesse, Markus (2012), "Suburbaner Raum - Annäherung an Gegenstand", in: *Suburbane Räume Als Kulturlandschaften*, Hannover: ARL Schriften, 13-24.

— (2014), "Just 'Dump and Borin', or 'Over'? Lifecycle-Trajectories, the Credit Crunch and the Challenge of Suburban Regeneration in the U.S.", in: O'Donoghue, Daniel P. (ed.), *Urban Transformations: Centres, Peripheries and Systems*, London: Routledge, 151-160.

Hesse, Markus/ Hoffschröer, Holger/ Mecklenbrauck, Ilka/ Polívka, Jan/ Reicher, Christa/ Tries, Daniel (2013), *Suburbaner Raum im Lebenszyklus*, Bonn: BBSR, 156.

Herfert, Günter/ Osterhage, Frank (2012), "Wohnen in der Stadt: Gibt es eine Trendwende zur Reurbanisierung? Ein quantitativ-analytischer Ansatz", in: Brake, Klaus/ Herfert, Günter (eds.), *Reurbanisierung. Materialität und Diskurs in Deutschland*. Wiesbaden: Springer VS, 86-112.

Holling, Clark S. (1986), "Resilience of Ecosystems; Local Surprise and Global Change", in: Clark, W. C./ Munn, R. E. (eds.), *Sustainable Development of the Biosphere*, Cambridge: Cambridge University Press, 292-317.

Jacobs, Jane (1961), *The Death and Life of Great American Cities*, New York: Random Publishing Group.

Jessen, Johann/ Siedentop, Stefan (2010), "Reurbanisierung zwischen Wunsch und Wirklichkeit", *disP*, 180/1, 16-23.

Kadono, Yukihiro (2010), "Kougai Juutakuchi no Hensen to Yukue" (Development and Future of Suburban Residential Areas), in: Akira Hirohara/ Yukihiro Kadono/ Kouzou Narita/ Teruo Takada (eds.), *Toshin, Machinaka, Kougai no Kyousei. Keihanshin Daitoshiken no Shourai (City Centre, Inner City and Suburbia Symbiosis - Future of the Kansai Metropolitan Area)*, Kyoto: Kouyou Shobou, 107-128.

Keil, Roger/ Young, Douglas (2009), "Fringe Explosions. Risk and Vulnerability in Canada's New inbetween Urban Landscape", *The Canadian Geographer*, 53, 4, 488-499.

Keppler, Steven (1997), "Industry Life Cycles", *Industrial and Corporate Change*, 6, 1, 145-181.

Klaasen, Leo H./ Seimeni, Gerald (1981), *Theoretical Issues in Urban Dynamics*, Gover: Aldershot, 8-28.

Knieling, Jörg, (2009), "Metropolregionen. Innovation, Wettbewerb und Handlungsfähigkeit, Metropolregionen und Raumentwicklung", *ARL*, 231, Hannover: ARL, 373.

Lang, Robert (2003), *Edgeless cities exploring the elusive metropolis*, Washington, D.C: Brookings Institution Press.

Lang, Robert E./ LeFurgy, Jeniffer B. (2007), *Boomburbs: the rise of America's accidental cities*, Washington D.C.: Brookings Institution Press, 212.

Li, Wei (1998), "Anatomy of a New Ethnic Settlement: The Chinese Ethnoburb in Los Angeles", *Urban Studies*, 482/35, 3.

Martin, Ron (2010), "Roepke Lecture in Economic Geography - Rethinking Regional Path Dependence: Beyond Lock-in to Evolution, Economic Geography", *Clark University, University of Illinois*, 86, 1, 1-27.

— (2012), "(Re)Placing Path Dependence: A Response to the Debate: Debates and Developments", *International Journal of Urban and Regional Research*, 36, 179-192.

Martin, Ron; Sunley, Peter (2010), "The Place of Path Dependence in an Evolutionary Perspective on the Economic Landscape", in: Boschma, Ron/ Martin, Ron (eds.), *Handbook of Evolutionary Economic Geography*, Chichester: Edward Elgar.

McManus, Richard/ Ethington, Philip J. (2007), "Suburbs in Transition: New Approaches to Suburban History", *Urban History*, 34, 2, 317-337.

Nierhoff, Sara (2008), "Entwicklungsperspektiven von alternden Einfamilienhausquartieren", in: *Quartiersforschung Zwischen Theorie Und Praxis*, Wiesbaden: VS Research.

Ourednicek, Martin (2004), "New Suburban Development in the Post-Socialist City: The Case of Prague", *Charles University*, Dept. of Social Geography, unprinted paper, Praha.

Phelps, Nicholas A./ Wood, Andrew M./ Valler, David C. (2010), "A Postsuburban World? An Outline of a Research Agenda", *Environment and Planning*, 42, 366-383.

Polívka, Jan (2013), "Suburban Life Cycles - Approching the Spatio-Temporal Varieties of Suburbia, Global Suburbanisms: Governance, Land and Infrastructure in the 21st Century. A Suburban Revolution?", Paper Presentation: Hesse, Markus/ Polívka, Jan, Toronto: The City Institute at York University, September 26, 2013.

Scott, Alister J. (2013), "Disintegrated development at the rural-urban fringe: Re-connecting spatial planning theory and practice", *Progress in Planning*, 83, 1-52.

Schnur, Olaf (2014), "Quartiersforschung im Überblick: Konzepte, Definitionen und aktuelle Perspektiven", in: Schnur, Olaf (ed.), *Quartiersforschung*, Wiesbaden: VS Verlag für Sozialwissenschaften, 21-56.

Schnur, Olaf/ Drilling, Matthias (2011), "Quartiere im demographischen Umbruch", in: Schnur, Olaf/ Drilling, Matthias (eds.), *Quartiere im demografischen Umbruch*, Wiesbaden: Springer VS, 11-26.

Siedentop, Stefan (2008), "Die Rückkehr der Städte? Zur Plausibilität der Reurbanisierungshypothese", *Informationen zur Raumentwicklung*, 3/4, 193-210.

Sieverts, Thomas (1997), *Zwischenstadt. Zwischen Ort und Welt, Raum und Zeit, Stadt und Land*, Braunschweig: Birkhäuser, 191.

— (2012), "Resilienz - Zur Neuorientierung des Planens und Bauens", *disP - The Planning Review*, 48, 83-88.

Siebel, Walter (2005), "Suburbanisierung", in: ARL (ed.): *Handwörterbuch Der Raumordnung*, Hannover: ARL, 1135-1140.

Simmonds, David/ Waddel, Paul/ Wegener, Michael (2013), "Equilibrium versus Dynamics in Urban Modelling", *Environment and Planning B: Planning and Design*, 40/6, 1051-1070.

Soja, Edward (2000), *Postmetropolis: Critical Studies of Cities and Regions*, Oxford: I. Blackwell Publishers, 440.

SSDI (2010), *Stadtentwicklungsstrategie Sachsen 2020*, Sächsisches Staatsministerium des Innern.

Swanstrom, Todd/ Chapple, Karen/ Immergluck, Dan (2009), "Regional Resilience in the Face of Foreclosures: Evidence from Six Metropolitan Areas", *Building Resilient Regions*, IGS, Berkeley: University of California, 66.

Teaford, Jon C. (1997), *Post-Suburbia. Government and Politics in the Edge Cities*, Baltimore: John Hopkins University Press, 249.

Tisdale, Howard (1942), "The Process of Urbanisation", *Social Forces*, 20, 311-316.

van den Berg, Leo/ Drewett, Roy/ Klaasen, Leo H./ Rossi, Angelo/ Vijveberg, Cornelis (1982), *Urban Europe: A Study of Growth and Decline*, Oxford: Pergamon Press, 162.

Vaughan, Laura/ Griffiths, Sam/ Haklay, Mordechai/ Jones, Emma C. (2009), "Do the Suburbs exist? Discovering complexity and specificity in suburban built form", *Transactions Journal Compilation*, 475-488.

Walker, Brian H./ Gunderson, Lance/ Folke, Carl/ Carpenter, Steve/ Kinzig, Ann/ Schultz, Liesen (2006), "A Handful of Heuristics and some Propositions for Understanding Resilience in Social-ecological Systems", *Ecology and Society*, 11, 1, 13.

Zimmer, Basil (1975), "The Urban Centrifugal Drift", in: Amos Hawley/ Rock, Vincent P. (eds.), *Metropolitan American Contemporary Perspective*, New York: Wiley, 23-91.

Interviews:

Biermann, E.L. (2012), Interview: *Development of the Resser Mark and projects of the Protestant Church on site. Protestant Church in the ecumenic church of St. Ida*, February 14, 2012, Resser Mark.

Beilein, A. (2013), Interview: *Mature Residential Suburbia in Lifecycles*, October 09, 2013, SSR Dortmund.

Braun, K./ Komm, S. (2012), Interview: *Urban planning strategies in the Leipzig metropolitan area*, July 06, 2012, City Planning Dept. Leipzig.

Dransfeld, E. (2014), Interview: *Market shocks and absorbtions in mature suburban family housing areas*, August 25, 2014, IfB Dortmund.

Feldmann, J. (2014), Interview: *Development of the Resser Mark statistical area*, June 12, 2014, Urban Planning Office Gelsenkirchen.

Freydank, P. (2012), Interview: *Local chief reprsentative Leipzig – Rückmarsdorf*, November 06, 2012, Leipzig Rückmarsdorf.

Planert, M. (2012), Interview: *Development of Borsdorf Parthenaue project*, May 07, 2012, Borsdorf.

Sommer, G. (2014), Interview: *Strategic development of the Landkreis Leipzig under the circumstances of maturity and demographic change*, August 11, 2014, Amt für Kreisentwicklung, Borna.

Schwarzlose, K. (2012), Telephone interview: *Urban planning strategies in the Leipzig metropolitan area*, June 05, 2012, City Planning Dept. Leipzig.

Vetterlein, J. (2014), Interview: *Development of Grimma Süd Area*, August 11, 2014, Grimmaer Bau- und Wohnungsgesellschaft mbH, Grimma.

Designing suburban infrastructure: The A 40/ B1 Bochum

Stefanie Bremer

1. An essential but unloved task

In Germany it still needs to be pushed that the design of motorways, public places and technical infrastructure are seen as a task of urban planning. Despite the fact that Germany is a land of motorways with one of the most elaborated transport networks in the world, there are still some reasons to be pointed out why Germany's design scene didn't cope with topics such as transportation and other infrastructures from 1945 onwards (BMVBS 2011: 6-10; Zellner 2002). Over the past years a first discourse was initiated (Hauck et al. 2011). Besides transportation infrastructure (motorways, traffic junctions), the topic of energy infrastructure has come into focus.

Despite these approaches, which often call for what is already common in other European countries, it should be noted that planning models that refer to the European City and transport policy objectives, like sustainability, make a stringent thematic approach without reservations difficult.

Introduced by the Darmstadt urban planning professor Thomas Sieverts 20 years ago, the debate on suburban areas and urban sprawl (Sieverts 1997) still hasn't reached the discourse of urban planners. It seems hard to explain suburban areas without using the codes of the European city. Therefore, everything different is seen as a fault, break or intervention in the aesthetic code of the old city. However, can we regard industrial estates and buildings, wide streets, motorways, solar parks and airports really per se as "non-places" (Augé 1992)? How much longer can we afford to swim against the tide of development and the reality of construction practice, and simply classify the habitat of a large population as a substandard building culture, without having any concepts in return? It seems that suburbia, as figured by Harald Bodenschatz (2004) in an exploratory work for the Bundesamt für Bauwesen und Raumordnung (Federal Office for Building and Regional Planning) has now "arrived, although with troubles and setbacks" in Germany (BBR 2004: 56) and that it urgently needs to be accepted as an issue for planners and architects.

Also, the reality of transportation planning and debates which are of major importance for the development of suburban spaces suggest a different future: A glance into the Federal Plan for Transportation Infrastructure (Bundesverkehrswegeplan) shows the need to widen existing routes. Current debates in mobility research show that the desire to abandon the car-friendly city is not realistic. Instead, the European Mobility Research makes rather clear that roads are part of new digital techniques, thereby providing efficient mobility. Roads and motorways form the "hardware" of mobility. They link and combine with intelligent vehicles, thus ensuring that the traffic of the future can be optimized (see EU research program "future roads"). Also, it can hardly be expected that all roads will be re-urbanized. These strategies will remain exceptions. Instead, one needs to accept and realize that spacious streets and highways with heavy traffic running through densely built areas will be persistent. These roads have to be coped with from different perspectives. Urban design could and should be one way to make life bearable with and close by to these major traffic axes. Even small interventions can improve people's everyday life. Looking even further ahead, one must realize that major traffic corridors also conceal important and challenging tasks. This especially applies to traffic corridors in dispersed settlement structures with low density. Streets there can function as conjunctions within heterogeneous and disconnected suburban spaces – an idea that the American architect Frank Lloyd Wright envisioned in the 1920ies (Bremer 2008). Today, landscape theorists such as J.B. Jackson in their concepts of "Landscape" and "Landscape Urbanism" understand motorways as important public places of modern society and hence demand them to be designed as such:

> "The infrastructure of a country equals its DNA. It can tell you more about one nation's cultural identity than any opera festival. A well-built street, a neat bridge, a spacious railway station have a huge effect on most of the people." (Sauerbruch cited in: BSVI 2011)

In the German Ruhr Area a few examples can be found of how the design of major suburban traffic arterias could enhance building culture within the "Zwischenstadt".

Figure 1: Without manual: This is how the A40/ B1 would look after construction works without the design manual (orange edge 2010)

Figure 2: With manual: This is how the motorway is going to look like (orange edge 2010)

1.1 A40/ B1 as an example

Crossing through the heart of the Ruhr area the A40/ B1 is an up to six-lane motorway. The line partly follows an old trade route, the so-called "Hellweg". Because of its historical background and its local value this road plays an important role in people's perception and regional identity. The A40/ B1 is often described as the lifeline of that particular region and is also topic of many books, films, poems and songs. In 2010, when the city of Essen was "European Capital of Culture", the motorway gained further attention as the core of a project called "Stillleben A40". For this purpose the traffic was blocked for an entire day and the longest public festival was held on a passage of 80 kilometers.

From a structural perspective, the transformation of the formerly heavily industrialized area is visible along the motorway. Technology parks, shopping centres and university campuses have emerged alongside the 100 kilometers passage.

Given the fact that for the next few years along the entire route a variety of expansion and renovation measures are planned, the neighbouring cities (Moers, Duisburg, Mülheim an der Ruhr, Essen, Bochum, Dortmund, Holzwickede and Unna) developed a design manual in close cooperation with Strassen.NRW and the Ministry of Construction and Transportation of the state of North Rhine-Westphalia.

The design manual consists of seven basic rules. In these rules, urban and traffic planning as well as economic aspects of the development of the route are integrated. As a result, the manual facilitates the transport planning practice. These basic rules also ensure that future renovations, upgrading and maintenance work will be linked with design aspects. The aim is to upgrade the road, make it more comfortable to use but also to improve its aesthetic appearance. Therefore all parties have agreed on using homogenous trees along the entire road between Moers and Unna. The tree species of choice turned out to be the Cypress Oak - on the one hand a perfectly resistant species, on the other hand rather slender in growth which allows it to exist in narrow environments close to the A40. For future noise barriers green has been set as primary colour. Its light colour is contrasting with the dark green oak leaves so that every single tree appears visible. At the same time the noise barriers are colourfully

decorated to make reference to specific urban spaces or simply to provide alternation within the monotony of the lengthy walls built up along the road. Connection points between motorway and urban spaces are highlighted in red.

Principally all noise barriers will be planted on the resident's side of the wall. On the road side, all residential areas will be shielded by groves. To display certain urban landmarks, transparent segments will be installed. Further, windows shall grant a view of the surroundings. As a special design feature short texts on selected bridges tell of the peculiarities of the cities. Under the slogan "I'm one of us" it is described what connects people to their region: the greenery, football, or the central geographical position in the middle of Europe.

The design manual provides a framework to enable the route to be experienced as a unit. Simultaneously, it generates creative leeway and the chance to react to local peculiarities. With the design manual at hand, councils are able to reintegrate large-scale traffic projects. Public places are being granted further meaning. The traffic space itself takes on a special significance. The road is recaptured as public space, while the design is also used as a traffic psychology tool.

1.2 Barcode A40

Prior to the development of the design manual, a pilot project was initiated by Strassen.NRW on the A40, with the road authority wanting to test what added value can be generated by the account of design issues. Already approved in height, material and location, one segment of the noise barrier was chosen to be artistically upgraded. No additional funding was involved, only the common budget at hand. The task of generating a design concept for the place was given to the architectural office Orange Edge. Orange Edge suggested to study and develop the design concept in a participatory process. First of all it was to be asked whether the residents actually wanted their noise barrier to be embellished or were indifferent about the visual appearance of such a profane architecture.

An interactive website was launched for the project, to enable anyone to design a personal pattern for a segment of about eight meters in length (www.barcode-a40.de). Basis of the site was the graphic of a white noise barrier, divided into twelve patches (strips). Each individual strip could be coloured directly on the Internet with a digital paintbrush. Before submitting his or her pattern, each participant was asked to explain his contribution in a short text.

The striped shape resulted from the construction. Noise barriers are constructed out of facing formwork made of aluminium, either applied vertically or horizontally. Each facing formwork is between 50 and up to 60 centimeters wide. Hence a cost-neutral way of colouring the wall differently every 50 centimeters was found. Due to the wall's construction, the element of altering colours becomes a quite natural design approach. It was then decided to make use of the wall's inner play of colours for the blueprint.

Around 160 individual contributions were needed to fill the space on the real barrier with the personal patterns submitted. The website was launched on a Friday. Supported by local media from the beginning, many submissions were sent in the first weekend. Within two month a total of 1290 contributions were submitted. This showed that the offer of participation was met with great interest. The evaluation of the colour pattern found that 80 percent of online participants linked their colour pattern directly to a personal story, so the colours and possible stripe patterns represented a specific topic. The majority of stories deal with characteristics of the Ruhr area or simply things that bring joy to individual people's lives. Whereas topics such as politics of the day or economy are represented rather rarely, traffic and the A40 itself are visualized a lot of times. Those who participated in the project used the wall as a communication space to tell their stories. Transliterated into strips, these stories make the wall a communication device.

The project was implemented in 2010. In 2011 it was part of Germany's contribution to the Biennale of Architecture in São Paulo. Also, the renowned Art Directors Club awarded the project in 2010 as a successful example for communication in public places and in 2012 it even won the city planning price and the engineering price of the BSVI. The barcode project can be interpreted as a lively proof that people do care about shaping their environmental surroundings, including those infrastructural spaces they usually only pass as major traffic arteries in suburban spaces. This might be one way to establish roads and motorways as public places that can give suburban areas an identity but also to implement the idea which Jackson envisioned by saying: "[r]oads no longer merely lead to places, they are places." (J.B. Jackson 1994: 190)

Figure 3: The barcode as a component of public spaces (orange edge 2010)

Figure 4: The interactive website (orange edge 2010)

References

Augé, Marc (1992), *Non-Lieux: Introduction à une anthropologie de la surmodernité*, Paris: Le Seuil.

Bremer, Stefanie (2008), *Broadacre City und die Zwischenstadt. Neueinordnung des amerikanischen Entwurfsmodells im Rahmen der aktuellen Debatte zur Qualifizierung der Zwischenstadt*, Dissertation, Essen: Universität Duisburg-Essen.

BSVI (2011): Ankündigung für eine Tagung, Plakat, unpublished.

Bundesinstitut für Bau-, Stadt- und Raumforschung/ Bundesamt für Bauwesen und Raumordnung (2004), *Suburbia: Perspektiven jenseits von Zersiedelung*, Bonn: BBR.

Bundesministerium für Verkehr, Bau und Stadtentwicklung (2011), *Infrastruktur in der Landschaft. Eine baukulturelle Herausforderung*, Berlin.

Bundesstiftung Baukultur (2014), *Baukulturbericht. Gebaute Lebensräume der Zukunft - Fokus Stadt. 2014/2015*, Berlin.

Hauck, Thomas et al. (2011), *Infrastructural Urbanism. Addressing the in-between*, Berlin: DOM publishers.

Jackson, John Brinckerhoff (1994), *A Sense of Place, A Sense of Time*, New Haven, CT: Yale University Press.

Landesbetrieb Strassenbau NRW (2010), *Barcode A40*, Gelsenkirchen.

Stadt Bochum (2010) (ed.), *A40/B1 Gestalthandbuch*, Bochum.

Zeller, Thomas (2002), *Straße, Bahn, Panorama - Verkehrswege und Landschaftsveränderung in Deutschland von 1930 bis 1990*, Frankfurt am Main: Campus Verlag.

Airport (Sub)Urbia - Transforming Berlin Brandenburg's periphery[1]

Johanna Schlaack

Introduction

While at the end of the 19th century the main railroad stations served as mobility hubs fuelling trade and (sub)urban growth in Europe's urban peripheries this key role has now been often taken over by airports as new global connectivity nodes. The rapid growth of aviation, as reflected in increasing numbers of both flights and passengers, has fuelled expansive spatial development in the airport area itself. However, these new forms of suburban growth often take place in the absence of overarching planning concepts and with little to no participation of communal and regional stakeholders. Despite the potential of becoming an integrated development hub in the city region the insufficient cooperation of planners, public institutions, airport authorities and private investors results in the well known image of today's airport areas: faceless business parks sprawling alongside traffic corridors and unstructured suburban residential areas. Obviously the unorganized, extensive growth around airports should rather be described as Airport Suburbia than as Airport City Development. Local and regional governments as well as airport authorities have increasingly sought to take advantage of the potential and the possibilities of strategic development around airports. As a result a clear shift has become evident in spatial orientation of city regions with a new suburban focus on the airport vicinity which increasingly plays a key role within regional strategies.

This can be observed for example in the Berlin-Brandenburg region. Berlin's airport system is undergoing massive transformation - three airports are being merged into one. The new Berlin Brandenburg Airport BER "Willy Brandt", blazoned as a hub for the capital region, will replace the existing multi-airport system. Thus, the spatial economic concept pursued by regional and local planning authorities supported by Berlin's airport authority Flughafen Berlin Brandenburg (FBB) aims at a strategically integrated axis from the new BER airport to

---

[1] This text is a revised version of the article "New Berlin Brandenburg Airport" that the author has published in Aerlines Magazine, e-zine edition Issue 53 in 2012.

Berlin's inner city and its new main train station. But how can sustainable development in the airport vicinity be encouraged in terms of urban quality, connectivity, economic balance, green development and quality of life? This article will discuss this issue and give an overview of the airport related development in Berlin Brandenburg and the pilot project "fAIRleben".

1. BER, TXL and THF: Three into one!

Since the reunification of Germany in 1990 and the designation of Berlin as the capital city, ambitious plans have been proposed to bundle Berlin's air traffic in one single airport which would be strong enough to compete with hubs like Frankfurt, Amsterdam or Paris. Projections for a 40% population growth to more than five million inhabitants and expectations of a strong economic boost, led to expansive plans for Berlin's residential and office development as well as infrastructure projects. However, Berlin's dreams of exponential growth burst like bubbles in the late 1990s. The financial downturn fuelled by the Berlin banking scandal around the turn of the millennium led to tight public budgets and limited planning policy of public authorities.

Due to Berlin's history as a divided city, the system of three airports Tempelhof, Tegel and Schönefeld was economically inefficient and transfer connections and intercontinental flights were severely limited in scope of operation. Especially Tempelhof, due to its outdated airport concept and its massive built structure was incapable of generating sufficient revenues in relation to the enormous maintenance costs. Therefore, in the golden era of reunification in the beginning 1990ies, the three airport shareholders, the federal states of Berlin and Brandenburg and the Federal Republic of Germany, decided in 1996 to expand the existing Schönefeld airport southeast of Berlin into a single-hub for the region (Berliner Abgeordnetenhaus (House of Representatives) 1996). The decision was strongly criticized especially by citizens' initiatives around Schönefeld and was brought to trial because the previous regional planning comparison process of three potential sites for the new airport clearly stated Schönefeld as the least eligible (Berlin Brandenburg Flughafen Holding 1994). Main arguments were the difficulties of further airport expansion with more than two runways and the rather densely populated surrounding area. Against

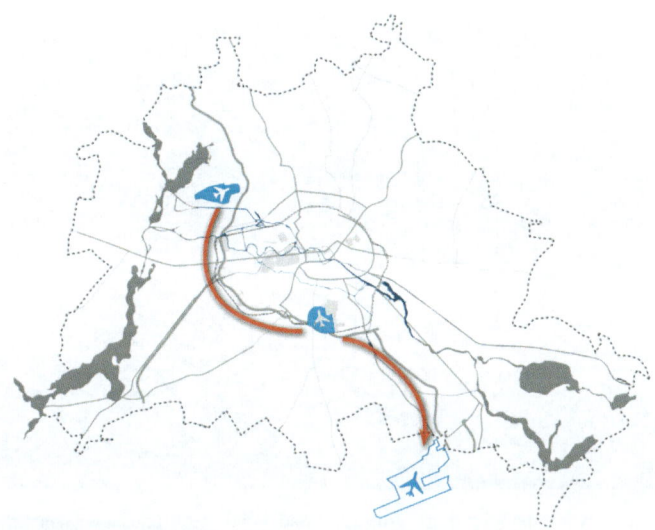

Figure 1: Scheme of Berlin's transforming airport system (Schlaack 2012)

the background of Berlin's proximity, potential revenues for the capital and public investments in a 100 hectare property close to Schönefeld the consensus shifted away from the two sites situated more remotely in Brandenburg to Schönefeld directly at the city boundary of Berlin. Following the hub concept, the two inner-city airports Tempelhof and Tegel needed to be closed in order to allow enough capacity to legitimate the mega-project BER and to mitigate the effects of noise and pollution for about 160,000 Berliners (GL 2006: 33). Tempelhof was closed in 2008 and Tegel will close with the opening of BER, predicted to be in (earliest) 2017. The original investment of 3.2 billion Euros is publicly financed, thereof 2.5 billion Euros for the new airport and 700 million Euros for rail and road access (SenFin 2009: 390 ff.). The postponement of the BER airport opening will increase the estimated costs over two billion Euros, including about 700 million for additional noise abatement and will force Berlin and Brandenburg to dip even deeper into their already empty pockets.

The process of transforming and relocating Berlin's airports equals a "castling" within the airport system, with expected winners and losers in the region. On

Figure 2: Re-use of Tempelhof airport terminal, Bread and Butter tradeshow (Schlaack 2009)

the one hand the northern part of Berlin will win quietness and comfort of living but will lose its important accessibility hub with Tegel's closing and therefore certain economic weight. In contrast, the south of the city region will gain in economic importance and prosperity but will be confronted with heavy airport noise pollution and its negative impacts on quality of life, above all the stress produced by this noise. Nevertheless, regarding the former tri-polar airport system in the region - the already closed Tempelhof airport, Tegel airport and the future BER - an integrated planning approach for these three important city-regional development poles is still lacking. The hotly debated conversion of Tempelhof's gigantic terminal building, the re-use of the airfield as a city park and the conversion of Tegel as business and industrial park for urban technologies are concepts broached in various plans and under discussion with the general public. Yet despite these plans, the implementation strategy, the profile and the concrete results in terms of urban built form, open space and impacts on the city are still rather vague. Transferring good planning process into a good outcome or "product" with high quality is therefore the current challenge. Besides the transformation in the air and on the ground in Berlin-Brandenburg, it can be argued that a kind of growth-triangle "BER - Inner City - Potsdam" with three main spatial-economic regional axes is evolving: First, the south-west axis

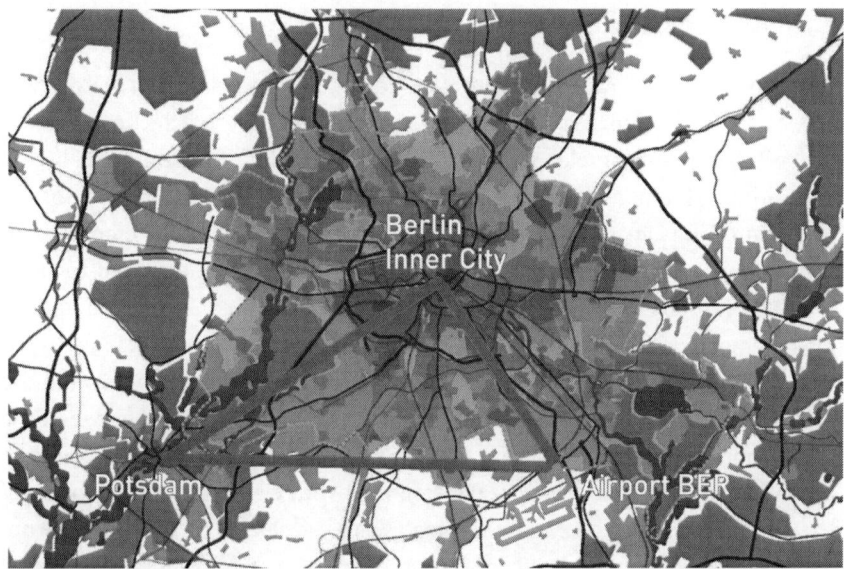

Figure 3: Spatial scheme of the evolving growth-triangle "BER - Inner City - Potsdam" (Schlaack 2012)

between Berlin's city center and Potsdam alongside the Schloßstraße, which has been prospering since the German Empire. Second, the south-east axis between the Berlin Hauptbahnhof and BER which is promoted and planned mainly through Berlin's political and administrative apparatus. This axis incorporates the technology media and science site Adlershof, the former industrial site Oberschöneweide, North Neukölln, a newly developing hub of the creative class and the former Media Spree site, another hub of creative industries in Berlin. And third, the axis between BER and Potsdam, incorporating the municipalities Teltow, Ludwigsfelde and Blankenfelde-Mahlow, which is developing in the absence of planning concepts alongside the B 96a road and north of Berlin's highway ring. The majority of Berlin-Brandenburg's economic development is currently already taking place within the depicted triangle and will be further concentrated there in the future. Unfortunately an overarching regional strategy to incorporate and balance the strength of the triangle in the region and to spatially qualify the three different development axes is still missing.

2. United we stand, divided we fall?

The airport BER will radiate out into the region and has already initiated high expectations on economic impulses on several sides. The much-cited study of Herbert Baum for example, predicts that 40,000 new jobs will be created by the new airport (Baum et al. 2005; 2009). Nevertheless, it neglects the local loss of jobs due to the closure of the two inner-city airports Tegel and Tempelhof. In Tegel alone, approximately 10,000 jobs will be lost or will be shifted towards BER (Baasner 2011). But the crux is, while BER is situated in Brandenburg, the main demand and passenger flow will be served from Berlin. This results in conflicts and competition for investments and economic development between the two federal states of Berlin and Brandenburg and on a lower level between the several municipalities around the airport as well as the southern boroughs of Berlin. To prevent an ambivalent development with clear winners and losers of the airport expansion, a variety of plans were developed to address the concerns and to mitigate imbalances. These plans, although exemplary for being planned across borders, still partly interfere with each other, and there remains a distinct air of strain between the large numbers of stakeholders involved.

In the following a brief overview of the related plans will be given. First, the so-called "Common Structural Concept" (Gemeinsames Strukturkonzept) (GL 2007) is the most complex plan with secondary layers for mobility and transport, business and industrial sites, residential development as well as natural and recreational areas. It was developed by the Joint Spatial Planning Department Berlin Brandenburg (Gemeinsame Landesplanungsabteilung) together with stakeholders of the "Dialogforum" including the federal states of Berlin, Brandenburg, twelve municipalities in the airport vicinity, three Berlin boroughs and administrative districts as well as the airport authority FBB. The concept, which is not legally binding, designates a total expansion area in the airport vicinity of 2100 hectares, thereof 1300 hectares for business and industrial development and 800 hectares for residential uses. Secondly, the "Masterplan Gateway" (Senatsverwaltung für Stadtentwicklung/ Gemeinde Schönefeld 2007) was jointly developed by Berlin, the airport community Schönefeld and the airport authority FBB. It contains the three key areas Airport City (FBB), Business Park Berlin (FBB, Berlin) and Waltersdorf (Schönefeld), which aim to function together as prelude for the development axis to Berlin's Inner City.

Thirdly, the jointly developed regional marketing concept "Airport Region Berlin-Brandenburg" by Berlin Partner and Brandenburg Economic Development Board (ZAB) incorporates the general economic clusters like industry, life sciences, clean technologies, media etc., whereas, fourthly, the "Stadtforum - Perspectives for Berlin" (Senatsverwaltung für Stadtentwicklung 2008) with the follow-up "BerlinStrategie" (Senatsverwaltung für Stadtentwicklung 2014) is rather more of a strategic vision for Berlin which shows the designated growth axis BER-Adlershof-Schöneweide. Fifthly, the "Planwerk South-East" (Senatsverwaltung für Stadtentwicklung 2008) is Berlin's overarching district plan which covers the area up to the BER in Brandenburg (Schönefeld). And finally the "Land use plan" (Gemeinde Schönefeld 2005) with 465 hectares designated area for business/industrial which equals the size of the whole airport site Tegel. Municipalities in Germany have the "planning authority/right" and therefore can hardly be restricted in their planning processes. According to the predicted demand per year in the airport area of BER of 25 hectares, Schönefeld alone has a 20 years buffer within the borders of their municipality.

Strong economic competition has evolved due to the oversupply of properties in the airport area and the long planning process of two decades. The ongoing delay in opening the airport sets uncertainties for potential investors and planning institutions and will exacerbate real estate competition and land speculation around BER. Hence the stated aim of an overarching urban development recedes into the distance. Although all airport municipalities continue to be organised in the Dialogforum BER and regularly meet in working groups, the institutionalised Berlin Brandenburg Area Development Company (BADC) - founded as equivalent to Amsterdam's Schiphol Area Development Company (SADC) - with eleven municipalities and two districts as shareholders, is restricted to environmental compensation measures instead of also promoting strategic airport area development. To foster the vision of a joint sustainable economic development around BER in Berlin's suburban periphery the idea of "First come, first served" should be contrasted with the idea of "Good things come to those who wait". Not only in regard to the delayed airport opening, but also in regard to strategic development of spatial economic clusters in the BER airport vicinity like exemplified in Schiphol and hence preventing further uncontrolled land speculation around BER as well as sustaining a spatial economic balance in Berlin's city region on a broader scale.

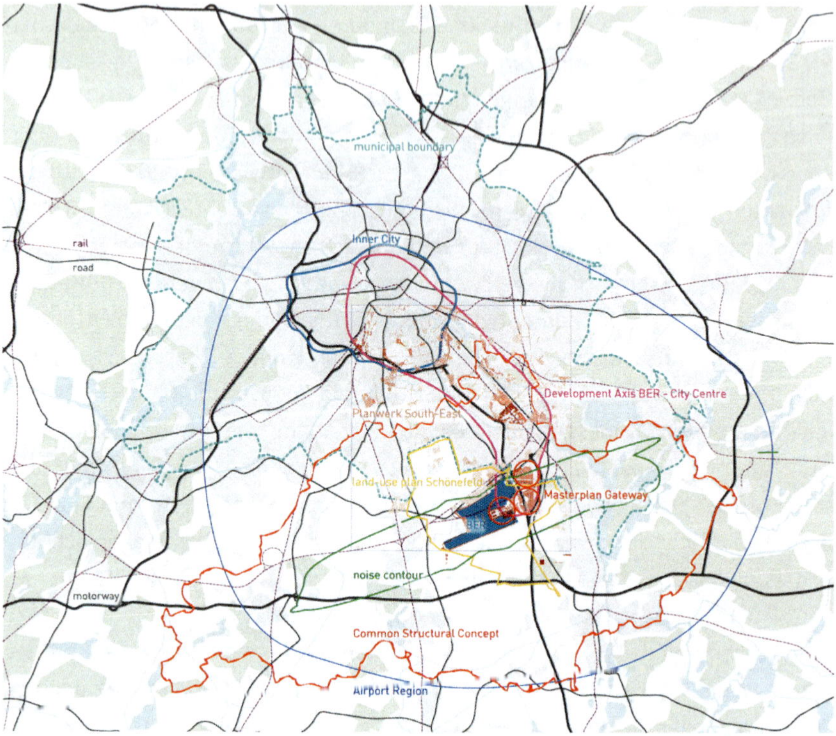

90   Johanna Schlaack

Figure 4: BER-related planning concepts for Berlin-Brandenburg region (Schlaack 2010)

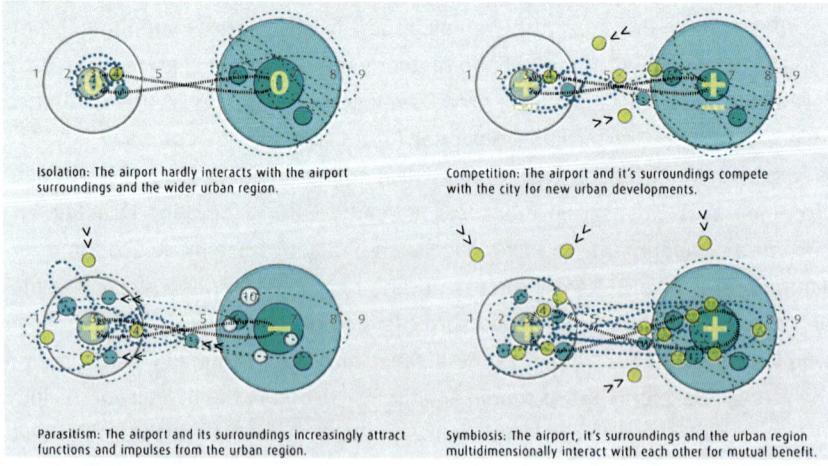

Figure 5: Types of interaction between airport and city region (Schlaack 2013)

Drawing on the conceptualized types of interaction between airport and city region: isolation, competition, parasitism and symbiosis (Schlaack 2015), the BER airport area still has the great potential to be integrated as a complementary development pole into the regional strategy in a symbiotic way. Due to the outstanding level of planning basis and the established cross-institutional framework, e.g. in the Dialogforum BER, the regional integration of airport and city in Berlin Brandenburg might on the long run become a model for sustainable (sub)urban development.

3. Pilot project "fAIRleben"

In order to deal with the above mentioned ambivalent threads and challenges as well as the variety of plans and concepts in the airport area, since beginning of 2010 the model project "fAIRleben - Sustainable development in close proximity to an infrastructure mega project" is jointly developed by several experts from the university, research and practise, together with the BER airport-neighbouring communities. In this regard the airport vicinity can be seen as a kind of prototype for extensive spatial development in the suburban periphery in a multitude of infrastructure and accessibility modes: air, road and rail. The neighbourhoods around BER are crossed by all three mobility routes on the ground and in the air and therefore provide a useful case study to illustrate the major chances and problems of dynamic contemporary mobility hubs. Since the direct airport proximity and each mobility mode already signify prosperity and urbanisation, the BER municipalities expect on the one hand rapid economic and (sub)urban growth. On the other hand, they will be confronted with major disadvantages related to the infrastructure mega project like spatial fragmentation, heavy noise emissions and exhaust fumes, large-area sealing, uncontrolled suburbanisation and environmental damage.

The principle goal of "fAIRleben" is to turn the transformation process in the airport vicinity to a positive outcome, a process that is to be approached in collaboration with the municipalities. To achieve this goal, "fAIRleben" seeks to support the airport area with scientific know-how in terms of noise management and handling of noise, green urban design and architecture, exemplary participation and education, sustainable economic development as well as profound evaluation of process and results. In this respect, the BER airport vicinity could become a kind of model project and exchange know-how in world-wide learning partnerships with international airport areas in comparable situations. The concept of sustainability with its three pillars - environment, economy and social issues - is complemented with governance and public participation as well as noise issues. The "fAIRleben" project outline incorporates therefore five pillars or guiding principles for a sustainable development in a liveable community:

- Reduction of noise: environmental noise in all living and working areas is perceived at least as tolerable;
- Green responsibility: ecological efficiency, reflection in airport community development and daily life;
- Quality of life: in the airport municipalities and in the community is outstanding;
- Economic balance: development and share of airport benefits support and secure the other goals of the municipalities and
- Governance: well-functioning cooperation of all involved stakeholders in the airport area in the sense of a joint benefit with an intensive public participation. Major local partners are the federal state of Brandenburg, the airport authority FBB, the districts Teltow-Fläming and Dahme-Spreewald, the Technische Universität Berlin as well as a broad variety of academic and non-academic institutions like the Competence Center City and Region in Berlin-Brandenburg (KSR), Leibniz-Institute for Regional Development and Structural Planning (IRS), Institute for Futures Studies and Technology Assessment (IZT) and Potsdam Institute for Climate Impact Research (PIK).

4. Good things come to those who wait?

The first suggestion then, is that patience is worthwhile and integrated airport area development needs time. As we can learn from Schiphol airport in Amsterdam, the efforts invested in coordination and cooperation of the involved stakeholders, in order to foster an internationally competitive and well-organized airport surrounding, are well worth the time and effort. The unfortunate coincidence of further delay of the BER opening and an airport area on its last legs after trembling over 20 years regarding the expansion in Schönefeld

Figure 6: Re-use of Tempelhof airport "Berlin - Home is where the heart is", Bread and Butter tradeshow (Schlaack 2009)

further intensifies the jostling but also leaves more time to put things on the right track for a sustainable future (Schlaack/Henckel 2011).

Which leads to the second principle implication: Sustainability in the airport area is essential. Conceptualized as "Airea" (Schlaack 2010), the airport vicinity bundles the challenges but also potentials of integrated urban development and growth like no other part of the contemporary metropolitan region. Therefore, they should be treated as "Better Aireas", as showcase for sustainable development within a complex regional setting (Schlaack 2015). In this context, the model project "fAIRleben" tries to address and incorporate these challenges in a close cooperation with municipal, private, public and academic partners in Berlin-Brandenburg.

The third implication is that the product is as important as the process, especially in airport-related urban development. Due to the variety of stakeholders involved, the process needs to be well organized but not at the risk of ignoring or diminishing the quality of output. The Brandenburg Ministry of Infrastructure and Agriculture stated at the beginning of 2011 that "Building culture" should be seen "as a locational factor" (MIL 2011). This seems to be a good maxim to act on when rethinking the airport vicinity itself and the evolving axes in the region, e.g. the airport corridor from BER to Berlin's inner city. Also, the conversion and controversial re-use of the two former airport sites Tempelhof and Tegel need to be discussed more with regard to urban qualities, building culture and their integration into Berlin's city fabric.

A fourth implication concerning the increasing economic imbalances in the region is the necessity of thinking big, since the region is the scale. The practical implementation of strategies to counterbalance the regional economic shift from north to south, as well as balancing the benefits in the airport area, need to be addressed in politics and administration (Think Berl!n 2011). A further economic downturn in the northern part of Berlin and a division of the region as well as the airport vicinity in obvious winners and losers needs to be prevented so that, in the end, good things can be expected by those who have the patience to wait.

A final more overarching implication is that the airport and its vicinity besides being a prominent part of the contemporary Zwischenstadt or In-between City (Hartwig 2000), are at the same time an important node in the global network following the Netzstadt or Network City approach (Michaeli et al. 2011). The airport node on an exposed scale level in the Netzstadt model is marked by a high density of people, goods and knowledge and is highly visible and accessible within the region. Thus this yet underestimated but prospering part of the (sub)urban periphery, the airport area, has the promising potential of being qualified in terms of urban planning, design and architecture to cope with its function as modern gate to the world and showcase of the region instead of leading a shadowy existence as plain Airport Suburbia.

References

Baasner Stadtplaner (2011), *Siedlungsstrukturelle Konsequenzen der Eröffnung des neuen Flughafens BER in Schönefeld*, Berlin.

Baum, Herbert/ Schneider, Jutt/; Esser, Klaus/ Kurte, Judith (2005; 2009), *Wirtschaftliche Effekte des Airports Berlin Brandenburg International BBI*, Köln: Institut für Verkehrswissenschaft.

Berlin Brandenburg Flughafen Holding (1994), *Flughafen Berlin Brandenburg International (BBI): Stand der Antragsunterlagen für das Raumordnungsverfahren*, Berlin.

Berliner Abgeordnetenhaus (1996), *Bericht über das Flughafenkonzept in der Region Berlin-Brandenburg*, Drucksache 13/624, Berlin: Deutscher Bundestag.

GL - Gemeinsame Landesplanungsabteilung Berlin-Brandenburg (2006), *Gemeinsamer Landesentwicklungsplan Flughafenstandortentwicklung LEP FS*, Potsdam: Ministerium für Infrastruktur und Raumordnung.

— (2007), *Gemeinsames Strukturkonzept Flughafenumfeld Berlin Brandenburg International (BBI)*, Potsdam: Ministerium für Infrastruktur und Raumordnung.

— (2008), *Gemeinsame Strukturkonzept Flughafenumfeld BBI*, Potsdam: Ministerium für Infrastruktur und Raumordnung.

Grassmann, Günther (2013), "fAIRleben - Modellprojekt für Forschung und Anwendung. Nachhaltige Entwicklung einer Kommune im Umfeld eines Großinfrastrukturprojekts Blankenfelde-Mahlow/Flughafen Berlin Brandenburg BER", in: *Zeitschrift für Lärmbekämpfung*, Band 8, Nr. 1/2013, 35-39.

Güller, Mathis/ Güller, Michael (2003), *From airport to airport city*, Barcelona.

Hartwig, Nina (2000): *Neue urbane Knoten am Stadtrand? Die Einbindung von Flughäfen in der Zwischenstadt: Frankfurt/Main, Hannover, Leipzig/Halle, München*, Berlin: Verlag für Wissenschaft und Forschung.

Michaeli, Mark/ Salewski, Christian/ Frei, Michel (2011), "Flughafen Zürich- Kloten: der Flughafen in der Stadt", in: *IzR Robustheit und Flexibilität. Neue Perspektiven für Flughafen und Stadt*, 1/2011, Bonn, 67-80.

MIL — Ministerium für Infrastruktur und Landwirtschaft Brandenburg (2011), *Baukultur als Standortfaktor im Umfeld des Flughafens Berlin Brandenburg International*, Potsdam.

Gemeinde Schönefeld (2005), *Begründung zum Flächennutzungsplan der Gemeinde Schönefeld*, Schönefeld.

Schaafsma, Maurits/ Amkreutz, Joop/ Güller, Mathis (2008), *Airport and City. Airport Corridors. Drivers of economic development*, Amsterdam: Schiphol Real Estate.

Schlaack, Johanna (2010), "Defining the Airea. Evaluating Urban Output and Forms of Interaction between Airport and Metropolitan Region", in: Knippenberger, Ute/ Wall, Alex (eds.), *Airports in Cities and Regions. Research and Practise*, Karlsruhe: KIT Scientific Publishing, 113-126.

— (2012), "New Berlin Brandenburg Airport. Good things come to those who wait?", *Aerlines Magazine*, e-zine edition Issue 53.

— (2013), "Zwischen Stadt und Flughafen - Die Berliner Flughafenrochade", in: Roost, Frank/ Volgmann, Kati (eds.), *Airport Cities. Gateways der metropolitanen Ökonomie*, Detmold: ILS, 109-130.

— (2015), *Flughafen und Airea. Impulsgeber für Stadtregionen*, Berlin. (forthcoming)

Schlaack, Johanna/ Henckel, Dietrich (2011), "Flughafenentwicklung und Stadtentwicklung: die Rolle von Robustheit und Flexibilität. Eine zusammenfassende Betrachtung", in: *IzR Robustheit und Flexibilität. Neue Perspektiven für Flughafen und Stadt*, 1/2011, Bonn, 89-98.

Senatsverwaltung für Finanzen (2009), *Beteiligungsbericht 2009*, Band 2 - Lageberichte 2008, Berlin.

Senatsverwaltung für Stadtentwicklung (2006), *Stadtforum Berlin. Perspectives for Berlin - Strategies and Pilot Projects*, Berlin.

— (2008), *Planwerk South-East*, Berlin.

Senatsverwaltung für Stadtentwicklung; Gemeinde Schönefeld (2007), *Masterplan Gateway BBI*, Berlin.

Senatsverwaltung für Stadtentwicklung und Umwelt (2014), *BerlinStrategie. Stadtentwicklungskonzept Berlin 2030*, Berlin.

Think Berl!n/ Bodenschatz, Harald/ Schlaack, Johanna/ Hofmann, Aljoscha/ Polinna, Cordelia/ von Oppen, Christian (2011) (eds.), *Berlin hat mehr verdient! Ist Stadtentwicklung nach der Wahl egal?*, Berlin: Think Berl!n.

Part II
Suburban Spaces - Global Variations

Unfinished suburbanization - Leipzig between Suburbia, Creative City and Shrinking

Arvid Krüger

1. Leipzig: a former metropolis or an upcoming creative city?

With hardly 500,000 inhabitants Leipzig might be Germany's smallest metropolitan town. Like Manchester, it was an important industrial town, but with a decreasing number of population almost all over the 20th century (Rink et al. 2013). Nevertheless, it is today the largest town in East Germany apart from Berlin which is situated 150 kilometers north of Leipzig. The distance to Prague is 200 kilometers and to Frankfurt 300 kilometers.

1.1 Leipzig's past as a European node

Leipzig has reached urban autonomy in 1165 and was one of the major nodes in medieval Middle Europe. The Leipzig fair made the town an outstanding trading place and Leipzig's university which was founded in 1409, is one of the oldest in entire Germany. Wittenberg nearby made Leipzig a place of the Lutheran reformation in the 16th century. Leipzig has also been marked by the presence of Johann Sebastian Bach who worked there in St. Thomas and Johann Wolfgang von Goethe who fostered the fame of Leipzig as "Little-Paris" (cf. Faust I, Scene in Auerbach's cellar [that still exists]). Also in military history Leipzig is famous for the defeat of Napoleon in 1813.

Industrialization has had large impacts on the town, it was e.g. terminus of the first German long-distance train connection to Dresden which opened in 1838. Leipzig's main station is still one of the biggest in Europe. From 100,000 inhabitants in 1871 the population rose to its peak of 750,000 in the 1930s. Economically, Leipzig gained importance for all traditional industry branches, media and trade. It was the capital of the central industrial belt which was focused on chemical and processing industry. For instance the mass production of color photograph film took place in this belt. In contrast to other German towns Leipzig was hardly destroyed in World War II, although the industrial belt surely was

Figure 1: Overview Leipzig, own revision based on Open Street Map (Drechsel, 2015)

a popular target for the allied bombs. Therefore the substance could be preserved.

Hence, Leipzig was deeply affected by the drain of company headquarters and adjacent functions induced by the belonging to the Soviet Zone. To name two examples, Frankfurt took over the largest German-spoken book fair and Hanover the largest industry novelty fair. Also the number of inhabitants never reached pre-war state again. Within the COMECON area Leipzig was still a major node: Brown-coal-based industry on the one hand and the largest East European trade fair on the other hand constituted remarkable metropolitan functions. One chapter of Leipzig's history in this context is the ecological impact of heavy industrialization. In the 1950s Leipzig's rivers were ecologically dead and the air pollution was continuously above average. It was only through the processes of de-industrialization after 1990 that the ecosystems recovered. Today, these large spaces of brownfields give shelter to ecosystems of the so called fourth kind (Sukopp 1998).

In 1989 Leipzig was one of the crucial places, where the peaceful revolution of the East-German citizens overcame divided Europe. Shortly after 1990 the

Population Development

	Area (km²)	Population	Population density (pop/km²)*1000
1699		15653	
1850	17.7	63824	1,8
1871	17.7	106925	6,0
1900	58.5	456156	8,8
1914	77.8	624845	8,0
1933	128.6	713470	5,5
1950	141.1	617574	4,4
1975	141.3	566630	4,0
1989	146.5	530010	3,6
1993	148.5	490851	3,3
2001	297.6	493052	1,7
2011 (Zensus)	297.6	502979	1,7
2014 (Stadt, 31.12.13)	297.6	531562	1,8

Figure 2: Population table own revision (population number 2011: Census Data, population number 2014: Freistaat Sachsen) (Nuissl/Rink 2003: 12)

"revolutionary town" of "L.E." became East Germany's "boomtown". As a kind of modernization backlog it was expected that heavy sprawl would boost the region. Shortly after 1989 this seemed to be a self-fulfilling prophecy (Nuissl/Rink 2003; Herfert/Röhl 2001). The rush and intensity of shifts of spatial patterns have been remarkable but there was sprawlish growth and erosional shrinking at the same time (Nuissl/Rink 2003: 7). First, Leipzig region was deindustrialized (Herfert/Röhl 2001: 151). 25 years later, the space between the town and the northern motorway A14 became an attractive company location e.g. for major plants of BMW, Porsche and Siemens, DHL's international logistic hub, the New Fair and the new airport of Leipzig. The western motorway A9 locates large shopping centres, among them the largest one of East Germany. Public employers of national importance, such as the National Court of Administrative Law, the National Net Agency, and the regional public media company (MDR), the Leipzig Energy Stock Exchange and certainly the large Leipzig University complete the economic structure. If there were not the former industrial quarters almost completely fallen empty, if there were not the destroyed mining landscapes in the south, if there was not the continuously high unemployment rate, Leipzig would be fine. However, this is not the case.

Eventually there is another spatial pattern that gives Leipzig a certain uniqueness: the block building apartments built during the period of industrialization between 1871 and 1939 slowly deteriorated after 1945. This was mainly due to the fact that there has been almost no preservation and renewal under the GDR regime. One of the major questions aroused by Leipzig's citizens in 1989, if Leipzig could still be saved, definitely had an urban dimension.

1.2 Spatial Patterns of Leipzig today

The region has been transformed completely throughout the first 15 years after the revolution. By 2004 the spatial pattern was more or less shaped:

- The central city as a "real" downtown with cultural offers, services in the tertiary sector and few, more expensive residential places. By 2006 this area still offered prominent brownfields. These voids have been filled over the last ten years e.g. with a second shopping center next to one in the main-station.
- The ring-shaped inner-city with its positively seen older stock from before World War II. This stock offers a mix of apartments from cheap and un-renovated up to higher middle-class standard, still affordable as the market prices are under pressure due to the ongoing loss of population.
- [1] By 2006 the problems of the non renovated "last quarter" are not solved yet. Especially the radial main-streets are places where emptiness concentrates, which affects the liveliness of the very neighborhood. The instrument of "guardian houses" is still necessary to save buildings of importance for the urban structures.
- Renewed quarters of residential settlements of the 1920/30s and the 1970/80s and the former municipal borders of Leipzig, often dominated by public and/or corporate housing and with a special emphasis on elderly population and, where there is public housing with an emphasis on the poorer. In terms of urban design these are the artefacts of the modern era of architecture, either from its starts or from its ends.
- Vast brownfields especially between the inner-city ring and the discrete several places of the modern residential quarters. These areas are extensively used, especially for creative industries, such as the workplace of Neo Rauch. These are the places, where Leipzig has been and stays deindustrialized.

---

[1] The turn of population development was around 2000, when Leipzig fell under the symbolic mark of half a million inhabitants. By 2004 the number of inhabitants rose to the mark of 1994, only by 2011 the mark of 1989 was reached again - but on a much larger space in 2012 than in 1989.

- New entrepreneurial zones especially along the motorway A14 in the north where Leipzig's economic successes can be found: TThere are typical suburban industrial sites like Porsche and BMW, typical shopping-centers and voids. With the fair, the airport and all the logistic industries that have been established around, there is also a partially elaborated edge-city function.
- In certain areas of suburbia there are well-functioning suburban residential sites, although compared to 1971 there are less inhabitants in these former rural areas from the industrial age (Herfert/Röhl 2001: 152). However, in 1971 they lived more densely together in the rural core towns. Suburbanization especially worked in the East, where there is quite a nice landscape (Nuissl/Rink 2004: 46). Later, the South also became a target, as step by step the re-cultivated mining landscape offered nice areas (e.g. the new Cospuden Lake in a former open-mine hole).

After 2004 there have been moderate but decisive dynamics, as Leipzig's development returned to normal and the market stabilized e.g. the mobility of tenants diminished (Steinführer 2004: 196). This happened not only in comparison to the extraordinary frame of development of the last 25 years, but also in comparison to the development back into the 1930s, when the industrial age growth stopped. The alterations in the housing schemes of the years between 1989 and 2004 have been a prerequisite for it. However, residential suburbanization has only been a partial aspect of this alteration-development.

Hence, the current news of Leipzig seems to contradict the development of the last 25 years:
- One of the "guardian houses" (see below), that has been suspended from the real-estate market has been transformed into luxury lofts;
- Several blocks along a main street with relevant car traffic have been bought and renewed by an investor - something that would not have been rational on the market since the 1920s;
- Debates on gentrification processes arouse as cases of people being expelled from their apartments due to risen rent rates became public, which is tremendously unusual for the 20 years after 1990;
- Some blocks of an area of residential inner city blocks that have been considered not to be developable anymore, the so called "last quarter" (see below) have been bought by investors. Additionally, some of the

long-term non-developable brownfields are now dedicated for townhouses, bringing detached houses into the inner city.
Leipzig's population is increasing since 2000, which is the first increase since 1937. The few suburban municipalities (most has been incorporated into Leipzig in 2000) are stable. However, the rest of Western Saxonia is still shrinking and awaiting the demographic echoes (more on this phenomenon see below). The spatial transformation seems to be done, as the current dynamics on the housing market are relevant on a small spatial scale; the general pattern has become stable after 2000.

2. Frame A: Development-phases of suburbanization after 1989

This article aims to give an overview of the period after 1989 trying to explain the different, sometimes even contradicting, developments that have affected Leipzig and therefore made it a genuine example for East-German development: One the one hand, it is a good example because the phenomena in Leipzig were typical for all other places in East-Germany. On the other hand, this certain uniqueness of Leipzig made it a kind of "avantgarde" for the general counterurbanization as well as for reurbanization trends. A description of the changed spatial patterns according to residential and entrepreneurial (commercial and industrial) localization will be given here. But beforehand this specific spatial pattern will be explained by reconsidering the phases of suburbanization by Nuissl and Rink (2003) and by an excursus on East-German shrinking.

First, a short overview of the urban and suburban development since the industrial age will be given in order to find a starting point for the phases according to Nuissl and Rink (2003): It is obvious that the industrial age meant a strong expansion of the former medieval core of Leipzig, which today represents the city center. Leipzig outstripped most other cities in Germany. Large estate companies developed industrial areas, especially west of the core. Additionally, a fringe of residential areas in a typical block-wise urban design was added, that today represents the liveliest part of a creative European city. These residential areas also were built between the core and the industrial outskirts (e.g. Plagwitz-Lindenau) as well as in the suburbs (e.g. Böhlitz-Ehrenberg). Altogether these residential areas formed a fringe that marks today the inner city of Leipzig. A second fringe which mainly consisted of industrial sites, sometimes interjected by outer block-wise residential areas. In the inter-war period these fring-

es were rounded off. Free spaces in between were often used to erect modern residential areas inspired by Bauhaus and other modern architects. The farsighted community built relevant parts of the infrastructure such as roads, trams end energy networks. Thus, the city was able to grow sustainably and therefore became one of the densest cities in Europe. Around 1930 one could identify the following parts with distinct spatial patterns each in Leipzig:
- the inner city and the functionally mixed 1st fringe;
- discrete residential settlements in the outskirts, also built before 1918 as modern residential areas (Bauhaus-driven);
- the industrial sites along the rail-circle for freight rail traffic (the passenger traffic used the largest central station terminus);
- garden cities and first evolving suburbs as an emerging 3rd fringe.

Today the first two fringes together are more or less considered as the inner city fringe. After World War II and the establishment of the GDR the inner city decayed and the fringes were petrified in different manners. On the one hand the region was exploited for brown-coal in open-mining. As a consequence the landscape adjacent to the town, especially in the south but, with a bigger distance to town, also in the north was altered and literally disappeared. On the other hand the large-scale settlements with industrialized pre-fabric building elements were erected as moderately comfort flats. In the 1970s and 1980s these were the only districts that gained population. One of the nice side effects of suburbanization were the dachas and garden colonies that rose wherever possible: in empty spaces between rail tracks, next to industrial sites and also in the suburbs. This was defined by Bernd Hunger as the triangle of jobs, slabs and dachas (in: Nuissl/Rink 2003: 18).

2.1 Phase 1: Wild East (1990-1992)

Nuissl and Rink (2003) divided these processes into several phases of development. In this report the first three phases will be explored. Departure point (or phase 0) was the compact dense - unrenewed - city of Leipzig and its surroundings which were either dominated by open mining in the north and south or by agriculture especially in the northeast and the east. As the industrial age spilled over also parts of the suburbs were densely populated. On the one hand there were places like Seehausen in the north with 67 inhabitants per square kilometers which is today part of the entrepreneurial belt in the north. Böhlitz in the

West, on the other hand, with 945 inhabitants per km2 is now legally part of the municipality and spatially part of the old industrial fringe of pre'45 housing stock. Therefore the potential for suburban development in these sparsely dense adjacent municipalities was there and has been used.

> "As soon as the German-German borders opened, thousands of investors [sometimes of doubtful reputation] flocked to the still existing GDR and endeavored to gain a foothold on the emerging market. [...] The activities in East Germany's emerging markets in the real estate and housing sector largely benefited from a combination of factors that proved to be highly conducive to the spatial expansion of cities, towns and villages. In the early 1990s the 'vacuum' regarding the power of public authorities to steer spatial developments was most pronounced. Representatives and employees of the public administration were often rather inexperienced as to the new forms of 'bargaining', and were also much focused towards growth. This gave private investors ample scope to get their own way. [...] The planning and development of such [commercial] sites with little internal differentiation could be pushed forward rapidly because their reduced complexity didn't place great demands on the investors, while their implementation was greatly facilitated by the weakness of the planning bureaucracy, which allowed concerns that usually have to be considered to be neglected." (Nuissl/Rink 2003: 34f.)

"Saalepark", a huge shopping center in the remote village of Günthersdorf at the A9 motorway, half way between Leipzig and Halle and with its 140,000 square meters shopping space still one of the largest in Germany, can be seen as the most famous spatial result (Herfert/Röhl 2001: 154). Its legal frame was established on October 2nd 1990 which was the last day before the Federal German regulations would be implemented on unification day, October 3rd. Surely, the legal frames of the GDR building law were not capable do deal with such an item. This was mainly due to the fact that the supply with shopping was strictly regulated in the centrally planned economy during GDR times. Additionally, the unification of Germany was also an extension of the European Union (by that day still: European Community). This meant, that the already existent freedoms of the European Common Markets were implemented in a region literally over-night (it was only twelve month earlier that the first large non-neglectable protest marches were held, only six month left since the first free elections in the GDR). The second biggest shopping mall was erected in Paunsdorf, an adjacent village in the East, which was then incorporated into Leipzig municipality. This shopping mall has an ambivalent character. It is a non-integrated spatial item in the urban landscape, however, it is accessible by tram, rail and bike and in near distance to a dense large-scale settlement (of the same name) and the residential areas of Engelsdorf (the neighboring village which is today also part of Leipzig municipality). An evaluation on three residential areas on an eastern axis by Heydenreich showed interesting results: The inner-city-one directly behind the central station, another one adjacent to the Paunsdorf center and a third one in the more outer suburbs all had in common to prefer the Paunsdorf Center for daily supply (Heydenreich 2000: 112). The preferred areas of development were around the A14 motorway north of Leipzig and the A9 motorway (Berlin - Nuremberg), crossing the A14 at Schkeuditz (cf. Usbeck 2002). The reason for this has been the availability of plain agricultural land (that might have become open mining a decade later) and the lack of planning regulations beyond a municipal level. Plus, rural communities like Seehausen had the power to decide over plans. Two typical developments could be observed: shopping centers and residential areas ("wohnpark", described more precisely below). These residential areas showed quite an untypical urban design for suburbs, as it reminded of dense postmodern urban architecture with its 3-4-storey buildings with rental apartments. Both phenomena happened in the suburbs while the first was more or less the establishment of western-standard consumer supplies and the latter a reaction on the housing market as a whole.

2.2 Phase 2: Postsocialist sprawl (1992-1996)

The second phase was dominated by the rapid increase of residential development in the suburbs; especially the so-called "wohnparks" (see below) went well on the market (However, their time was already over in phase 3). Untypically rental apartments built by large companies were dominant (some 70%), instead of the typical suburban way to a "home of one's own". Thus, large parts of the motivation to build in suburbia were company-driven. Available space the companies were looking for in order to realise new housing projects, could only be provided on suburban sites and therefore competed with the product with the urban still un-renewed housing stock of the core city. Thus moving to suburbia was a mixture of motives with push and pull factors and more typical for movements of tenants within a city or between different segments of a town's housing market (more of it below). One might say that the "wohnparks" in the suburbs won this competition of push- and pull-factors. Development seemed to follow an usual suburbanization process: people moving out of town because they wish to leave behind urban structures in favor of smaller scales, landscape and space (a garden and a house instead of an apartment i.a.).

2.3 Phase 3: The resurgence of the city (1996-2000)

When the increase of residential suburbanization stopped in 1997, this marked a significant turning point; it increased further, but on a slower level than before (cf. Herfert 2002). Furthermore, the urban design changed. The "typical" (semi-)detached houses became more common, although often still developed by companies and then sold to customers instead of self-built by the owners. But what happened in the city at this point was more important: urban renewal became effective and housing markets levelled out. The price of a rental apartment, a comparative advance of suburbia, disappeared and even more, later on the situation should turn differently. By renewal in the inner city on the one hand and still new-built "wohnpark" houses in the suburbs on the other hand, the competition became tougher, as Leipzig's continuous population loss since the mid-1930s hasn't stopped, although the losses in phase 3 have been not that dramatic as in phase one. Certain mitigations of the core city were made in these years, especially the advantage of an urban inner-city apartment in comparison to the same type of residential living somewhere else in the region became sustainable. Due to cultural activities (which has always been an existing factor in favor of Leipzig in all its history) and an emerging street life the first visible successes of the area-wide renewal could be seen. As a consequence the target group for multi-storey-apartment tenants became spatially clustered in the "gründerzeit" housing stock of the inner city fringe.

However, suburban development was definitely not finished yet. The late 1990s were the years where large projects whith relevance to the city were finished: Terminal C of the airport was opened, which led to the refurbishment of the older terminals to what is now the second largest freight hub in Germany. Additionally, in 1996 the new fair opened. In these years, the two car companies Porsche and BMW decided to open completely new plants in the north of Leipzig, which were completed in 2002 respectively 2005. Alongside with these activities suburbs were completed infrastructurally. First of all, the rail- and tram-lines to the fair and the airport were established. Furthermore minor streets and several suburban areas that were newly incorporated into Leipzig's municipality were equipped with a good bus service comparable to the one in older parts of town. To sum up, phase 3 was characterized by growth-oriented development in all parts of the region.

3. Frame B: Shrinking and "Stadtumbau"[2]

The Post-industrial phenomenon certainly does not only occur in former East Germany. However, there is a definite unique situation, namely the German reunification in 1990. This meant a clash of two different economic ideologies - and a takeover by the western economic, legal and social system in the East.[3] Due to these regulations and the immediate introduction of the market economy the eastern economy broke down. Therefore the degree of industrialization and employment belong irreversibly to the past. East Germany's "peoples' property", accumulated by expropriation and investment from tax-income of the GDR was flogged and sold out by western administrators of the Treuhand society, allegedly because there were no investors found. The East German population was not able to take over a lot as they had no credit at the bank, neither financial nor confidential one. As a consequence enterprises and estates not sold deteriorated or were dismantled (Schulz 2004: 205f.). There was a total trust of policy in market economy as motor for economic growth - in contrast to the West German success story after World War II, when major industrial state property was created.

After a successful growth of these enterprises they were privatized step by step. Noé concluded in 1990 that the new federal property - the former "people's property" - was the only chance to preserve the indispensable industrial base of East Germany (Noé 1990 in: Schulz 2004). However, this advice was not followed. If there had been investments into the industrial cores after 1990, they were punctual and only under certain (subsidy) circumstances. The West-German economy did not want to establish competitors to them in the East. Even worse they encouraged the East German people to move to the West: Labor agencies in Bavaria have changed strategies and now offered package solutions (e.g. labor, apartment, children care) for whole families to make them

---

[2] This chapter is completely based on Krüger 2006, reviewed for this article.
[3] July 1, 1990 - monetary, economic and social conversion in the GDR to the FRG system, October 3rd, 1990 - "unification", e.g. constitutional and legal extension of the FRG into the area of the GDR (cf. Art.23 Grundgesetz).

move from the East to the West, commuters become settlers. The German essayist Wolfgang Engler (2001: 4f.) refers the cynic attitude of industrials he met:

> "To avoid unwanted competition from the East is part of our enterprises' strategy for the sake of our stakeholders and for the state. This is not especially philanthropic, but politically rational ... Instead of mourning [about the westward migration] one should be happy with them. Sure, that way East German towns and villages thin out more and more and so they become less and less attractive locations. I don't see a convincing alternative to this process." (Engler 2001: 4f.)

The results of de-industrialization in Schwedt, a small-town at the Polish border stands for many: the Petrochemical Company (PCK) was among the largest companies in the GDR with 8,700 employees in 1987. After being transformed into a "western" company and investments of 1.3 million Euro the number of employees has been reduced to 1,400. Related research and development branches have been completely closed down in Schwedt (Beer 2002: 49f.).

As the empty housing phenomenon became more apparent shrinking entered the public discourse. At a first stage, the public just recognized too less tenants for apartment houses. It was only at a second stage that the demographic and economic dimension of shrinking was noticed. Between 1990 and 1998, the number of inhabitants of East German towns decreased by 17.7%. According to this loss of population the number of empty premises increased tremendously to an average of 16.5% (Hunger 2000: 168). The public debate arouse because the situation became economically serious: in general, 15% of empty premises means a critical turn for an estate company, from 20% upwards a clash is predicted (Kil 2002). In fact, towns in Eastern Germany reach these numbers! Since the mainly public estate companies announced these scenarios, shrinking became an angstful reality within society.

As a consequence, the stadtumbau program has been developed that forced municipalities to work out Integrated Urban Development Concepts. These concepts can be seen as a crossing between formal development respectively zoning plans and informal bottom-up development concepts. As a prerequisite for a donation of subsidies the municipalities must present their demographic and economic forecast up to 2015 or 2020. Besides they must name areas of preservation, areas where urgent transformation is necessary and areas where long-term transformation is necessary. This spatial division was first executed in Leipzig and turned into a best practice of the stadtumbau concept. Leipzig's urban development agency divided the town into basically three types of quarters. First, there are preservation sites, among them the downtown and the more successful southern and western inner city neighborhoods from the "gründerzeit" era. Consolidated areas are mainly living-oriented quarters, as well as of "plattenbau"-typology as other urban forms, where there is a stable population. These stability roots either in a certain urban attractiveness, e.g. a good proximity to the inner-city and to green areas or in a milieu bounded to its neighborhood, e.g. "first-movers" that moved in during the 1960s/1970s as young families. They use the enlarged space in their "empty nester" apartments and stay in the neighbourhood as pensioners. However, a subcategory of that are areas of long-term observation in anticipation of the alteration of a rooted milieu that may come one day. The category of areas in transition (or: restructure areas) leads to the problematic neighborhoods with high shares of emptiness. Stadtumbau measures will reduce the number of empty houses and thus give the quarter a new urban quality. This urban form of the future will create a tension between new spaces available with more attractiveness and tooth gaps in the urban structure finalized in the "perforated city" leitmotiv (Lütke-Daldrup 2001).

Leipzig's way inspired the national stadtumbau competition to think in urban structures of transition. Within the Integrated Urban Development Concepts (IUDC) there must be a detailed statement on the most urgent neighborhoods, where action of destruction and renewal must be located. Renewal with relevance for the whole municipality is possible everywhere. The term of destruction not only refers to the physical demolition of apartment buildings (except to the ten sites in Berlin only housing is possible to be pulled down) but also to a tenant-oriented social work aiming to help the people who have to move from the condemned houses. Renewal measures based on traditional renewal and revitalization concepts should improve the whole neighborhood in order to keep it alive. Generally it is not planned to tear down complete neighborhoods. Therefore it is absolutely necessary to attract people to stay in the neighborhood, even when several buildings and maybe even "the own one" (where there has been the rented apartment) will not exist any further. This punctual surgery in the neighborhoods validates the attempt of several municipalities in order to stay relevant nodes. An "amputation", e.g. the demolition of whole neighborhoods, might give inhabitants and municipal actors the impression that the municipality gave up its role. On the other hand municipalities have no other chance to deconstruct relevant parts of their municipality area because their functional relevance has already been regressed. Thus a new vision needs to be found, following the example of the community of Schwedt. Within the stadtumbau process Schwedt followed the principle of "breathing out"; Neighborhoods at the edge of town physically disappeared, as 60% of the population already had emigrated from these neighborhoods (Beer 2002: 49ff.). The historical inner city and other more consolidated "plattenbau" neighborhoods will be renewed and will therefore definitely meet the future housing needs of Schwedt. By the way, Schwedt was the first town to demolish a "plattenbau" apartment block with 748 apartments in 1998 (Beer 2002: 49ff.). Their actions show a fair degree of radicalism, because the punctual surgery in other towns does not necessarily solve the estate problem.

Within the federal funding scheme 350,000 apartments should be torn down until 2009 (BMVBW 2003; BMVBS 2004; Haller/ Liebmann 2001). This is one quarter of all empty apartments today. Those concepts deal with 25%, but if the economic growth keeps passing by large parts of East Germany it might be nessecary to talk about 100% or maybe even 125% and await what remains of the present towns and urban structures (Bohne 2004: 62). The question is wether this is too pessimistic or the municipal IUDCs are too optimistic. The fact is that unfortunately there has been a history of too optimistic concepts in the East. A regular phenomenon in East-Germany are IUDCs explaining less zoning needs in a heavy contrast to valid formal zoning plans, that serve new areas to develop (Nuissl/Rink 2004). There is already now a legality debate about the take-back of zoning and the retransformation of approved reserved building land into the green areas they are in reality, respectively in order to establish temporary zoning. The empty housing stock is necessarily part of the urban form of the town. Tearing down the neighborhood may reduce the stock to a more market-adequate amount but what happens to the urban design? Again, Leipzig takes a role pars pro toto by elaborating the leitmotiv of the "Perforated Town" (Lütke-Daldrup 2001). One the one hand this is a formal opposition to the paradigm of the compact European City. On the other hand this concept aims to achieve a form between the preservation of the general structure of the European City and the opportunities of torn down houses, namely qualified spaces in the neighborhood. These perforated forms are resulting from a punctual destruction of buildings. Consequently the traditional dense form of the European City will be altered: green spaces will be next to housing blocks, streets and squares will not necessarily be bordered by buildings, different housing forms - e.g. multi-storey blocks and detached houses - will coexist next to each other. The ambivalent term of "city landscape" returns. Within this context Iris Reuther (Leipzig) and Michael Bräuer (Rostock) interrogate: Is there bravery for the gap? Will there be a backlash to rows? Will the cultivation of an inner periphery be able to compensate the loss of the traditional margins (Reuther/Bräuer 2001)? Inner-city brownfields are no longer reserved areas for building, but possible fields of adventure. In order for this to happen, the associative link of "brown-field" with "depravity" has to be replaced by an associative link of brown-field with "wild urban nature" and more urban life perspectives (cf. Rink 2003). As an example, in Leipzig-Plagwitz wheat was sowed on an industrial brownfield.

The empty housing problem has definitely consequences on the estate economy. If one can say that four rented apartments finance a fifth, more than 20% empty stocks may ruin the company. Hunger (2000) gave a scenario what will happen if the situation does not change: Due to the continuing construction in suburban locations and a decreasing population the competition will get tougher. Public companies as main players will dramatically lose their financial power. Besides they still have to carry the so-called old-debts, namely regulations coming from of the unification treaty. It is their task to serve the transfer-dependent poor population. This is especially the case when the social service pays the rent directly to the public company so they have to attract more solvent tenants. The companies definitely face insolvency and several have already been ruined (Hunger 2000: 169). This point of view becomes more and more common (Bernt 2002: 11ff.; Kil 2002). The best complex description of the shrinking process has been originally created in Schwedt. As pointed out by Beer (in: Hannemann 2003), it is a vicious circle of socio-economic consequences of East German shrinking. It was originally created to consider the specific development of Schwedt, where shrinking processes started fairly early. Eventually Schwedt can be seen as a kind of East-German avant-garde. The correlation of a negative economic development and a decreasing population in connection with a correlation of the population development with the increase of empty premises summarizes how East-German towns developed after 1990.

4. The "spatial struggle" of suburbanisation and reurbanisation

4.1 The change of residential quarters in Leipzig

Probably nine out of ten inhabitants of Leipzig changed their apartment at least once in the 10-15 years after German unification. Steinführer (2004: 199) proved this data for two inner-city quarters of Leipzig. Assuming that - if not nine of ten - still the overwhelming majority of inhabitants changed its residence at least once it can be said that the situation of Leipzig has been extraordinary between 1989 and 2004. So if one takes the recent heavy debates on an upcoming housing shortage into consideration, this era has to be accounted.

Before 1989 there was a qualitative housing shortage: On the one hand there was the stock, built before 1945 ("gründerzeit stock"), which was un-renovated and often literally stood into ruins. On the other hand there was the "plattenbau", the moderately comfort flats of the GDR era, which meant substandard in terms of the housing in Western standards of unified Germany. In 1995, after the housing market was freed, it offered (within the municipal borders of Leipzig according to 1990) 61% pre-1945 stock and 36% of pre-1989 stock (Steinführer 2004: 165). Therefore it definitely lacked segments.

In order to tackle the problem by quantity new houses had to be be erected. This was mainly due to the fact that the renewal - of both majoring stocks - would take at least a decade to function spatially beyond a single renewal project. Surely those sites were situated in suburbia as this was the only available space after 1989: juridically, monetarily, and spatially. Houses with a dense urban design with three to four storey houses and rental apartments were built, which can be characterized as a special suburban architecture of East-Germany (Nuissl/Rink 2003: 50). These so-called "wohnpark" sites were built quickly by investors who wanted to take profit of the "Sonder-AFA", a special tax rule to induce economic development in the so-called new lands of Germany. This implied the possibility to reduce taxes to factually nothing by erecting something somewhere else in East-Germany (Nuissl/Rink 2003: 29; Herfert/Röhl 2001: 153).[4] For the village of Borsdorf, east of Leipzig, Heydenreich (2000: 64) evalu-

---

[4] Even more, the economic funding was blind against spatial demands, so especially easily available agricultural land was developed for anything that might have induced development in the quickly deindustrialised East (Nuissl/Rink 2003: 29; Herfert/Röhl 2001: 153).

ated, that 83% of the tenants moved there because of the facilities and the type of the apartment especially because something comparable could not be found in the older stocks. Only 26% of the tenants named the place as a reason to move there. Even more surprisingly, only 14% named the proximity to their labor place as a reason to move there. Before 1994, Borsdorf's population was shrinking as everywhere in East-Germany. The main reason was the enormous labor-driven migration from East to West (Nuissl/Rink 2003; Engler 2001; Tiefensee 2003; Kil 2001). However, in the short period from 1994 to 2000 there has been a considerable population growth in Borsdorf (Heydenreich 2000: 54). Between 1995 and 1997 3,000 apartments per year were built around Leipzig (county Leipziger Land). However, in 1998 and 1999 only 1,200 apartments were built p.a. - the amount was cut in halves (Steinführer 2004: 168). Among the people who moved at the same time to the Eastern Inner Cities[5] 82% named the apartment facilities as a reason to move there (they moved to the first renewed apartments of the "gründerzeit" stock, thus early reurbanites). Furthermore 74% mentioned the place and 43% the proximity to labor as pull factors. This case is explanatory: moving to Suburbia these days did not mean to move to the countryside. Furthermore this did not mean a spill-over effect caused by a general growth that would have been typical for suburban development (Nuissl/Rink 2003: 20; Herfert/Röhl 2001: 154). Often it only meant to move to a new apartment somewhere in a region, where most of the housing stock was un-renewed (Nuissl/Rink 2003: 37+52). In the early 1990s, the few renewed apartments were much more expensive than suburbia. Especially for downtown apartments no high-class demand could be found on the market. Therefore the movement to Suburbia was almost completely facility-driven and not place-driven, as the standard of an apartment mattered more than its address. Theoretically this is the continuous implementation of dissatisfaction with the own living eventually turning into residential mobility (Steinführer 2004: 299). Throughout the 1990s the areas and sites in suburbia stayed the same, but their relative position on the market and their formal integration changed. Their growth was limited to only some years and they lost almost all of their dynamics. By 2000 most of them were incorporated into Leipzig municipality, which today means e.g. better public transport services than outside. At least they are sites one would call ex post sustainable devel-

---

[5] More precisely Neustadt-Neuschönefeld and Graphisches Viertel, both are neighborhoods in the large "Leipziger Osten", the Eastern Inner city.

opment, as detached housing has been kept to inner-urban sites where they fit into a greater planning scheme - as long as if that would not contradict to the story of their formation.

This certain spatial pattern as not only a result of this, on the other hand there is the restitution problem. As the free market was reestablished the claims of pre-World-War-II became relevant after 60 years; with all German history in mind, it was a long-lasting task to find out all the owners and their predecessors (Nuissl/Rink 2003: 25f.).[6] This has been a relevant push factor, making tenants leave because of uncertainties (Heydenreich 2000: 43). On the other hand there is the serial character. Due to its tremendous growth during the industrial age Leipzig consists mainly of "gründerzeit" housing stock (see above). However, an overall renewal of this stock would take an extremely long time. Hence, renewal became effective after 1995, also because of the end of the "Sonder-AFA" tax mentioned above and another tax regulation scheme that allowed investors to bet off 40% of renewal investments against the taxable income (Heydenreich 2000: 39). In the same year the housing markets of the inner city and suburbia levelled out (Heydenreich 2000: 45). As a consequence suburban multi-storey housing ceased to be cheaper than the same standard inside the pre'45 inner city fringe. So place took back its predominance. The inner-city became attractive as inner-city; and suburb as suburb. Hence, in the late 1990s there was the peak for detached housing in the suburbs (Nuissl/Rink 2003: 56). Also some of the "wohnpark" sites that have not been completed yet were replanned as detached housing areas. On the other hand many new inhabitants (re)located themselves in the city. These were often younger generations who were establishing a first household, but also the people of Leipzig who moved again to the city, this time due to the attractiveness of the place. For instance, in 1999 only 43% of the population in Gohlis, which is situated northwest of the central station, lived there for 20 years and longer. 51% of the population were

---

[6] Often new "old" proprietors lack the necessary financial resources for renewal after being detected, the finding often took longer than assumed. Tenants were often elbowed out by restitution claims. Not knowing if the place will be renewed and how this will be done and which market-segment should it meet after renewal, rose a tremendous insecurity among tenants. Therefore it was often easier for tenants to actively look for a new flat (often in the urban fringe). Furthermore local retail facilities often were hindered in their development, thus letting a neighbourhood deteriorate, as in the mixed-use areas not only the residential use was affected but also the street-shops on the ground floor (Nuissl/Rink 2003: 25f.).

newcomers from the last five years (Steinführer 2004: 143). They represented the new Leipzig, the resurgence of the core city and the European urban housing stock from the industrial age that is linked with the reurbanization phenomenon. Nevertheless, there was still the existence of the "last quarter" (Lütke-Daldrup 2003): Even after the great efforts that have been made in the decade after 1994/95 (when renewal started to boost) one quarter of the stock has not been affected by renewal. This quarter of the stock is spread all over town, not clustered in one last quarter.

In the 1990s reurbanization was only interpreted as something symbolic. It has been only in 2001 that it was a statistically proven phenomenon (Steinführer 2004: 300) and until today it is still valid to describe Leipzig. Another term that was raised around 2000 was the one of the "perforated city" (Lütke-Daldrup 2001, Lütke-Daldrup 2003), imagining this "last quarter" to disappear. Of course this was not possible, as it often were corner houses and houses along main streets. For instance, the urban design of the whole neighborhood would have been negatively affected by the disappearance of even a single house there. Therefore, Leipzig became famous for its "guardian houses": Within this concept empty houses are used by neighbors for cultural activities, crafts, galleries and alternative livings, being the guards of the physical substance. Surely at the beginning one would not imagine such a guardian house to become luxury apartments. But when it happens (cf. Rink et al. 2013; Herfert 2003) the fear of gentrification is spreading among the citizens although the overall data does not give proof on this (see more of this below).

Back to the starting point and to another residential segment: the "plattenbau" stock of the 1960s-1980s. The quarter of Grünau, which has been erected between 1976 and 1988, is the largest neighborhood of this type in East-Germany. At its peak in 1989 there were 85,000 inhabitants in Grünau. For the sociologist Alice Kahl, who started a (still ongoing) long-term sociological research on that neighborhood, this place was a privilege for the non-privileged after its erection. Neither the poor people nor the "rich" (e.g. artists, owners of craft firms, directors of companies and clinics, higher officials of the state party) lived in Grünau. The poor lived in the shabby "gründerzeit" stock, the others in designated areas. Ordinary people came to inhabit Grünau in the 1970s and 1980s (Steinführer 2004: 183). In 2002 the population of Grünau compared to the time back then halved (Steinführer 2004: 165). A deeper analysis of this stock requires a differenciation between the public housing company (LWB) and the housing corporations. The latter had comparative advantages. Firstly, because they could start earlier with the renewal of their stocks, secondly, because of their corporative model, they had more loyal tenants who were as well shareholders of the housing company. The LWB had severe economic problems. Thus only by 1993 they could offer their apartments on the free market (Heydenreich 2000: 43f.). By then already a certain number of tenants had moved away, partly because the demand was steered into the suburban "wohnparks" mentioned above. So the "plattenbau" was most heavily affected by suburbanization (Steinführer 2004: 184).

Additionally the prices were very low for un-renovated "plattenbau" flats. This meant a noticeable increase of the rent after renewal, which was mainly a retrofitting of the technical facilities such as water, sewage and electricity and energetic conditions such as facades, insulation and windows. Again, tenants were for the first time able to choose. Whether a renovated "gründerzeit" flat has been to cheap these days or a renovated "plattenbau" one too expensive - the result by all means has been, that not only the suburbanites left the "plattenbau" stock outside the city, but also reurbanites left to adjacent neighborhoods (Steinführer 2004: 202).[7]

This did not necessarily go along with a higher increase of emptiness in the "plattenbau" neighborhoods than elsewhere (emptiness also increased in other parts of Leipzig), because the apartments became a preferred target for poorer households. This could be seen as a well-performed counteraction against segregation as these neighborhoods from the 1970s and 1980s were well-functioning. However, this also meant a negative push-factor for the established milieu described by Kahl (see above). Surprisingly most of the Leipzig people were unsure about their preferred living area when they became mobile: circa half of the interrogated persons in Steinführer's study were unsure where to move (2004: 218). This image became more and more crucial as an argument for the direction of a planned movement.

After 1990 both types of older stocks had negative images. However, after 1990 the image of the "plattenbau" deteriorated even more rapidly as it was a projection of the fallen-down GDR system. The negative image of the "gründerzeit"

---

[7] According to the rent index the pre'45-stock became cheaper according to diminished demands, while the plattenbau stock rose to adequate prices according to the standard (Steinführer 2004: 172).

stock derived from its ruin-like atmosphere and its substandard, and also because of the quickly aborting, though remaining remarkable pollution of inner city quarters as a remain from the industrial age (Nuissl/Rink 2003:37). It is interesting to observe that by 2004 Grünau, a "plattenbau" stock and Connewitz, a "gründerzeit" stock, were caracterized by the same image (Steinführer 2004: 193). Today, Connewitz is one of the inner-city neighborhoods where first traces of gentrification can be found even statistically (not only politically). Grünau, on the contrary, is a quiet, but poor neighborhood with a bad image and unclear perspectives for the future. However, only ten years ago both neighborhoods were shrinking.

By 2000 it seems, that almost every Leipzig citizen has moved at least once before having found an adequate place to be:

- in the renovated stock of the "plattenbau" type in well-renewed high-rise buildings with a well-equipped infrastructure. For instance, two of the biggest shopping centers outside the inner city are located in Grünau and Paunsdorf, the largest and second-largest neighborhood of this type. Besides, schools, kindergartens and social services are well-equipped in these quarters since their erection, as well as public transport with light-rails and streetcars;
- in the inner city "gründerzeit" stock built before 1945, whether in a renovated apartment or in an un-renovated one. The un-renovated appartments offer very cheap rents as well as alternative ways of living;
- in the suburbs in detached houses or multi-storey houses (3-4 floors).

The overall shrinking phenomenon (see excursus below), that challenged all of East Germany since the 1990s and which is still occurring, made it very easy for tenants to move. Whole small-towns and whole regions became actually dispensable (Kil 2001). In some regions it were not only deindustrialization phenomena but de-economization (Hannemann 2003). Leipzig managed it to reinvent its economic base - spatially spoken with one hand in the suburbs, where BMW, Porsche and the fair are located and one hand in the inner city and its tertiary sector (see below). The whole shrinking phenomenon is described thoroughly (see above), but for Leipzig it meant that the housing market was only driven by the diminishing demand in every segment:

- renovated and un-renovated "plattenbau" stock has been taken from the market, as the technical term of the respective funding scheme named their deterioration;

- for the "gründerzeit" stock one spoke of the "last quarter" (see above) and in the Eastern Inner City a new pocket park (named Rabet) was installed, as it was possible to cluster some empty houses, which usually were spread all over the neighborhoods;
- in Suburbia premises fell empty (Nuissl/Rink 2003: 42; Heydenreich 2000: 42), especially the multi-storey houses built in the early 1990s as they had spatial disadvantages and were not competitive anymore to the renewed houses with their facilities;
- new land development ceased at most sites, already equipped with technical infrastructure, the term of "illuminated cow-meadows" (Herfert/Röhl 2001: 151) named them precisely.

Approximately 69,000 empty premises could be counted in Leipzig around 2000. This was the peak (Rink et al. 2013). Until 2011 the number decreased to 38,500, of which ca. 30,000 (2000) respectively 17,500 (2011) were not active on the market e.g. because of their bad condition. They shrank either because of their deterioration or because of the substantial revitalization, which often meant an actually new building behind the original facades. The reorganization phase has started in Leipzig, but as the stock is so huge the last quarter may have shrunk to a last fifth or sixth today. Nevertheless two decisive aspects are relevant. As in many other places around the world the image of the "gründerzeit" stock changed significantly into a positive one; and Leipzig became one of the cities labelled as "creative". With its culture, its university and its history it became an attractive place to be for a younger, more urban-oriented generation. They were attracted to the city of Leipzig as the housing stock there was cheap and of adequate standard as there was many of it.

4.2 Entrepreneurial Suburbanization: The location of commerce and industry

The typical driving force for an entrepreneurial suburbanization was totally absent in Leipzig: economic growth. Even in contrast, during the five years after 1989 some 70-90% of the jobs in the industry vanished (Nuissl/Rink 2003: 22). New entrepreneurial sites were not developing to fulfill any growth demand. However, they were developed to induce economic activity. Old industrial sites were not considered as suitable for the reestablishment of an industrial fundament of the region by the administrations (they were called conversion sites).

As explained below it was commercial suburbanization that dominated the first years after 1990. North of Leipzig, along the motorway A14 a new spatial pattern emerged (Herfert/Röhl 2001: 159). The A14 became a new east-western motorway. In 1990 it only connected Dresden with Leipzig; quite soon it was extended north-west-bound to Magdeburg and connected with the important A2 between Berlin and Cologne. A further extension was executed towards Hamburg and the small portuary town of Wismar, thus connecting the Leipzig region with the largest German gateway to the North Sea as well as to the Baltic Sea.

The big names along the A14 from East to West are: BMW, the Leipzig New Fair, Porsche, DHL and the Leipzig-Halle airport, all of them new suburban developments after 1990. As the region has been an industrial district since the 19th century one can imagine that there have been already several industrial areas convertible to commercial zones. Around 2000 the supply of commercial zones have been three times larger than the demand, according space (BBR 2002) Even acknowledging the increased demand that has emerged due to the new creative industries also coming to Leipzig it is unlikely that since 2000 it has been necessary to develop new commercial zones - the lack of it in 1990 has been overcompensated in the first decade after German unification.-With approximately 600 employments per 1000 inhabitants and the location of the airport, the municipality of Schkeuditz is insofar the most relevant employment place in the region (Leipzig 2005: 425, first suburban ring altogether: 375, second suburban ring altogether: 350); Schkeuditz is an exceptional case; compared to the 1980s it has increased its employments by 18%, whereas the region lost 40% (Usbeck 2002). Schkeuditz is a place where people commute in (to work), whereas the other suburban towns are places of out-commuting, mainly to Leipzig (Nuissl/Rink 2003: 54).

A general view on the spatial pattern of employment and commercial zones in the region shows that 80% of the dedicated zones are being used. However, there have been only marginal positive effects on the labor market (Herfert/Röhl 2001: 155). And there are still 800,000 square meters empty office space (Herfert/Röhl 2001: 155). A more details analysis on the spatial structure has been done by the city of Leipzig in 2005 (Leipzig 2005), describing the result of the change of the spatial pattern.[8]

- non-built areas of a large scale are demanded in the north along the A14;
- built areas are demanded between the city and the north, especially along the B2 route (between the main station in the city and the fair in the A14 corridor), or in the "old west" - the creative industries after 2000 prefer the "old west", most famous is the painter studios of Neo Rauch in former industrial buildings (e.g. former cotton wool fabric "Spinnerei");
- there is a continuous shift from commercial units from inner city to un-built, hence infrastructurally developed zones in the suburbs;
- the highest share of brownfields can be found in newly developed peripheral suburban sites (not situated in the A14-corridor and in problematic old industrial sites in the city);
- shortages of supply are predicted for high-value unbuilt industrial sites (Porsche and BMW took almost all sites available with 330ha altogether) and a future shrinkage of empty office lots is predicted (in the decade between 2005 and 2015 there is a chance to fill all the built respectively converted office space from the 1990s).[9]

The Leipzig municipality is aware of the peril that a predicted (or hoped for) economic growth might not follow a sustainable manner. The city has been named "boom-town" already three times in the last 20 years. First, as "L.E." after 1990, then as the German Olympic Candidate for 2012 and recently as the Creative City replacing Berlin. Leipzig's employment shrank from 100,000 in 1989 to 37,000 in 1993 (Leipzig 2005), and since then there has been very little growth. Leipzig is still one of the biggest German towns with a high unemployment rate. Only in the recent years a turnaround may be visible. The result of deindustrialization can still be found in the town's physical structure:

> "The mix of living and working that dates back to the industrial revolution, leads to brownfields in the middle of the urban physics. Their conversion challenges the ur-

---

[8] The analysis was made just before BMW and Porsche developed their sites in Leipzig, afterwords there has been a growth of demand by local sub-suppliers. Additional demands have been articulated by creative industries. But the general spatial pattern has not altered.

[9] BBR 2005 gave the data of 24% empty office lots in 2000, but 35% in 1998 and a sign of rising rents after 2000, which made them also predict a possible turnaroung especially in the very inner city.

ban renewal additionally. The competition between newly developed greenfields and inner city commercial zones is tough for those old zones." (ELD, in Leipzig 2005)

5. Regional development between growth and shrinking

At first, this meant for Leipzig a balanced development of Leipzig's former suburbia, now incorporated outskirts and the inner-city. Growth was over, beyond the larger projects such as BMW and Porsche all big projects have been completed recently. Even more, Saalepark closed in 2003, but reopened as Novaeventis with a reduced shopping mall of 76,000 square meters enhanced by entertainment facilities in 2006. The real-estate markets altogether calmed down.

This development was confronted with the rapidly increasing and thus again dramatic population losses in East-Germany. This meant for Western Saxony that Leipzig's shrinkage was more or less moderately compared to the losses of the provincial towns some 50 kilometers away from Leipzig. Until 2000 only some sort of first ring around Leipzig, approximately 25 kilometers away from the city hall in any direction, has been affected by suburbia, the provincial towns were dedicated to be sustainable cores of a possible second suburban ring. Now they depopulate - and the first suburban ring would do the same if there were not the population gains from the 1990s. Leipzig transformed into a kind of stable island in a negatively dynamic region.

For the housing market it meant that rents fell to an incredibly low level because of the emptiness rates that rose everywhere. An analogue development can be observed concerning the office rates. As a result even Leipzigers could easily move between the neighborhoods as it was a quite rational effort to move. In certain cases it was even possible to lower the overall rent by a move within the same segment according to standard and place of the flat. This meant that the market was dominated by low demand and the consumers. As the renewal schemes and funds were increased and differentiated after 1999/2002 the core city was developing a little better than suburbia. The development there turned into stagnation. In the dense "plattenbau" settlements from the 1970s and 1980s a lot of flats were taken from the market, as deterioration was euphemized. Other parts of the settlements were qualified, especially public space and infrastructure. The two largest plattenbau neighborhoods are close to the largest shopping centers. These areas have been refitted and serve as a mixed area with a large amount of social housing. They are a typical segment for a European City that is able to get along with social segregation - not because there is social housing, but because of the mixture and the functional integration of those areas with social housing in town. During the decade after 2000 it did not play a role as rents were low everywhere, but on the long run Leipzig will profit from those efforts into these half-urban, half-suburban settlements.

The other big effort of renewal was, that the "gründerzeit" housing stock was not only renewed, but then accompanied by a social monitoring and community projects (note: in GDR time the poorest lived in the old stock, as rents never rose that much after 1989, those creative "pre-gentrification" areas were spots to observe in terms of social cohesion) as well as by a renewal of the public space. As also here flats were taken off the market it was possible to create a more broadminded public space e.g. with the creation of the Rabet park or the transformation of the industrial sites close to the Karl-Heine-Canal. So Leipzig took the chance to enhance the western parts of the inner city fringe by some waterfront sites. Tu sum up, what looked like a decade of stagnation after 2000 changed the town in certain relevant details, which led to the reurbanisation and gentrification debate of today, mentioned in the first chapter.

References

Beer, Ingeborg (2002), "Wohnen und Leben im Wartestand. Ein Quartier in Schwedt zwischen Abriss und Aufwertung", in: *Berliner Debatte Initial 13/2002*, Berlin: Gesellschaft für sozialwissenschaftliche Forschung und Publizistik, 34-48.

Bernt, Mathias (2002), "Risiken und Nebenwirkungen des Stadtumbau Ost", *Umweltforschungszentrum Leipzig-Halle (ed.)*, discussion paper, Leipzig.

BMVBW (Bundesministerium für Verkehr, Bau- und Wohnungswesen) (2003), *Auswertung des Bundeswettbewerbs Stadtumbau Ost*, Berlin.

— (2004), *Dokumentation zum Kongress 'Zwei Jahre Stadtumbau Ost' am 27. November 2003 in Berlin*, Berlin.

Bohne, Rainer (2004), "Das Phänomen Stadtschrumpfung verändert den Charakter der Städte in Deutschland, Was its zu tun?", in: Schröder, Roland (ed.) (2004): *Stadtumbau Ost, Eine Zwischenbilanz*, Berlin: Technische Universität Berlin.

Engler, Wolfgang (2001), "Friede den Landschaften! Impressionen und Phantasien zur politischen Geographie Ostdeutschlands", *Blätter für deutsche und internationale Politik 07/2001*, Bonn: Blätter-Verlag, 872-879.

Haller, Christoph and Liebmann, Heike (2001), "Vom Wohnungsleerstand zum Stadtumbau", in: *Berliner Debatte Initial 13/2002*, Berlin: Gesellschaft für sozialwissenschaftliche Forschung und Publizistik, 34-48.

Hannemann, Christine (2003), "Schrumpfende Städte in Ostdeutschland, Ursachen und Folgen einer Stadtentwicklung ohne Wachstum", *Aus Politik und Zeitgeschichte 28/2003*, Bonn: Bundeszentrale für politische Bildung, 16-24.

Herfert, Günter (2002), "Kleinräumige Wanderungsprozesse in Westsachsen - Trendwende zur Reurbanisierung?", in: Leipzig Municipality (ed.), *Statistischer Quartalsbericht*, Leipzig, 13-18.

— (2003), "Between Gentrification and Downwards Spiral", *Raumforschung und Raumordnung 03/2003*, Bonn: BBR.

Heydenreich, Susanne (2000), *Aktionsräume in dispersen Stadtregionen, ein akteursbezogener Ansatz zur Analyse von Suburbanisierungsprozessen am Beispiel der Stadtregion Leipzig*, Passau: L.I.S Verlag.

Hunger, Bernd (2000), "Strukturschwache Regionen der neuen Länder. Die schwierige Situation der Kommunen und Wohnungsunternehmen", in:

Raumplanung 91, Dortmund: Informationskreis für Raumplanung, 168-172.

Kil, Wolfgang (2001), "Redundant Population, Redundant Cities. Leitgedanken zu einer nicht mehr aufschiebbaren Diskussion", *Deutsche Bauzeitung 06*, Nürtingen: Konradin Medien/Kohlhammer, 58-63.

Kil, Wolfgang (2002), "Schattenland des Neoliberalismus. Überlegungen zum Schrumpfungsprozeß ostdeutscher Städte", *Archplus 163*, Aachen: Archplus Verlag, 4-5.

Sukopp, Herbert (1998), *Stadtökologie: Ein Fachbuch für Studium und Praxis*, Jena: Gustav-Fischer-Verlag.

Krüger, Arvid (2006), *What happens in East-Germany? The demographic change and its relevance for the spatial development in the Baltic Sea Region*, Stockholm: Kungliga Tekniska Högskolan.

Leipzig Stadt (2005), "Stadtentwicklungsplan Gewerbliche Bauflächen", *Beiträge zur Stadtentwicklung*, 46, Leipzig.

Lütke-Daldrup, Engelbert (2003), "Die perforierte Stadt - neue Räume im Leipziger Osten", *Informationen zur Raumentwicklung 1-2/2003*, 55- 67.

— (2001), "Die perforierte Stadt - Eine Versuchsanordnung", *StadtBauwelt 24/2001*, Gütersloh: Bertelsmann.

Nuissl, Henning/ Rink, Dieter (eds.) (2003), "Urban Spawl and Post-Socialist Transformation, the Case of Leipzig", *UFZ (Umweltforschungszentrum Leipzig)*, Leipzig.

— (2004), "Schrumpfung und Urban Sprawl, Analytische und Planerische Problemstellungen", *UFZ (Umweltforschungszentrum Leipzig-Halle)*, Leipzig.

Reuther, Iris/ Bräuer, Michael (2001), "Shrink positive? Zur Einführung in ein brisantes Thema", *Der Architekt 04/2001*, Bonn: Bund Deutscher Architekten, 1-3.

Rink, Dieter/ Haase, Annegret/ Schneider, Andreas (2013), "Vom Leerstand zum Bauboom? Zur Entwicklung des Leipziger Wohnungsmarkts"; in: Stadt Leipzig, Amt für Statistik und Wahlen (ed.), *Statistischer Quartalsbericht I/2014*, Leipzig.

Rink, Dieter (2003), "Ersatznatur Wildnis Wohnstadtfaktor, Soziale Wahrnehmung und leitbildhafte Vorstellungen von Stadtnatur", *UFZ (Umweltforschungszentrum Leipzig)*, Leipzig.

Schulz, Klaus-Dieter (2004), "Stadtumbau Ost, Ergebnis gravierender profitorientierter Fehlaktionismen im West-Ost-Spannungsverhältnis?", in: Schröder, Roland (ed.) (2004), *Stadtumbau Ost, Eine Zwischenbilanz*, Berlin: Technische Universität Berlin.

Steinführer, Anett (2004), *Wohnstandortentscheidungen und städtische Transformation: vergleichende Fallstudien in Ostdeutschland und Tschechien*, Wiesbaden: Verlag für Sozialwissenschaften.

Tiefensee, Wolfgang (2003), "Stadtentwicklung zwischen Schrumpfung und Wachstum", *Aus Politik und Zeitgeschichte 28/2003*, Bundeszentrale für politische Bildung, 3-6.

Usbeck, Hartmut (2002), "Die Entwicklung kleiner und mittlerer Zentren im mitteldeutschen Verdichtungsraum, Schkeuditz im Zentrenvergleich", in: Moser, Peter/Thiele, Kathleen (eds.): *Entwicklung kleinerer und mittlerer Zentren im suburbanen Raum, Einordnung des Mittelzentrums Scheuditz*, Leipzig: UFZ (Umweltforschungszentrum Leipzig), 53-74.

A Big Gamble for "Greater Paris"

Elodie Vittu

1. The other side of "the fabulous world of Amélie": Social and spatial fragmentation in the suburbs of Paris.

Paris is not as romantic as its reputation suggests. The dramatic riots in 2005 and the tensions expressed by the media by violent young people without hope is a stark contrast to "Amélies´" world, a film that "[...]represents fully the myth of Paris" (Schüle 2003: 178). The fact that people burnt their own neighbors' cars was incomprehensible to those who were unaware of the situation of the peopleliving in the so-called "banlieue"[1]. To those people I would recommend to watch the film "La Haine" (The Hate 1994) by Mathieu Kassowitz, which shows the point of view of the young people living there. While there are huge social problems (e.g. unemployment, migration) and a dramatic housing situation in the "banlieue", some suburbs[2] are like traditional cities with central functions and other suburbs are economical hubs or rich residential areas. In the Paris´ suburbs, there are both spatial and social inequalities in terms of incomes, the housing situation or facilities. This article deals with different administrative scales to show the fragmentation of urban space around the inner-city and to discuss planning projects like "Greater Paris" as an answer to the uneven distribution of social facilities, transportation and housing issues.

Paris´ suburbs are not homogenous and host different social and spatial situations. The non-existent "spatial justice" (Soja 2010) and the gap between some peripheral areas and the inner-city fixes the people to the place they come from (Eckardt 2007: 36). The highway around Paris ("périphérique") along the lines of the historic wall of Fermiers Généraux which was built 1784-1791 during the French Revolution (Benevolo 1993: 78f.) is experienced as a barrier, a radical frontier between "in" and "out". To pass the "périf" (abbreviation from "périphérique") is a psychological step for the citizens of Paris. On the other

---

[1] In everyday language, the term "banlieue" is synonymous for areas with social problems, although it can represent both rich and poor neighborhoods outside the core city (cf. chapter 2.3.).

[2] In relation to the case study of Paris, I will speak about "suburbs" as a peripheral area around the inner-city.

side of the "périf", there are the "banlieues" with their problems: social disadvantage, ethnic diversity, infrastructure under-development and political disinterest (Eckardt 2007: 34). Since the 1980s, French urban politics have tried to implement positive discrimination in these neighborhoods, but the urban violence persists (Bachmann/Leguennec 1996; Bacqué/Sintomer 2001; Beaud/Pialoux 2003). Later, the program Agence Nationale pour la Rénovation Urbaine ANRU (National Agency for Urban Renewal) was created by the Act of August 1st, 2003. It changed strategies of city renovation by implementing a massive demolition of housing units in areas selected by criteria such as poverty, migration, social housing and unemployment. These demolitions concerned mostly concrete massive buildings from the 1950-60. Results of this high-cost program are disputed (Le Garrec 2006; Fijalkow/Lévy Vroelant 2014; Peigney/Allen 2014).

Following the six attributes[3] of the European City from Walter Siebel (2012), the city of Paris as well as some of Paris' suburbs can be seen as the European city par excellence. Its identity and culture, and the power of its history, the quality of its public space, its urban landscape and of course its French cuisine give tourists and selected inhabitants a pleasurable way of life. This image corresponds to the Ile de la Cité in the middle of the inner-city, but also to the Cathedral of Saint-Denis or the Castle of Versailles. However, Paris is also a global metropolis whose development needs to be controlled. The Kyoto-Protocol established new goals, namely to reduce greenhouse gas emissions by 2020 and cut down carbon emissions. In this context, a vision of the metropolitan area named "Greater Paris"[4] was launched in 2007, initiating discussions about governance and architecture, but also about planning issues. To better understand the city and the current vision for the metropolitan area of "Greater Paris", I will first investigate the frontier between the centre and suburbs. I will further present a hypothesis of non-homogenous but multi-centred suburbs, situated at the periphery of the core city. This article makes a case for a spatial and so-

---

[3] These attributes are emancipation, the presence of history, the urban way of life, the "Gestalt" (form, design), the city as a political subject and urban development focused on growth (Siebel 2012).

[4] The common translation in English of "Grand Paris" is "Greater Paris" with the use of the superlative "Greater" to match "Greater London". This appellation does not highlight the wordplay of "Grand Pari(s)": a homophone that simultaneously means "Big Paris" and "Big gamble". In the following article, the term "Greater Paris" refers to the project, launched 2007 by Nicolas Sarkozy to redefine the metropolitan area.

cial fragmentation between Paris and its periphery. After a presentation of the spatial structure, governance and planning issues will be accentuated. Finally, I will focus on central challenges of development and conflicts of the "Greater Paris" project, such as social issues, the housing question and the transportation system.

2. Spatial structure of Paris and its periphery

2.1. From Paris to other French cities: the "desert"

In his book "Paris and the French desert" (1948), Jean-Francois Gravier explained the distribution problems and inequalities between the capital and the rest of the country. At its time, the Gravier's thesis implied that Paris is responsible for the decline of the countryside. This title, labelling the French provinces as a "desert", was and still is a term that caught on. Bernard (2001) established a strong critic, showing that the growth of Paris is not responsible for the lack of development in the provinces. They are responsible for themselves as spatial planning in France is decentralised since the 1980s. French laws of decentralization and the new territorial law, in application in January 2015[5], define big cities situated in the province as "metropolitan areas" because they are economically competitive. In 2015, it is thus not acceptable to speak about these French cities as a provincial desert.

The development from Paris to other big French cities is a challenge to take off pressure of the capital city. With the far-distance train called TGV (Train à Grande Vitesse), metropolis like Rennes, Rouen, Lille, Marseille, Lyon can rapidly be reached from Paris' train stations and allow commuting. A new vision for the development around Paris, introduced through the "Greater Paris" competition in 2008 by the architect and urban planner team of "Grumbach & Associés" foresaw a development from Paris to Le Havre, a city with around 175,000 inhabitants which was rebuilt after the war by August Perret. This large-scale frontier saw the "Valley of the Seine" as a maritime axis from Paris river to Le Havre Harbour. The aim of this project was to promote the position of the French capital in a global world with a development to the coast (AMC Le Moniteur 2009: 129). To that end, a high-speed train line was planned to con-

---

[5] This law, applied from January 1st, 2015 creates metropolis in big cities inside an urban area and shrink the 22 "régions" into 14 "metropolitan regions" (AFP Liberation, January 23rd, 2014 and July 23rd, 2014).

nect Le Havre to Paris (200 kilometers) in one hour and fifteen minutes (instead of two hours). Furthermore, this project also saw the future of transportation by water, along the Seine river (Jacquand 2010b: 419).

Even if the economic objective is still important and was achieved with projects in other cities in the past, thanks to the modern technology of the TGV, the idea of developing Paris to the Baltic Sea with a connection to Le Havre seems to be more an image, a vision, than an actual, real project. A far-distance train connection could be possible, but not a realistic urban project on this scale. The area is too big and has far too many inhabitants. The challenge is to upgrade the actual transportation system in the suburbs rather than to further improve the attractiveness of the capital. The problems of development are bigger within the Paris conurbation than for commuters around France.

2.2. From mono-centralism to poly-centralism

In the collective imagination, Paris is known as the centre of a strongly centralized country; there is Paris and there is the desert. However, it has been showed that this vision is a prejudice against economical strong cities in the province. Furthermore around Paris it is difficult to distinguish between what is called "centre" and "periphery".

Many satellite towns outside the core city of Paris have central functions: commercial streets and malls; metropolitan infrastructure such as airports (Roissy, Orly), railway stations (regional train RER, but also the TGV in Marne-la-Vallée), universities (e.g. Paris Est, Nanterre), employment hubs and economic centres (Plaine Saint Denis, la Défense), hospitals and malls (Evry, Créteil Soleil). Inside these cities, there are also local elements of centrality: a city hall, where weddings are celebrated, mostly in a designated building, post office, local markets and shopping axis, church, theatre and schools. The population density is very high in these cities. This means that, on the one hand, there are a lot of inhabitants and, on the other hand, there is also a density of employment possibilities in these areas. These satellite towns are clusters of jobs and places for living. They are independent from the inner-city with regard to commuting: in general, workers stay in the "labour market region" they live in, especially inside the cities located in the first ring around the inner-city (Devillers et associés 2014: 2).

Figure 1: Centralities and Densities (Atelier parisien d´urbanisme 2013: 52)

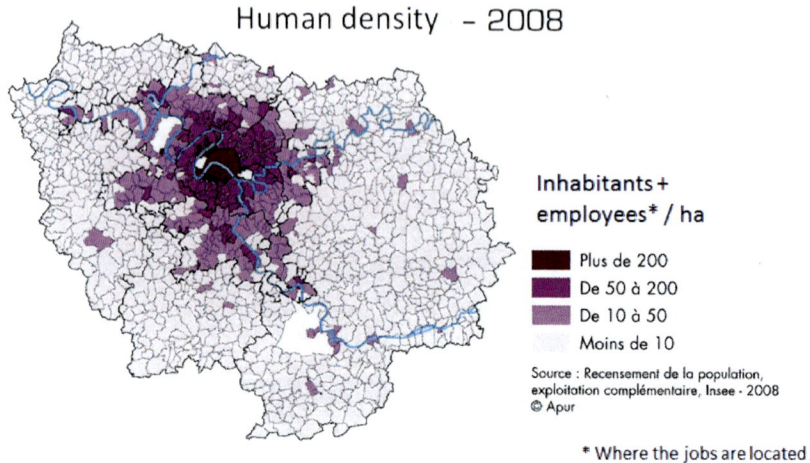

Figure 2: Human density (Atelier parisien d'urbanisme 2013: 15)

Because the discussion of poly-centralism around a Paris with heterogeneous cities is quite new, there is no term to distinguish these satellite towns and the other cities, which are economically developed; for the people they are all considered as periphery. Even though in Paris there is no governance area like Greater London, the multi-layered administrative organization (see next chapter) does not clarify the situation. In this text the economical centres around the city core are called satellite towns and all other peripheral cities "suburbs".

The Paris Urban Planning Agency proposes a new reality for this poly-centralism created through economical satellite towns around the capital of Paris: the so-called "hetero-polarization" (Atelier parisien d'urbanisme APUR 2013: 50f.). It means that there are many nodes around Paris with different functions. Considering the map of "centrality" connected with the "human density", there are "centralities everywhere" (Dominique Alba, Director of the Parisian agency of Planning APUR[6]). The challenge for the development of Paris Metropolis is to strengthen this poly-centralism but also to give a diversified response to these centralities, and to consider the heterogeneity of the local situations.

---

[6] Alba, Dominique, "Conférence territoriale sur la métropole parisienne", January 10th, 2014, conference paper, available at: http://www.driea.ile-de-france.developpement-durable.gouv.fr/conference-territoriale-sur-la-a4419.html (Accessed August 8, 2014).

Compared to "edge cities" according to the US-American model (Garreau 1992) in term of density, "satellite towns" and "suburbs" both are located inside a statistical area with a homogenously dense area, where people live and work. This area is called "urban area" (unité urbaine, see figure 6). According to the National Census of Population (INSEE), "urban area" includes towns with more than 2,000 inhabitants, where the houses are built without discontinuity.[7]

The border of the urban area follows the human density: from ten to 200 inhabitants and jobs[8]/ha (general Census of the population, INSEE 2008). Consequently, there are only a few spots with a concentration of jobs outside the urban area.

Despite their uniform density of population and jobs in the urban area, there is a sprawl phenomenon in terms of land uses outside the ring. This is similar to buildings spreading around roads taking over green spaces. However, in peoples' minds a transition from the perception of mono-centralism to polycentralism can be perceived. The "urban area" as a statistical area is the right point of reference to discuss when considering suburbanization topics and tensions between the centre and the periphery. In fact, in this area, the famous "banlieues" exist in their imagined variety.

2.3. Degression on the meaning of "banlieues"

In Paris, "banlieue" indicates both rich and poor neighborhoods. As early as 1891 the "beaux quartiers" were equipped with sanitary facilities, when the north-east areas in and around Paris were still under-equipped (Pinol/Garden 2009: 112f.). Many "banlieues" were affected by the massive construction policies of the 1960s-1970s with mono-functional, monotonous urban planning and architecture, named "grands ensembles", meaning a vast complex of housing buildings. However, "banlieue" also refers to affluent residential areas. The "red banlieue" is one traditionally governed by communist mayors, inhabited by workers since the 1930s (Pinol/Garden 2009: 112f.)

There is also a territorial dimension to "banlieues", especially in the north and east of Paris, where a stigmatization of these urban places is prevalent. Some segregation mechanisms in terms of finding a job with an address from a social disadvantaged area are taking place (Orfeuil/Wenglenski 2004). Mostly, the

---

[7] Meaning that there is no more than 200 meters between buildings.
[8] INSEE considers "job" to be the location of the job, not the location of the employee.

Figure 3: Mission Banlieue 89: water colour. Landscapes of "Greater Paris" (Atelier Castro-Denissot 1983)

term "banlieue" is synonymous with areas with social problems, called "sensitive urban zones", where migration and unemployment rates are extremely high and education levels very low (Eckardt 2007: 34). Historically, when Paris became a so called "département" after the French revolution in 1790, the "banlieue" was considered as the "granary" and the "lungs" (Fauré 2010: 73) of the city. Many years later, in 1920, Henri Sellier also proposed a metaphor of the body for the relationship between the capital and the "banlieue", but the "banlieue" is no longer the "lungs" but the limbs, albeit separated from the torso. The term "banlieues" acquired a negative meaning after industrialization, because of poor conditions of housing and commuting (Fauré 2010). From 1985 onwards, the word "banlieue" is not relating anymore to a spatial situation, but to a specific population - mostly poor migrants with large families - who lived in buildings from mass construction (Fauré 2010: 76), leading to the creation of mental images, such as "ghetto", "zone", "rabbit, chicken cage" (Volpe 1994).

The word "banlieue" is a trivial term for many different situations around a big city, by creating such mental images (Schüle 2003: 378f.). Political urban programs such as Banlieue 89, which aimed to increase the acceptance of the "banlieues" (Texier 2005: 226f.) did not succeed. Because of this deeply negative meaning, a new term to define the suburbs is needed. Fauré (2010) proposed "quartier" meaning neighborhood.

3. Governance and planning in Paris

Thus, "Greater Paris" is a development project which, in 2007, began to redefine the future of the capital. Actually, questions of governance and architecture were more debated than urban problems such as social polarization or urban fragmentation. To define the question of frontiers, a discussion about competencies, planning structures and historical planning projects is fundamental: in the project of "Greater Paris", the issue of scale determines which actor will govern the metropolitan area. Political conflicts are directly linked to administrative issues. After this chapter, it should be obvious that the project "Greater Paris" is not only a planning strategy but also a question of power.

3.1. The French territorial administration: a multi-layered system

Following the 1980s laws of decentralization, the "régions" gained more competences and responsibilities. Nevertheless, France remains a centralized state with different administrative entities: the smallest territorial division is the "commune" - France has about 36,000 of these cities - having a limited but nevertheless real autonomy (Benovolo 1993: 95). Then, there are the 101 "départements" and the 22 "régions" in mainland France.[9] An ironic slogan speaks of an "institutional mille-feuille", referring to a creamy cake with many layers to describe the multi-layered organization of French administration.

The "région" is not responsible for city planning. However, it organizes spatial planning on a regional level through Master Plans called SCOT (Schemes for territorial coherence). The competencies for urban and housing questions are distributed among the city and the "département". The key planning document is the local plan of urban development (PLU). It is both an operational document with land use orientations and a strategic instrument. Both PLU and

---

[9] July 2014: the parliamentary debate began about a territorial reform, planning to replace the 22 "régions" into 14 "metropolitan regions". It was adopted by the parliament on July 23rd, 2014.

Competences of authorities	région	département	City
City planning	∅	Gives a statement for some parts	Adopts the P.L.U. = local plan of urban development (// B-Plan) → Obligatory
Spatial planning	Makes the Shéma Directeur (master-plan) SCOT (Schema for the territorial coherence) → Obligatory	Give a statement	Prepares the master-plan
Housing	Gives Priorities Offer Subvention	Housing construction	Social housing
Transportation	Makes the Regional transportation Plan, Manages the airports, trains, canals	Gives a statement Makes a departmental transportation Plan, Public transport	Gives statements Organizes school transport
Infrastructure	∅	Constructs and maintenance of departemental streets	Constructs and maintenance of municipal streets and passes
Social services and public health	∅	Regulates social infrastructure and services	Finances welfare

Figure 4: competences of authorities in France (own translation from german, Barth/Lang 2003: 48)

SCOT should have the same objectives. Infrastructure, social services, such as welfare and public health fall under the responsibility of the "département" (e.g. the maintenance of main streets or the regulation of social infrastructure) or the city (e.g. the construction of municipal streets and the welfare payments). Transport and housing competencies as well as education are divided into a regional, departmental and local level.

3.2. Paris: a city, a "département" and part of a "région"

The "région" of "Ile-de-France" represents the specific administrative unit in and around Paris, with its own council. This "région" represents one sixth of the French population and one third of the gross domestic product. At the same time, perhaps surprisingly, it is three-quarters rural. The "région" consists of both: really dense urban areas and rural areas. The population is concentrated around the city-capital. The city of Paris is divided into 20 "arrondissements"

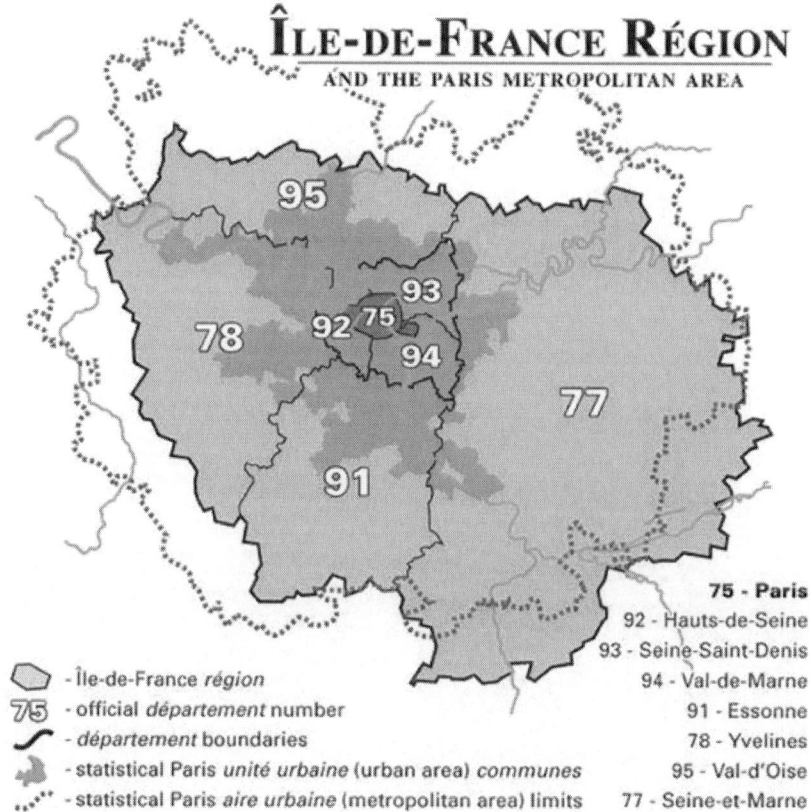

Figure 5: Paris administrative and statistical areas (Atelier parisien d'urbanisme 2013: 12)

each of which has its own council that, however, has no competencies in terms of administration. Instead it could be described as a level that creates local identity e.g. where people register or marry. The "arrondissements" follow the historical development of the city: The first "arrondissement", actually situated in the middle of Paris, reaches back to the medieval origins of the city, all following 19 "arrondissements" spiral outward around this historical node. All the main tourist attractions - except the airports, Disneyland Paris, the parks and castles such as Vincennes or Versailles - are located inside the city, within these 20 "arrondissements". But the city inside the peripheral ring road counts only 100 square kilometers (Berlin: 900 square kilometers, London: 1,500 square kilometers). It is even possible to cross the city on foot or by bike with a north-

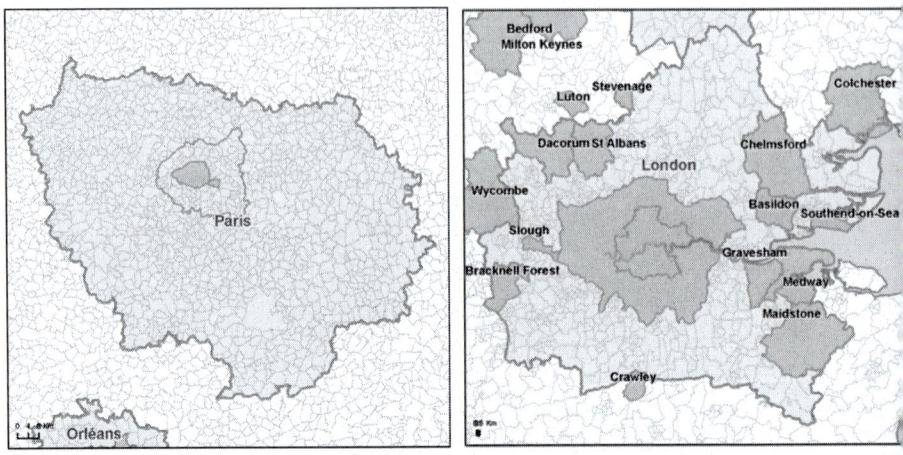

Figure 6: Core city and LUZ for Paris (Eurostat 2004). **Figure 7:** Core city and LUZ for Berlin (Eurostat 2004).

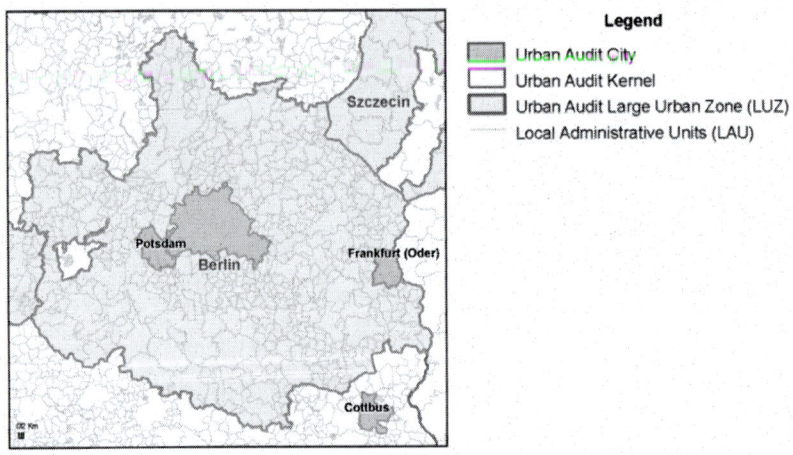

Figure 8: Core city and LUZ for London (Eurostat 2004).

Eurostat Data 2004	Paris	Paris LUZ (Ile de France)	Berlin	Berlin LUZ	London (Great London)	London LUZ
Superficy	105 km²	12.080 km²	891 km²	17.405 km²	1.579 km²	8.920 km²
Relation Superficies City:LUZ	1:115		1:19		1:6	
Population (inh)	2.151.853	11.089.124	3.387.828	4.971.331	7.429.200	11.917.000
Relation Population City:LUZ	1:5,1		1:1,5		1:1,6	
Density of population	205 inh./ha	9 inh./ha	38 inh./ha	3 inh./ha	47 inh./ha	1 inh./ha

Figure 9: European Metropolis in comparison (Database: Eurostat 2004, analysed by B. Trostorff and E. Vittu).

south distance of only 15 kilometers. Thus, taking into consideration only the inner-city, Paris is a quite small capital. However, it is one that includes a lot of economic activity, offices and a high population density.

These "ring road" limits are also the borders of the "département" identified by the number 75. This metropolitan area is bigger than the core city. Since the 1964 administration reform, the "région" Paris has eight "départements", divided into the "inner circle" (three "départements" around the "département" Paris) and into the "outer circle" (four "départements" in a second ring around the inner circle).[10] Given that the "départements" have no competences in urban planning, a general debate asks, in the context of a new reorganization of the metropolis, if and why they should be kept. Eurostat defines the "core city" as an administrative unit with an enormous dataset; in this case, Paris with its 20 "arrondissements". The Larger Urban Zone (LUZ) is an approximation of the functional urban zone centred on the city. Comparing this data from Paris with other European metropolitan areas, the LUZ is the "région" Ile-de-France. Berlin´s LUZ sprawls into the State of Brandenburg, as far as the Polish border on the east. On the city scale, London´s LUZ
concentrates approximately as many inhabitants as that of Paris. Looking at the relationships between the LUZs and their cities, the statisticcal comparison does not make sense (see figure 10). Moreover, the LUZ is too large to discuss

---
[10] Translations are taken from Breuillard (2012: 45).

about urban fragmentation in terms of population density, workplaces, infrastructure and transportation.

3.3. Master Plans for the "Région Ile-de-France": an historical overview

Historically, there have been many plans for the development of the Paris region. The Cornudet law in 1919 presented a plan for the beautification and extension of the satellite towns and created the first restrictions on development. It tried to constrain the natural topographic growth of the cities using territorial boundaries. In 1934, Henri Prost initiated special zones around the city centre by a network of motorways constructed in the landscape and through the forests (Orfeuil/Wiel 2012).

Based on the administration reform in 1965, the first Master Plan of Urban Planning created the "New Towns", with their architecture of concrete, car-oriented urbanism and the installation of universities. They were connected to Paris by a rapid transit system, which was a commuter railway system that offered a regular timetable. This was the first attempt at polycentrism (AMC Le Moniteur 2009: 12f.). This 1965-plan was responsible for the current situation of the metropolis. It happened in the context of the Cold War when the French state wanted to demonstrate its power over the municipalities. Therefore, the idea was not to develop the existing suburbs, but to build ex nihilo new cities around the capital. This merely slowed down the construction of the metropolis and did not prevent its development into the suburbs (Jacquand 2010b).

From the 1960s, with the opening of a Planning Office affiliated to the Regional Council, namely the Institute of Urban Planning in the "région" (IAU Ile-de-France), the government promoted the spatial planning of metropolitan Paris. In 1976, IAU Ile-de-France proposed a new Master Plan. With this second Master Plan of Urban Planning, realized by the IAU Ile-de-France, landscaping and spatial development became more important than land use planning. The next Master Plan for the "Région Ile-de-France" was established in 1994 and positioned urban planning against the natural expansion of the city and in favour of a connection between Paris, the New Towns and the airports.

Finally, the most recent Master Plan (2008) has been established by the "région" and acts as counter-plan to "Greater Paris", offering another approach to planning. Following an architectural competition with internationally famous

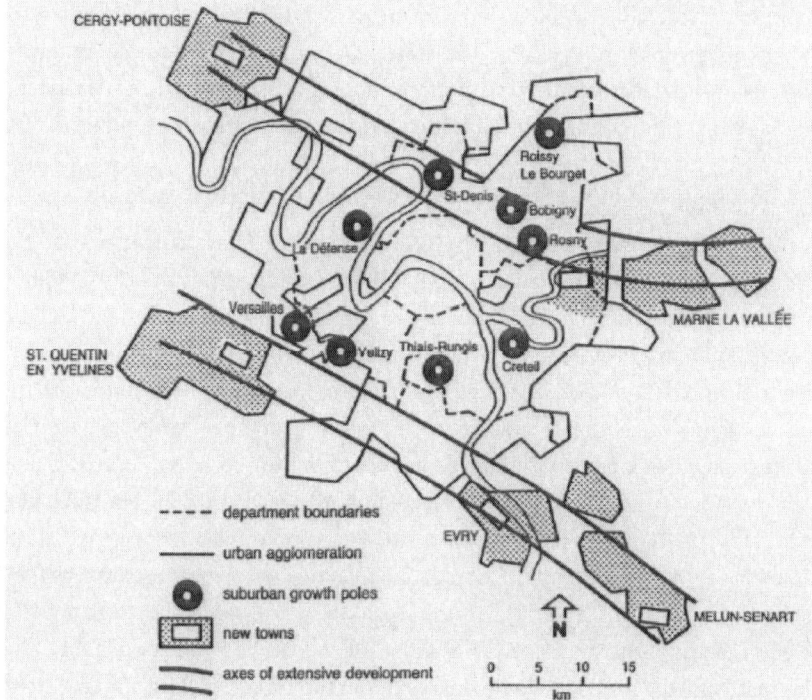

Figure 10: Paris Masterplan 1965 (Schüle 2000)

teams, the two high-profile ideas for "Greater Paris" were the following: first Grumbach´s idea to connect Paris to Le Havre and second, an idea to construct a sort of regional subway, called "big 8". This project was defended by Christian Blanc, state secretary of Nicolas Sarkozy, with the aim of quickly connecting 40 new railway stations, which should be constructed on agricultural areas and on fallow land inside the "Région Ile-de-France". Both plans shared the idea of quitting the radial-concentric development.

At the same time, to affirm its disagreement with these huge projects, the "région" adopted a new Master Plan in 2008 based exactly on radial-concentric planning with projections of development up to 2020. Many rings should be connected by a circular subway, the "Arc Express", with a budget of 6 milliard Euro (Bodenschatz et al. 2010: 378). It was a project directly in competition with the "Greater Paris"' project "big 8". The discussion about the future generated two opposing political visions: the state wanted to develop a number of economic clusters (multi-polarism); the "région" preferred the development of many centers (poly-*centralism*). The state wanted a "super automatic metro", partly underground, connecting airports and the economic poles (Jacquand 2010a: 252); the "région" wanted fast connections for the existing suburbs.

3.4. Confrontation of political visions in different administrative levels

Paris and the "inner circle" (75-92-93-94 - see figure 6) are considered as the Paris Metropolis but they have no joint political existence. Besides these administrative borders, the metropolitan area is defined by economic and political factors. The European Spatial Development Perspective from 1999 defined just five metropolises, namely London, Paris, Milan, Munich and Hamburg, as "the only dynamic areas of integration in the world economy", which have to be strategically developed. With European expansion, the focus of European policies moved towards a polycentric development (Paragraph 25 and following the Territorial Agenda 2020). Another important point of discussion would be to criticize the concentration of spatial planning into metropolitan regions through Master Plans (Faludi/Waterhout 2002).

In the case of Paris, the issue is not whether the city is a metropolis, but how the metropolitan area should be developed in the future. In contrast to "Greater London", which is a vision for the future of London, Paris has got many Master Plans (see 3.5.) but no common vision.

Since 2001 the City of Paris, and since 1998 the "région", have been under left-wing government. In 2003 a number of mayors from the "red banlieue" (see 3.3.) together with the Mayor of Paris founded a "metropolitan conference" to coordinate projects, but nothing concrete emerged from this. Because the personalities in power took a passive role, they opened the way for President Sarkozy when he arrived in power in 2007. Right at the start of his presidency, he initiated the "Greater Paris" project and tried to win back the "Région Ile-de-France", as well as the city of Paris, to his centre-right Party (UMP).

All actors agreed on the need to have one vision. "Greater Paris" is a plan to control and regulate the development of the metropolitan area, independent from the administrative borders. In June 2007, Nicolas Sarkozy, by that time President of the French Republice, initiated the project for many reasons:

"It was time to start a new, large-scale way of thinking, it was time to awaken thought in cities (...) diametrically opposed to utopia, fundamentally anchored in the reality of metropolitan areas." (AMC Le Moniteur 2009: 5)[11]

The motivation of the French politicians who initiated the project was to maintain Paris' position on the global stage and to reform the metropolitan area. The ambitious aim was to be competitive, not only as a European Metropolis but also as a global Metropolis, like New York or Tokyo and,

"to permit France to maintain its place in the competition between countries by making its capital an open, dynamic, attractive "world city", a creator of wealth and jobs." (Statement of intent by Christian Blanc, Secretary of State for the Development of the Capital Region)

Between 2007 and 2011, there was a real expectation to rethink the metropolis but no consensus on the way to develop the specific project launched by Sarkozy. In this period, the deception, created by "unsatisfying answers" and "exaggerated ambitions" was high (Orfeuil/Wiel 2012). It was a subject of political dispute during the presidential election and a renewed discussion about suburbs.

With the new presidency in 2012, the "région"-state conflict vanished since both were controlled by the same party. We will see later that the current status of the transportation discussion under the Hollande government is a mixture of both approaches. However, this duality of thinking ignores the important roles of the municipalities: during the time of the project, new alliances are being built which explains why, up to today (2014) nothing really has happened in practice.

Despite the administrative boundaries (city, "département" and "région") - because the cake is really multi-layered - many satellite towns can cooperate inter-communal on various questions, such as waste management. A good example of such co-operation in practice is, in the north-east of Paris, the 354,000 inhabitant grouping of satellite towns named "Plaine Commune", created in 2000, which is going to be an inescapable economic stakeholder in metropolitan Paris. A second form of an inter-communality/inter-municipal cooperation exists between the local and regional authorities, such as "Paris métropole". It

---

[11] Unless otherwise noted, all citations from French and German sources have been translated by Emrys McNeill. At this moment, I would also like to thank Hazel Slinn (Language Centre, University Jena, Germany) and Tatjana Zemeitat for the time they took to review the article.

was created in June 2009 with 193 authorities, consisting of various political and territorial stakeholders on different levels and takes a consultative role.

Because of the political competition between the state on one hand, and the "région" and the left wing mayors, including the Mayor of Paris, on the other hand, all stakeholders have defended their different governance models: the "région" wants to secure its competences through a project named "Région capitale". Some politicians inside the municipality have proposed abolishing the "départements" and creating one big city, constisting of Paris and the inner circle. The "région" has advocated for poly-centralism with a project named "development petals", focused on six to eight communities of cities, responsible for urban development. Every petal would represent an economic centre, such as "Plaine Commune".

4. Some actual challenges for the metropolis

4.1. Social inequalities

Basically, the city of Paris has a majority population of senior citizens (aged 65 and above) and the suburbs are inhabited mostly by young people under 18. The particularity of the "Région Ile-de-France" is that it includes the richest and the poorest "département" of France. For example, the incomes in Neuilly-sur-Seine ("département" 92) are five times higher than in Clichy-sous-Bois ("département" 93). The median income in Paris Ile-de-France is 956 EUR/unit of consumption[12] (Insee 2010). On average, 15% of households have low income[13] in the urban area, rising to 25% in the "département" Seine-Saint Denis in the north-east or in the 18th, 19th and 20th "arrondissements" inside the peripheral highway.

This poverty and the resulting inequalities are associated with the housing market. Because of the high prices of the real estate market, people cannot choose where they want to live, but they live where it is affordable. In their analysis about mobility and access to the market, Wenglenski/Orfeuil (2004) explained

---

[12] The "median income" is the calculation of an income where 50% of the population earns more than it and 50% earn less than it. It differs from the average income. A "unit of consumption" is an adult up to 18 years old. Children below 14 years count as 0.3 of a unit and youth between 14-18 years count as half a unit of consumption.

[13] "Households with low income" earn less than 60% of the median income per unit, this means less than 2,000 EUR/month for a couple with two children below 14 years.

the inequalities in accessing employment for the citizens of Paris´ outer suburbs and offer two possible ways to resolve this situation: the first one would be to improve the public transportation and the second proposition would be to develop housing policies that would create less "unequal competition in that [housing for less affluent households] market" (Orfeuil/ Wenglenski 2004: 125). "Greater Paris" approached matters in exactly this way.

4.2. Centralized transportation system

The competences in the field of transport are distributed among the different levels of administration. Although the "région" makes regional transport plans, manages the airports, trains and canals, the "département" gives advice on these plans and also the city has input on the plans.
ome inequalities arise from the inefficiency of the transport system. All transportation plans for Paris are focused on the city. In 1968, to relieve the housing situation in the city of Paris, the government built the "new towns" and connected them to Paris with the RER (cf. figure 5). The current problem is, that all the connections go to the station "Les Halles" in the centre of the city. Thus, it is impossible to go from "banlieue" to "banlieue" without passing through the centre. Due to this transportation system, only the people living or working in central Paris can benefit from short commuter times. This dense city within short distances is a model for creating an advantaged minority.
Commuters profit more from the long distance fast trains, such as the TGV than they do from the regional transit system. For example, it takes less time to go from Paris to Lille (200 kilometers), than to Trappes (30 kilometers). A lot of areas have no railway station and no access to public transport. For the inhabitants, there is no alternative to using a private car. Politicians and Lobbyists facilitated a car-oriented planning, with the construction of fast roads
and highways in the suburbs. Also by bus, commuting takes a lot of time inside the metropolitan area. Even if there are rental systems for bikes (vélib) or for electric cars (autolib), they are only available inside the city of Paris and in a few streets around the ring road. A new transportation system is obviously needed. To resolve these transportation problems, "Greater Paris" proposes a development project trying to curtail the hyper-centralism of Paris and to facilitate the poly-centralism around Paris with the development of growth poles. Although the government has affirmed the solidarity and territorial equality as a political ambition, Enright (2013) analyses the improvement of financial and

Figure 11: The project of Les Halles under construction in mai 2014 (Baumgärtner 2014)

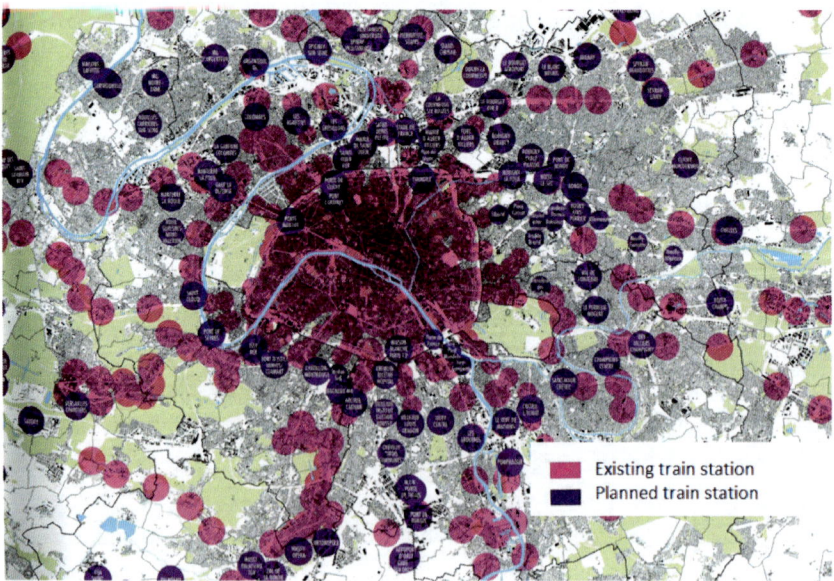

Figure 12: Train stations: existing and planned from "Greater Paris" (Atelier parisien d´urbanisme, 2013: 27)

technologic clusters around proposed transit stations as neoliberal strategies which do not resolve territorial inequalities. The Grand Paris Express should become a public transport system that connects the various sites of economic activity, the airports and the TGV station, and the residential areas. The Grand Paris Express is an improvement in the transportation situation but it is not radical enough. Thinking about mobility means thinking about more than transportation. For example, there is no initiative for car-sharing (e.g. such as in Germany) or designated lanes on highways for fully-occupied cars (e.g. such as in Los Angeles). The project of Grand Paris Express for 2030 was officially accepted in 2012, but there is no information available about more recent decisions.

4.3. A Housing market in tension

The housing situation is a result of different periods of urban policies after World War II, oriented to the construction of individual housing in the suburbs of Paris. After the war, the French government had a number of reasons to build a lot of flats quickly: the loss of houses due to war damage, the rural exodus and the miserable quality of the existing housing stock. Residential areas were heavily developed and, from the 1960s, tower block apartments began to be constructed. The satellite towns of the "banlieues" gained population through the massive construction of housing estates or housing projects. From the 1970s, the government promoted wider access to home ownership, with funding for the middle-class to become owners. There were no conditions on the location and type of housing. Real estate developers used this opportunity to build large numbers of individual houses with gardens. Even in the metropolitan area of Paris, with its various qualities, the dream of the house with a garden was supported by housing policies. Since the 1980s, housing policies have been oriented towards urban renewal: this has meant increasing housing density and constructing the city in the city. Thus, individual houses continue to eat up a lot of natural areas.

In the field of housing, the "région" can set priorities and offer subsidies. The "département" is responsible for housing construction; the city constructs and manages the social housing. The "French Social Housing Model" (Driant/Li 2012) sees social housing policies as a function of the welfare state with changing conditions since 2000 (e.g. promotion of home-ownership, cost of housing construction, etc.). For example, the "Solidarity and Urban Renewal Law" from 2001 obliges every town with more than 3,500 inhabitants (1,500 households) to have 20% social housing over all. Despite this, there is still no spatial equality of social housing inside the city of Paris and in the region. Some districts have a high rate of rented social housing (Seine Saint Denis, 32% in 2012), while many town councils (Neuilly-sur-Seine, 4% in 2012) in the suburbs do not fulfil the minimum requirement of social housing.

Given that the social housing market is very difficult to access, a lot of people are forced to find flats on the private market, where the prices have been exploding for the last ten years, and to live increasingly far from the city centre. Will the real estate bubble burst? Between 2005 and 2010, the prices for housing in Paris increased by 35% and in the "départments" around Paris by 20 - 35%. With regard to the levels of occupation and the types of housing in the "Région Ile-de-France", there are both rented and owner-occupied housing, individual houses and apartments. The tendency in Paris and the "inner circle" is for rented apartments. The further away from the centre, the more individual housing can be found, and in apartment blocks there are multiple owners.

The current target is to build 70,000 new housing units per year in the next 25 years in the metropolitan area Paris. This means 1.5 million housing units more in total (Grand Paris Law 2010), probably built around the new railway stations of "Greater Paris". A major challenge for the future metropolis is to intensify social housing policies to aid the suburbs.

5. Suburban "Greater Paris"?

5.1. The big phases of "Greater Paris" 2007-2012

The beginning of the revision of the Master Plan of 1965 during the year 2007 was politically motivated in order to launch a new development concept for the region of "Greater Paris". "Greater Paris" began with an architecture and urban competition in 2008 (Consultation du Grand Pari(s), in which multi-disciplinary teams proposed preliminary schemes. Ten teams[14] were invited to submit second proposals, which were presented in a public exhibition. Since 2010, the At-

---

[14] The teams are: "MVRDV", "Atelier Castro Denissof Casi", "LIN", "Studio 09", "Nouvel, Duthilleul, Cantal-Dupart", "Atelier Portzamparc", "l'AUC", "Atelier Lion - Groupe Descartes", "Rogers Stirk Harbour & Partners" and "Agence Grumbach & associés". All the projects can be downloaded under: http://www.ateliergrandparis.fr/aigp/conseil/consultation2008.php (Accessed July 29, 2014).

elier International du Grand Paris[15] with its architectural teams has been responsible for going further into the results of this competition to develop a vision projected for 2030.

On June 3rd, 2010, the "Greater Paris" Law[16] was passed, giving the state, through the relevant minister, the responsibility for this project of "national interest". The cooperation with the local and regional authorities is to be effected through agreements that have quantitative and qualitative objectives; the construction of a total of 1.5 million houses (70,000/year over 25 years) and the creation of a public company (Société du Grand Paris) to be responsible for the development of the regional subway, called the "Grand Paris Express".

> "Greater Paris" is an urban, social and economic project (...) that promotes a sustained and solid economic development that creates employment. It aims at decreasing social, territorial and fiscal imbalances to the benefit of the nation as a whole. The regional authorities are involved in the elaboration and realization of this project." (Article 1, Law "Greater Paris", June 3rd, 2010)

The architects involved in the "Greater Paris" expert group regret the lack of an urban project behind the law and the precipitate commitment. M. Perreau-Bezouille, Mayor of Nanterre, a university-town in the inner circle, introduced the "right of centrality" in his vision for "Greater Paris":

> "In the face of social and territorial inequalities, the only project conceivable is one that is guided by the resolve of guaranteeing access to the right of centrality to the greatest number of people possible." (Perreau-Bezouille 2013)

In 2010, a new competition focused on the transport system; the big improvement was to connect the suburbs. Finally, in early 2012, before the elections, the few first projects started in the economic, cultural, health and education fields. While Jean Nouvel's big tower project in La Défense (Tour Signal) was abandoned, some sites, such as the new Philharmonic by the same architect, began in the Parc of La Villette near the Tschumi´ Folies and the "cité of the music" from Portzamparc. The first achievements of "Greater Paris" have been hailed as architectural masterpieces rather than successes of master planning. With the election of Francois Hollande in 2012, the Minister for Housing and Territorial Equality took responsibility for the "Greater Paris" plan and called it

---

[15] Booklet in English under: http://www.ateliergrandparis.fr/ressources/AIGPgb.pdf (Accessed July 29, 2014).
[16] Law n° 2010-597

the "new "Greater Paris", establishing distance from the original project. Unfortunately, since the date of publication (August 2014), there has been no literature or reports on public debate available. Focusing on three sectors of urban development (social issues, transportation and housing) would now give keys to understand the challenges of development for Paris.

5.2. "Greater Paris" as a solution for suburban problems?

As previously presented, there is no homogenous suburban area around Paris because of an urban and social fragmentation in the periphery of Paris,. Even before industrialization, Hausmann, the famous Préfet, used the term "suburban" (in French: suburbain) (Fauré 2010: 74) to describe Paris´ "banlieues". Can we speak about suburbanization in the case of Paris? Yes, there are forms of suburbanization on the periphery of Paris, because of individual houses which eat up natural areas, and mono-functional areas in the "grands ensembles". Because the housing market is unaffordable inside the city core, many inhabitants choose to live outside the city and prioritise the car. Although public transportation is efficient in the core city, it does not function well in the suburbs and, at the moment, every type of transport uses the transport hub "Les Halles" in the centre of Paris. Otherwise, suburbanization is not visible in terms of density and quality of services, in the urban area. There are many towns with elements of centrality; but the so-called "hetero-polarity" cannot be defined as a suburban phenomenon, when it is understood negatively as sprawl, with a low density and no functional mix (Bodenschatz/Schönig 2004). Even the "région" is dense in comparison with other European metropolitan areas. And "hetero" means variety; the various social situations give the metropolis a diversity and multi-culturality. Finally, because of the poly-centralist system of towns inside a dense area, there is a kind of hybridization of many urban realities.

"Greater Paris" is a set of projects in many fields: economic, cultural, housing, public health, to name the most obvious. Above all, "Greater Paris" has generated a debate about territorial organization; it should be used as a new planning instrument, a concept for urban development, and not only as another level of administration. The challenge is to acknowledge the diversity of situations between Paris and the "banlieues", not with a specialization in economic clusters, for only a small part of the population (Fijalkow 2010), as the earlier

"Greater Paris" projects intended. Instead a harmonious planning is needed that connects residential areas with working places and public services, to allow Paris Metropolis to become a European City in the positive sense: a city of integration and social justice.

References

AMC - Le Moniteur Architecture (2009) (ed.), *Le Grand Pari(s). Consultation internationale sur l'avenir de la metropole parisienne*, Paris.

Atelier parisien d'urbanisme (2013), "Atlas du Grand Paris 2013", *Paris projet 43*, Paris: APUR.

Bachmann, Christian/ Leguennec, Nicole (1996), *Violences urbaines. Ascension et chute des classes moyennes à travers cinquante ans de politique de la ville*, Paris: Albin Michel.

Bacqué, Marie-Hélène/ Sintomer, Yves (2001), "Affiliations et désaffiliations en banlieue: réflexions à partir des exemples de Saint-Denis et d'Aubervilliers" *Revue française de sociologie*, 42(2), 217-249.

Barth, Hans-Günter/ Lang, Annette (2003), *Nachhaltige Stadtentwicklung in Deutschland und Frankreich. Instrumente und Umsetzungsmöglichkeiten in ausgewählten Themenbereichen des Umweltschutzes*, Frankfurt am Main.

Beaud, Stéphane/ Pialoux, Michel (2003), *Violences urbaines, violence sociale: genèse des nouvelles classes dangereuses*, Paris: Fayard.

Benevolo, Leonardo (1993), *Die Stadt in der europäischen Geschichte*, München: Beck.

Bodenschatz, Harald/ Bräuer, Michael (1994), *Stadterneuerung im Umbruch*. Arbeitsheft ISR, Berlin: TU Berlin.

Bodenschatz, Harald/ Gräwe, Christina/ Kegler, Harald/ Nägelke, Hans-Dieter/ Sonne, Wolfgang (2010), *Stadtvisionen 1910/2010. Berlin, Paris, London, Chicago*, Berlin: DOM.

Bodenschatz, Harald/ Schönig, Barbara (2004), *Smart growth - new urbanism - liveable communities. Programm und Praxis der Anti-Sprawl-Bewegung in den USA*, Wuppertal: Müller + Busmann.

Breuillard, Michêle (2012), "From Grand Paris to "Greater Paris": An Old Project, a New Approach", *Croatian & Comparative Public Administration*, 12, 41–69.

Devillers et associés (2014), "Les bassins de vie du Grand Paris" in: *Atelier international du Grand Paris* (ed.), Paris, http://lesbassinsdeviedugrandparis.fr/ (Accessed August 3, 2014).

Driant, Jean-Claude/ Li, Mingye (2012), "The Ongoing Transformation of Social Housing Finance in France: Towards a Self-financing System?", *International Journal of Housing Policy*, 12(1), 91-103.

Eckardt, Frank (2007), "Frankreichs Schwierigkeiten mit den Banlieue", *APuZ*, 38/2007, 32-39.

Enright, Theresa Erin (2013), "Mass transportation in the neoliberal city: the mobilizing myths of the Grand Paris Express", *Environment & Planning A*, 45(4), 797-813.

Faludi, Andreas/ Waterhout, Bas (2002), *The making of the European Spatial Development Perspective: no Masterplan*, London, New York: Waterhout.

Fauré, Alain (2010), "Banlieue" in: Topalov, Christian/ Coudroy de Lille, Laurent/ Depaule, Jean-Charles/ Marin, Brigitte (eds.), *L´aventure des mots de la ville. À travers les temps, les langues, les sociétés*, Paris: Robert Laffon.

Fijalkow, Yankel (2010), Urban Strategies and Collective Memory. An Upper-Middle Class Municipality in the Grand Paris Project. *Journal of Urban and Regional Analysis*, 2(2), 7-18.

Fijalkow, Yankel/ Lévy-Vroelant Claire (2014), "Making new from old in France: urban change through housing renewal in two Parisian districts", in: Turkington, Richard/Watson, Christopher (eds.), *Renewing Europe´s Housing*, Bristol: Policy Press.

Garreau, Joel (1992), *Edge city. Life on the new frontier*, New York: Anchor Books.

Jacquand, Corinne (2010a), "Grand Paris, eine Herausforderung für die Zeit nach dem Kyoto-Protokoll", in: Bodenschatz et al. (eds.), *Stadtvisionen 1910/2010*, Berlin: DOM, 248-253.

— (2010b), "Grand Paris: bürokratische Idee oder städtebauliches Projekt? Interview mit Paul Chemetov", in: Bodenschatz et al. (eds.), *Stadtvisionen 1910/2010*, Berlin: DOM, 416-421.

Le Garrec, Sylvaine (2006), *Le renouvellement urbain : la genèse d'une notion fourre-tout*, Paris: Plan Urbanisme Construction Architecture.

Marchand, Bernard (2001), "La haine de la ville : « Paris et le désert français » de Jean-François Gravier", *L'information géographique*, 65(3), 234-253.

Orfeuil, Jean-Pierre/ Wiel, Marc (2012), *Grand Paris: sortir des illusions, approfondir les ambition*, Paris: Scrineo.

Orfeuil, Jean-Pierre/ Wenglenski, Sandrine (2004), "Differences in Accessibility to the Job Market according to Social Status and Place of Residence in the Paris Area" *Built Environment*, 30(2), Alexandrine Press, 116-126.

Peigney, Fabrice/ Allen, Barbara (2014), *Regards croisés sur l´évaluation de la rénovation urbaine*, Paris: La documentation francaise.

Perreau-Bezouille, Gérard (2013), "Tribune: Métropole du Grand Paris: les rendez-vous manqués du gouvernement", *Nanterre-infos*, Nanterre.

Pinol, Jean-Luc/ Garden, Maurice (2009), A*tlas des Parisiens. De la Révolution à nos jours ; population, territoire et habitat, productions et services, religion, culture, loisirs*, Paris: Parigramme.

Savitch, Hank (1988), *Post-industrial cities. Politics and planning in New York, Paris, and London*, Princeton: Princeton University Press.

Schüle, Klaus (2000), *Paris: Vordergründe - Hintergründe - Abgründe, Stadtentwicklung, Stadtgeschichte und sozialkultureller Wandel*, Grabenstätt: Aries.

— (2003), *Paris: die kulturelle Konstruktion der französischen Metropole. Alltag, mentaler Raum und sozialkulturelles Feld in der Stadt und in der Vorstadt*, Opladen: Leske + Budrich.

Siebel, Walter (2012), "Die europäische Stadt", in: Eckardt, Frank (ed.), *Handbuch Stadtsoziologie*, Wiesbaden: Springer VS, 201-211.

Soja, Edward William (2010), *Seeking spatial justice*, Minneapolis: University of Minnesota Press.

Texier, Simon (2005), *Paris contemporain. Architecture et urbanisme de Haussmann à nos jours, une capitale à l'ère des métropoles*, Paris: Parigramme.

Volpe, Evelyne (1994), *Côté banlieue: récits du bord des villes*. Paris: Autrement.

Don't trust the idyll. Meritorious objectives and arguable substance in Dutch suburbia

Holger Gladys

Introduction

In April 1995, beneath the arcade of the Netherlands Architecture Institute (NAi) in Rotterdam, students of the Delft University of Technology set up a vast model of a ribbon city to the scale of 1:300, consisting of 800,000 houses with a density of 60 houses per hectare, and thereby producing a housing tapestry of 13,500 hectare or a city of 60 x 2.25 kilometer. The provocative outdoor exhibition lasted only one hour and was the opening event to the main exhibition "Adriaan Geuze - West8. In Holland there is a House". The actual exhibition presented a range of 500 pictures with comparable day-to-day situations, systematically taken in more than 100 suburban neighborhoods. According to the landscape architect and urban designer Geuze, the show was an unbiased photographic record of the Randstad suburbia anno 1995. The architecture critic Hans van Dijk probably felt vertiginous when he commented: "It is a sobering look at the cacophony of banality" (van Dijk 1995: 9).

The seemingly abstract number of 800,000 referred to the amount of houses that according to the 1992 national governmental "Fourth Memorandum on Spatial Planning Extra" (in Dutch: Vierde nota over de ruimtelijke ordening extra or with its acronym "Vinex") was to be realized between 1995 and 2005 in the Randstad conurbation and elsewhere.

Even though Geuze's show was ostensibly set-up as an even-handed view on the Dutch suburban condition, the exhibition was a critical, passionate statement and a severe call to reconsider the decisions made to create this flooding spread of houses. The professional concern was with the uninspired spatial and political organization of the Vinex implementation. The legitimate worry was about questions of how and where to realize these new developments in an already densely populated, sprawling Dutch environment. There was also concern about the Dutch landscape and particularly the green heart as a cultural property, which would be put under pressure.

Figure 1: 800.000 houses, exhibition at the NAi (van Dijk 1995)

The discomfort with Vinex consolidated with the notion that the open green areas in the heart of the Randstad would be partially built over and that characteristic rural qualities, counterbalancing the urban environment, might be lost forever.

In anticipation of the following discussion, it can be said that, what had been intentionally introduced as a distinct break with the anti-urban developments of the 1960s and 1970s policies, in fact turned out to be the continuation, if not the acceleration in the production of suburban landscapes. The physical appearance of the newly build areas split the professional world of politicians, architects, planners and users. While some lauded the new textures as honest and legitimate answers to the posed questions on urbanity, others disapproved the new neighborhoods as unimaginative and tedious. The developing consortia were criticized for their lopsided market-orientation. The overconcentration of one single kind of land use and the esthetic monotony of the housing patches caused irritation. Whether the Vinex housing districts were built on greenfield or brownfield sites, or on newly claimed land, most of the brand-new neighborhoods had no urban character whatsoever. Apparently, there was a tremendous gap between intention and implementation. Cor Wagenaar got to the heart of the issue:

> "Apart from the intention to promote the so-called 'compact city' there is nothing 'metropolitan' about the last wave of large-scale housing estates that washed over the Low Lands since the middle of the 1990s. Although the density of the new neighborhoods is usually higher than was common in the 1950s and 1960s, their character is decidedly suburban. [...] One look at the map of the Netherlands makes clear that the compactness that is officially part of the program is entirely fictitious; in practice, suburban sprawl never ceased." (Wagenaar 2011: 541)

Although there is immense professional talent present in the Netherlands, the Vinex policy and implementation brought the low lands on the verge of losing its international reputation in urban planning and design. Throughout the 20th century, the Netherlands developed a highly sophisticated and efficient planning regime that gave control to the upper- and lower-tier governments and its public housing corporations. The planning culture proved to be original and capable of allowing architects, planners and politicians engaged alike, to create innovative and sensitive plans for new neighborhoods and city expansions. Famous examples of large-scale plans of the first half of the century include the 1915/17 Plan Zuid (Plan for the expansion of Amsterdam South) by Hendrik Petrus Berlage and the 1934/35 Algemene Uitbreidingsplan AUP (General Expansion Plan) for Amsterdam West by the Town Planning department of Amsterdam (dienst Publieke Werken, afdeling Stadsontwikkeling) under guidance of Cornelis van Eesteren. During the past hundred years, the Dutch planning system always worked hand in hand with the building industry. And particularly during the post-World War II period, this intense tie added importantly to the financial well-being of the country and consequently established the building industry as an economically and politically powerful force.

1. Suburban landscapes

The concept that guided the process of renewal during the post-World War II period up to the 1970s aimed at progress and welfare, combined with the ideal of the collective. The moral concept of the welfare state is rooted in the understanding that the state plays the key role in the protection and promotion of the economic and social well-being of its citizens. The comprehensive political model aims at producing socially inclusive environments based on the principles of equality of opportunity and equitable distribution of wealth.[1]

According to this moral concept and political model, governmental policy focused on a nationwide dispersion and decentralization of settlement and prosperity. The Dutch researcher and advisor on spatial planning Jelte Boeijenga explains the two arguments that figured prominently, "the desire to achieve equal opportunities for all and the fear of excessively large concentrations of people in the cities, particularly in the west of the country" (Boeijenga and Mensink 2008: 11).

---

[1] Website of the Encyclopedia Britannica: Welfare State:
http://www.britannica.com/EBchecked/topic/639266/welfare-state

Since the late 1950s, the Dutch Ministry of Housing, Spatial Planning and the Environment (Ministry of VROM) in an irregular rhythm of approximately every five to ten years released policy documents that gave direction to the developments planned.² The 1966 and 1974 memorandum aimed at relieving the pressure on central cities, to support cities in coping with growing environmental and social problems, and to absorb or redirect the predicted urban growth. "In the urban core zones, congestion and environmental degradation were the major problems. In the peripheral areas, connections were inadequate. Both problems needed to be addressed. [...] Polycentric development was the preferred method reflecting this view" (Černe 2004: 91).

The ideal conception was given form by spreading houses and businesses, services and commerce, governmental facilities and educational institutions throughout the cities, regions and provinces, thereby organizing the new Dutch urban landscape. The policy of concentrated deconcentration,

> "this oxymoronic term referred to allowing people to live in suburban environments, but concentrating new developments in and around existing towns and cities and in a number of designed overspill centers. [...] Concentrated deconcentration was to take place within the framework of city regions comprising both donor cities and overspill centers. So the city region became the complement of concentrated deconcentration." (Faludi 1994: 133ff.)

The spatial organization of this new environment created two kinds of patterns, many small-scale scattered dwelling units and some medium-scale nuclei, creating points of reference and structural support.

During the mid-1960s and up until the mid-1980s, the Netherlands built sixteen medium-sized new towns as areas dedicated to receive developments. The measures for the implementation of the growth scenario were established in the Urbanization Policy Document from 1976. The share of these overspill centers in overall building production grew from 7% in 1972 up to 18% in 1982. Until 1990, nearly 230,000 dwellings were built in polycentric developments. Latest since the 1960s, the production of large numbers characterized the day-to-day practice of the efficiently top-down organized Dutch planning and building

---

2   Since 1958, Dutch spatial planning is organized by a series of policy documents that each establishes a national perspective on how to facilitate and develop the country's built environment. In 2006, the Balkenende III Cabinet broke with the centrally organized and controlled spatial planning policy. With the last report, the ministry decentralized the subject matter and empowered the municipalities and regions to conduct spatial development policies from regional and local perspective.

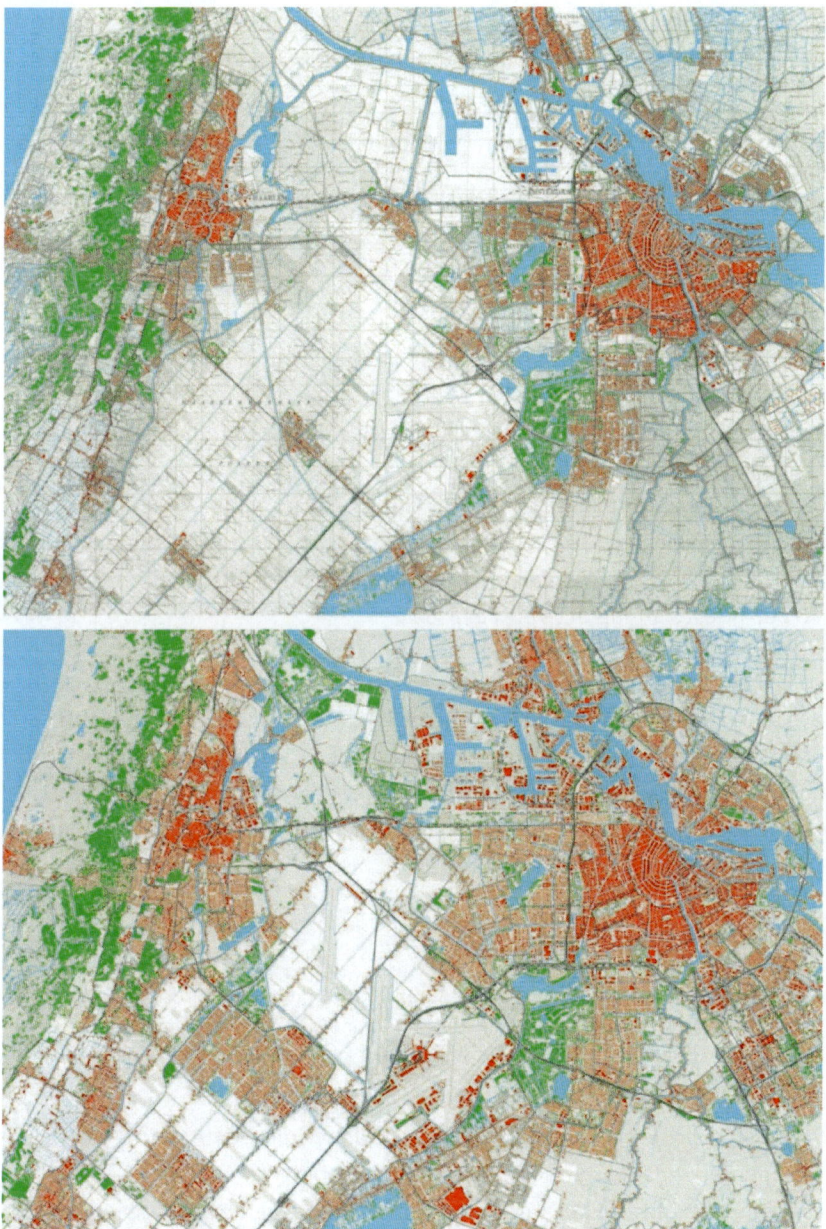

Figure 2: The south-western part of the Amsterdam Metropolitan Area including Schiphol, Haarlem and Haarlemmermeer in 1970 and 2011 (Planbureau voor de Leefomgeving, PBL Den Haag)

industry. National governments coordinated the main sectors and interests, provinces translated land claims in provincial plans and municipalities, armed with subsidies and proactive land policies, implemented the plans, and finally, developers and the building industry realized whatever number was to be build.

Thus, the 1995 Vinex task of building 800,000 houses may have felt ambitious to begin with, but looking at the successful production rate of production in the second half of the last century, it didn't seem overly ambitious. From the mid-1970s to the 1990s, the building industry produced annually more than 100,000 houses with a peak around 1975, realizing throughout a period of three years around 450,000 homes in total. The rationally organized Dutch building industry worked extremely efficiently and the production of numbers at this scale were considered normal. In 1985, the housing stock counted for approximately 5,400,000 houses, in 1995 it grew up to 6,200,000 and reached by 2005 6,900,000 - which is a growth of 800,000 houses for the first decade and 700,000 houses during the Vinex decade.

The building production from the mid-1980s on to the mid-1990s was in retrospect even larger than that of the mid-1990s to the mid-2000s.[3] While the post-World War II paradigm was still defined by a centralized planning system, this top-down approach significantly transformed during the 1970s to the 1990s into an intricate, decentralized planning system with many different stakeholders and participants involved (Brands 2010).

2. New markets

> "Over the past two decades neoliberalism has been the dominant discourse in the formulation of housing policies in Western societies. Across national boundaries, state intervention in social affairs has been reduced, especially in North America and Western Europe." (Sleurink 2012: 7)

Both, privatization and deregulation aims at downsizing state control. Privatization and deregulation is the process of transferring government interest and responsibilities towards private interests and opportunities. Classical liberalism and neo-liberalism, thus politics of privatization exists as early as the industrial

---

[3] Centraal Bureau voor de Statistiek 2011.

revolution, starting in England at the end of the eighteenth century. Already the classical liberalism and the neoliberalism in the 1930s and 1940s called for a widespread retreat of the state from the economic activity. Countries such as England and Germany, with a strong industrial past and present, were particularly receptive to this argument. Privatization policy is often justified by the economic liberal conviction that the share of the public sector has to be pushed back or curtailed in favor of the private sector; as private sector performance, as being governed by market forces and laws of the market, is basically more efficient than any other.

Similar to most Western-European countries, the Dutch political climate in the 1980s and early 1990s was fairly conservative. Cold war politics and the economic recession of 1979 to 1984 had left their marks.

> "During this period, policymakers and politicians tried to define what spatial planning could contribute to an economic recovery. The central theme of the Fourth National Policy Document on Spatial Planning was internationalization, economic perspectives, opportunity development and improving existing qualities."
> (Netsch/Kropman 2013: 1093)

With campaign slogans such as "more market, less government", Ruud Lubbers, the Prime Minister from 1982 to 1994, prepared the ground for a policy shift towards the withdrawal of the welfare state that entailed extensive cutbacks in public spending, and the liberalization of market with far-reaching deregulation and privatization programs.[4]

Until 1990, governmental housing policies generally focused on the supply, with the production of homes and particularly social rental housing. "Social rental housing in the Netherlands expanded from 12% of the housing stock in 1945 to 44% in the early 1990s" (Willem Korthals Altes 2008: 15). From the 1990s onwards, the proportion between home ownership, private rental and social rental of the total housing stock changed significantly "with neoliberal politics stimulating home ownership by providing easy access to mortgages, loosening regulations and sometimes by providing tax benefits for home buy-

---

[4] During the twelve years of the Lubbers' government (from 1982 to1994), three cabinets were formed by the CDA (Christian Democratic Appeal) and the conservative-liberal VVD (People's Party for Freedom and Democracy), with the VVD being replaced in 1989 by the social-democratic PvdA (Labour Party). Ruud Lubbers was regarded by many during his time in office as an ideological heir to Margaret Thatcher.

ers. Government schemes and regulations brought purchasing a property within reach for a growing number of households." (Sleurink 2012: 8).

Along with the human geographer Marijn Sleurink, it can be stated that the increased commodification has a strong impact on the spatial development and the living environment. The share of private housing property increased from 8% in 1982, to 46% in 1990, and to more than 60% in 2010. At least for the period between 1982 and 2001, home owners could count on a year to year increase in real-estate prices, with a total increase of approximately three hundred percent for the period of thirty years.

> "This had led to a situation where, on average, housing were being sold every five to ten years after buying it. The profit made on sale of the house was then used to buy a new and more expensive house. This process has been the engine behind the strong real-estate market for at least two to three decades, but the engine is no more. " (Netsch and Kropman 2013: 1093)

In general and official language of municipalities and developers, homeowners became consumers; in market terms, people would go for a housing career, or according to the omnipresent Dutch term, for "wooncarrière". Armed with bold slogans, government housing policy would seduce the middle class homeowner sector to engage parallel to family and job careers into a consumer mobility of moving from small to medium to large to extra-large, from affordable starter units to costly up-market homes. This newly developed career path became substantial to the realization of Vinex. Marijn Sleurink further explains the spiral movement that led to the burst of the bubble:

> "The flourishing economy during the 1990s and the increased household incomes also intensified the demand for owner-occupied housing. This combination of factors together with the low interest rates, which contributed to the attractiveness of borrowing large amounts of money, resulted in a large pool of potential home buyers. The massive inflow of capital into the real estate market drove up the prices. Purchasing a property became an interesting investment because of the assumption that real estate prices would rise indefinitely. Up till a certain point in time, large increases in house prices indeed led to financial benefits for buyers. However, the commodification of housing goods and the speculation on the housing market has pushed up prices to an unbearable level, which in the end contributed to the bust of the housing bubble." (Sleurink 2012: 8)

Many studies from the early 1990s anticipated a reorientation of the real-estate market, away from the grand planning narrative towards individualization and diversification. Building in large numbers has always been connected to serial production, and especially in the Randstad, there was hardly any space reserved for individual architecture with private clients. With so-called housing experiments, such as the 2001 BouwExpo "Gewild wonen" (Wanted Living), the municipality of Almere aimed at the weaned consumers (and aspirant residents) to express their personal preferences and have a voice in the layout, size and appearance of their homes. One might expect that the most recent developments in suburban Netherlands would have taken up these timely issues and engage into polyphonic models, eventually incorporating the diverse cultural qualities present in suburban conditions. However, though appreciated in the media, most liberating proposals stayed on paper. Instead, the market-driven competition played the game according to its economic principles and continued the unbroken tradition in mass production, the reproduction of sameness.

3. The Grand Projet

In many ways, the 1990s were politically, economically and culturally a challenging period. The collapse of socialism in the late 1980s and early 1990s had been a most crucial geopolitical event, and since that very momentum "the free market has achieved worldwide dominance" (Wagenaar 2011: 510). In a short lesson on global economy, Wagenaar reminds us on the fact that globalization is an ongoing process, "which departed in the sixteenth century (mapping and colonization), radically intensified in the nineteenth century (new infrastructures and technologies), accelerated in the 1950s (air traffic) and increased in the 1980s as a result of the revolution in communication technology" (Wagenaar 2011: 510).

In short, what changed over time, is first the pace of communication that at some point last century was even able to replace physical traffic, and secondly, the increase of competition on regional and international scale. Recent trends in globalization are very much connected to the consolidation of neoliberal politics, and the Netherlands, like most welfare states, attuned to the international trend of increasing deregulation and privatization. Wagenaar describes globalization as political phenomenon:

> "What is new is not the scale of the economy, but the retreat of national governments. For ideological reasons, the nation-state has delegated part of its authority

to lower administrative levels (provinces and municipalities), to higher administrative levels (for example the European Union) and, most importantly, to the market. Global space became an open field of business opportunities" (Wagenaar 2011: 510)

How did all this effect physical planning? With the 1988 Memorandum on Spatial Planning, the Dutch government anticipated the cultural change from territorial to translocal, from orthogenetic to heterogenetic, and from inward to outward looking. Without anybody having been able to foresee the 1989 political bang and its economic consequences, a changed point of view towards renewed perspective on urban culture was in the air. In the light of an international economic and cultural perspective, politicians and planners desired strong cities and the ongoing depopulation and the shrinkage of the urban base was recognized as being unsatisfying and counterproductive to take up the predicted competition between cities and regions. Consequently, the Memorandum prepared an armamentarium of opportunities. The politicians and planners involved reconsidered in general lines "the role of the Netherlands in a changing world and to the Dutch economy in particular, envisaging the country as a distribution hub, thanks to Schiphol and the port of Rotterdam, with Amsterdam as a financial center" (Boeijenga 2011: 27). The policy document designated a series of thirteen urban nodes for places of preferential treatment. Next to that it introduced the massive task of building approximately 800,000 houses to fight the existing and estimated housing shortage until 2010.

Due to political circumstances, the fall of the second Lubbers government and the forming of new political coalitions, the fourth report got revised in the years between 1989 and 1992 and published as the "Supplement to the Fourth Memorandum on Spatial Planning" or shortly "Vierde nota extra", the "Vinex". The main revisions of the Vinex concern the topics of environmental awareness and the limitation of growth in automobile traffic. Importantly, the Vinex put an official end to the earlier policies and abandoned the policy of dispersal and new towns, thereby promoting the compact city.

4. Quo Vinex?

How is the Vinex implementation realized? In 1994 and 1995 the State authorities signed individual agreements on implementing the Vinex program with the seven largest city regions and eighteen smaller urban regions (each represented by the provinces. Since the implementation was meant to happen on regional level, the national authorities were counting on cooperation between the municipalities. The covenants specified for large parts the locations and numbers of houses to be built; 455,000 at assigned places, plus 190,000 elsewhere in the provinces, a total of 20% less than imagined earlier. Out of the total of 645,000 houses, only 25% were to be built on inner urban sites. For each region that committed itself to the national target, the national government pledged itself to financially support land purchases, soil remediation, and public transportation infrastructure. Boeijenga knows that although many topics were highly fixed, the covenants decisively left space for alternative routes and loopholes in building dispersed settlements without losing national funding:

> "It never quite came to that, but even so, this high degree of freedom reflects the primary goal of Vinex and the covenants, namely, to ensure the construction of as many homes as possible within the urban regions. Less importance seems to have been attached to the principle of building in the city if possible, and otherwise adjoining it, and further away only after that." (Boeijenga 2011: 29)

The Vinex Atlas specifies that within the given timeframe of ten years, the initial amount of 830,000 houses were realized, with 290,000 houses on inner urban sites, thus the percentage of inner urban developments increased to 35%.[5] Although the general numbers per region is published, the survey particularly stays vague on what has been considered an inner urban site. The Region Amsterdam (ROA) together with Almere[6] for instance claims that they have built 31,500 of the 34,500 houses appointed on inner urban locations. Knowing the low-rise and low density of the Almerian fabric, however it seems rather unclear, what is described or understood as being urban.

5. The commodification of the home

In his article "Design Dispatch; The Dutch Retouch Suburbia" Christopher Hawthorne critically remarks on Vinex developments:

> "The Netherlands, a country that has set the international design standard for everything from glassware to corporate headquarters, made its first comprehensive attempts to grapple with suburban sprawl. [...] Along with a few real-estate scandals,

---

[5] The Vinex Atlas offers detailed tables on the agreed and achieved numbers of housing.
[6] Almere is the new town in the southern Flevoplolder, 30 kilometers away from Amsterdam. The city has been built in the 1960s on reclaimed land, in 1984 Almere became a municipality. The city has around 200,000 inhabitants and its fabric mainly consists of suburban districts, vying with Amsterdam for the favor of the inhabitants.

the guidelines have produced plenty of unremarkable architecture. [...] the new houses look for the most part like those in a conventional American suburb, with rows of reassuringly old-fashioned homes and patches of lawn." (Hawthorne 2004: 1)

Out of the approximately one hundred Vinex locations that had been agreed upon for implementation, Leidsche Rijn is one of the better rated places. Leidsche Rijn is a large scale extension in the west of Utrecht and planned around the existing villages Vleuten and de Meern. The urban plan by Riek Bakker (BVR) and Rients Dijkstra (Maxwan) was originally meant for 30,000 houses, which later had been adjusted to 20,000 households. According to the survey in the Vinex Atlas, approximately half of the program has been built until today and the construction period is extended until 2020 and beyond. The planning of Leidsche Rijn is subdivided in four sectors with a central park as the fifth sector. The urban plan basically defines the building zones and landscape areas, incorporating at its best existing landscape elements, archeological places, existing villages and particular farms, thereby creating a potentially rich landscape for living. Particular attention received the motorway at the edge of the Vinex area towards Utrecht, a barrier that partially has been covered to better connect with the old city. The plan missed out to determine the atmosphere of the various places, possibly hoping that the introduced framework would be sensitive and strong enough to stimulate diversity in building and neighborhood. The master plan was presented in 1995 and execution started in 1997. Beside all the interesting ingredients, Leidsche Rijn doesn't differ from other Vinex locations and contains all the typical Vinex properties, similar to others one would mostly find places of great uniformity, too much of the same.

Each sector in the huge area of Leidsche Rijn is again subdivided in easy-to-supervise projects of a few hundred houses, and each patch is usually executed with the same or similar types of houses. In their colorful marketing brochures, municipalities and developers alike pretend to be sensitive and build what people want. Basically, it is the other way round, the market system tells the developer what commodity sells, and the choices for people are limited to what the market produces.

The landscape architect and urban designer Bart Brands summarizes the difficulties in planning and building urban areas:

"In the 21st century, it is still difficult to fit unplanned elements into our urban plans. The Dutch urban planning tradition is deeply based on control, commitment and contracts. To reduce each party's risk over time, programmatic and spatial agreements are fixed legally and financially. Before a project starts, most decisions are made and contracted among the stakeholders (housing types, density, program, exploitation), or are indirectly and unconsciously defined by the (sometimes conflicting) regulations of different governmental levels. Essential changes or fresh insights are at some stages of the planning process difficult to incorporate. As one can imagine, changes might affect liabilities and commitments and might demand revising contracts; a process could easily become a political, and strategic game rather than a discussion about spatial qualities, and developers mostly have better lawyers. ... The spatial appearance of the Netherlands is eventually more defined by an intricate network of private developers, builders, (semi-)public organizations, rules, market mechanisms and politicians, rather than by urban planners and designers. For those working in the field, it might be obvious, that this process in most cases leads to simplification and standardization and to a loss of diversity and complexity in urbanism and landscape architecture." (Brands 2010: 274)

Out of the little more than 80 Vinex locations mentioned in the publication "Via Vinex", 45% of the designs have been produced by five urban planning offices only (van't Hoff et al. 2006: 121). The average size of a Vinex location covers 3,700 houses with a density of thirty-six houses per hectare, ranging from fourteen to eighty-two houses per hectare. Clearly, the realized low densities belong to suburban or rural developments. There are only a few areas that work with higher densities. In that respect, eighty-two houses per hectare are very exceptional. But not only density, the type of houses is decisive for the character of the development too. A particular weakness of the Vinex program is that it mainly is targeted at young families longing for starter houses with small gardens. The average Vinex-spread of housing types is 10% single-family houses, 20% detached family-houses, 50% row houses and 20% multi-family houses. Interestingly enough, Leidsche Rijn exactly reflects these average numbers (van't Hoff et al. 2006: 114f.).

As anywhere else in the building sector, houses are mainly executed with standard construction bays of 5.40 or 7.20 meters. What happens behind the façade hardly seems to be of interest. The housing typology offers a limited palette of floor plans only, variations are organized per cluster and differentiation is a matter of style and decoration. Traditional, conventional, revival-style, neo-eclectic architecture, generic building styles, supermodern types and façades, anything goes in Vinex-land. Apparently, the commodity Vinex-house

Figures 3+4: Housing at Leidsche Rijn (Gladys 2014)

Figures 5+6: Housing at Leidsche Rijn (Gladys 2014)

sells through its skin. "Since most houses were built to be sold, their architectural finishing was part of the developer's marketing strategy." (Wagenaar 2011: 451) The national institute for strategic policy analysis in the field of environment, nature and space, the Planbureau voor de Leefomgeving and the Amsterdam School of Real Estate recently published an astonishing study, stating that neo-historical styles of any kind sell best. According to the report, neo-style houses are most wanted and have per definition, depending on the amount of façade details, a significant higher value than others (Buitelaar 2014: 6). The same study addresses the issue of a conspicuous rising market concentration in the Dutch, but particularly in the Randstad housing market. The study quotes a survey done by Property NL and the Centraal Bureau voor de Statistiek dating from 2006, revealing that 34% of the housing production is developed by the top five developers[7]; in 2004 the share had been 30%.

All Vinex estates mainly offer standards and little space for neighborhood facilities such as shops or cafés. Only larger Vinex districts explicitly serve central city functions with mainly shopping. Work places are hardly provided, thus the daily work-home commuters keep contributing to the motorway congestions with the seemingly unavoidable consequence of being the traffic jam twice a day, in the morning and in the evening.

One of the few highlights found in the Vinex at Leidsche Rijn is a series of small bridges, designed by the office of Maxwan. The very individual look and the delicate finish of these simple artifacts create a sense of joy in an otherwise uncharismatic environment.

6. Desires for a compact city

In 2010 the Dutch state architect Liesbeth van der Pol invited an illustrious group of fourteen business men, politicians and university teachers to engage into a debate on urban densification.[8] The round table talk was introduced to elicit common positions, fresh statements and critical remarks on the desire of compacting urban fabrics. Liesbeth van der Pol was in search of a jointly sup-

---

[7] The Top Five mentioned are Bouwfonds, AM Vastgoedontwikkeling, Heijmans, Dura Vermeer and Rabo Vastgoed.
[8] The transcript of the round table talk is published in Prachtig Compact Nederland.

ported agenda as a basis for meeting the incessantly rising housing demand and qualifying Dutch cities as livable places. Beside all the commonplace and aspiring opinions and assumptions that were expressed during the meeting, the most fascinating part concerns some remarks on the financing and the realization of urban plans relating to the Vinex-period and to urban planning after the 2008 economic crisis. To some extent, the statements offer alternate insights to the question, of why the housing production during the past 20 years happened mainly in greenfield sites instead of working on inner city developments. During this round table, Apeldoorn alderman Jolanda Reitsma briefly elaborates on the financial trouble her municipality is facing.

> "Fifty-five percent of the new housing stock should be created within the inner city fabric, but the situation is getting more and more complex. Actually the biggest profit is made with greenfield sites. The municipal development company (grondbedrijf) is now hopefully close to being financially stable with a zero balance. In the past year, 60 million Euro profit forecast evaporated. Now that the State support is shrinking as well, I have no idea from where to take money for inner city developments."
> (Werkgroep Binnenstedelijk bouwen 2010: 117 - own translation from Dutch)[9]

It seems to be an astonishing fact that to build on inner city locations is more expensive and therefore less attractive than greenfield developments. How does this come? According to Reitsma, the assumption that with building in inner city districts, infrastructure doesn't need improvement or adjustment, is a great misunderstanding.

> "Compaction has major implications on traffic planning. The difference is: with inner city developments, infrastructural costs are paid by the municipalities, with developments outside the city fabric, infrastructural costs are passed on to the State."
> (Werkgroep Binnenstedelijk bouwen 2010: 117 - own translation from Dutch)[10]

Reitsma's statement might be a key in understanding the general motivation to build on the edge of cities rather than in inner cities. In the discussion, Henk Ovink, at the time the director of National Spatial Ordering at the Ministry of

---

[9] "Wij willen 55 percent binnenstedelijk bouwen, maar het is wel steeds ingewikkelder aan het woorden en: wij verdienen het geld in uitleglocaties. Het grondbedrijf staat nu hopelijk op nul. In het afgelopen jaar is 60 miljoen winstverwachting verdampt. Nu ook van het rijk weinig geld komt, heb ik geen idee waarvan wij het geld moeten halen voor binnenstedelijk locaties."

[10] "Verdichting heeft grote consequenties voor de verkeersplanning. Het verschil is: binnenstedelijk draait de gemeente op voor de kosten, buitenstedelijk worden de kosten afgewenteld op het rijk."

VROM, spontaneously objects whether it shouldn't be reverse: "[...] to recognize intra-urban costs as societal costs and to pass on investigations outside the city fabric to private parties". The discussion suggests that there is a distortion of competition between greenfield and brownfield developments. Did the national governmental financial support for land purchases, soil remediation, public transport and general infrastructure during the Vinex-period influence the choice for building at the fringes of cities? Were municipalities in planning and executing Vinex properties more cost-effective or profitable, just because of national governmental subsidies received?

The issue touched upon might come down to the critical question of where in land development and real-estate business the big money is made and where subsidies are spent. The actual problem might suggest that the dedication and distribution of state subsidies during the planning and execution phases goes pretty much along with traditional, rather defensive patterns of decision-making and vested interests, not necessarily related to commonly recognized long-term goals, but as a lubricant that keeps business-making in the comfort zone of criteria previously used and affirmed problem solving strategies.

7. After the game is before the game

Since the early 1990s, we are witnessing new forms of commercialization in urban developments. And this commercialization comprises suburbia as well. The story of the Dutch suburbia is very much the story of the neoliberal thinking and practice. Neoliberal politics is not just a short firework of a ruling elite, but a system that implies and builds on commitment and cooperation of the masses. Neoliberal politics caused significant shifts in the perception and expression of cultural values, away from the collective towards the ideal of the individual, of the self. In the interview, "Only Losers Cooperate" ("Nur Verlierer kooperieren"), the German philosopher Peter Sloterdijk contours the changes and concomitant consequences as follows:

"Neoliberalism had the ideological merit, to let down the bashful mask in front of consumerism, it has been very frank in declaring consumerism a central life-motive." (own translation from German)[11]

And Sloterdijk continues his evaluation of what politically happened during the past fifteen to twenty years:

"We have been entangled in a large-scale experiment on psycho-political frivolity - but what was on the menu, was not any more aristocratic frivolity, but mass frivolity, carelessness and selfishness for everyone. During this period it has been argued that common-interest-thinking had failed. So there was the anti-social, which we politely called individualism, to commit ourselves with better feelings to it [neoliberalism]." (own translation from German)[12]

And despite or because of the ongoing economic crisis, the neoliberal swing is not at its end. Just last year, the Rutte administration confirmed its position in the first throne speech of King Willem-Alexander and proclaimed that the welfare state is at its end and will be substituted by an undefined "participative society".[13] The governmental call for a "participative society" might be an interesting challenge in economically steady times, but in the midst of the economic crisis, it might be considered a doubtful move. Therefore it is not surprising that the announcement attracted immediate critic and became the buzzword of the year. Among others, it is feared that in the long run, private initiative and engagement becomes a surrogate for considerate politics and planning.

Politics before and during the economic crisis keep moving in one direction: demounting and redistribution of what had been called state responsibility. It is very much standard that financial cuts and redistribution of responsibilities in first instance hit the vulnerable health, social and cultural sectors. But national governmental rearrangements do not halt here. In October 2010, after almost

---

[11] "Der Neoliberalismus hatte das ideologische Verdienst, die schamhafte Maske vor dem Konsumismus fallen zu lassen, er hat ihn geradewegs zum zentralen Lebensmotiv erklärt."

[12] "Man hat uns in ein psychopolitisches Großexperiment über Frivolität verwickelt - aber was auf dem Programm stand, war nicht mehr aristokratische Frivolität, sondern Massenfrivolität, Leichtsinn und Egoismus für jeden. Man hat in dieser Zeit behauptet, Gemeinwohldenken sei gescheitert. Also blieb der Asozialismus, den wir höflicherweise Individualismus genannt haben, um uns mit besseren Gefühlen zu ihm zu bekennen."

[13] "De klassieke verzorgingsstaat verdwijnt" (The classic welfare state will disappear), The first throne speech of King Willem-Alexander as head of state. Dutch daily newspaper De Volkskrant September 17, 2013.

65 years of integrated housing and spatial planning, the Ministry of Housing, Spatial Planning and the Environment (VROM) has been dissolved and the tasks got distributed between the Ministry of Infrastructure and Environment (IenM) and the Ministry of the Interior and Kingdom Relations (BKZ).

In the revised set-up, the ministry only organizes and structures the general building process. The actual planning of land development since 2006 is fully in the hand of provinces and municipalities. It is striking that the national government decided to reorganize the responsibilities of the ministries at a time, where lower-tier structures were very much pressured with severe financial shortcomings and with limited means to keep an eye on interregional developments.

The urban planner Stefan Netsch particularly addresses the financial situation of municipalities: "As a result of the economic crisis combined with the financial risk governments took on the Dutch real-estate market, there are now roughly sixty municipalities facing bankruptcy." (Netsch/Kropman 2013: 1095) According to Netsch, municipalities miscalculated and invested during the strong economic period in land development that today needs to be considered as risky activity, due to the uncertainty of the market in changing economic conditions and long project life spans. Investing within the economic stable Randstad under regular circumstances isn't considered to be risky, but especially in economic weak areas in the periphery of the country, this might be problematic. Netsch and Kropman recognize that the crisis produced a country of two speeds: the conurbation of the Randstad versus the rest. The economic imbalance between the Dutch regions cannot be considered a new phenomenon, but especially in the today's situation, it might be a central factor for completed urban and suburban developments that took place outside the Randstad, and it might become a crucial issue in the decision-making of any future development.

Though some developments such as Leidsche Rijn are not completed yet, and others are even built out, according to the current political situation, the Vinex implementation was most likely the last state-controlled housing program in the Netherlands.

During the past five years, the entire Dutch building sector is under the impression of the economic recession and the housing production significantly slowed down. When in fall 2014, some Dutch banks announced a light recovery of the global markets, the mood rose up again and the real-estate sector with its many investors, developers, architects, operators, builders, and realtors prepares to continue business as usual: producing more of the same kind of houses for the urban and suburban buyer's market. After the game is before the game. Without wanting to over-simplify the matter and insinuating lack of interest, it feels as if the market hasn't learned much from the previous years. The production of arbitrariness and insignificance continues. The unbridled consumption lives on.

References

Boeijenga, Jelte/ Mensink, Jeroen (2008), "Vinex Atlas", Rotterdam: 010 Publishers.

Boeijenga, Jelte (2011), "Vinex: a compact city policy?", in: Boelens, Luuk/ Ovink, Henk/ Pálsdóttir, Hanna Lára/ Wierenga, Elien (eds.), *Compact City Extended, Outline for Future Policy, Research, and Design, in:* Design and Politics #4, Rotterdam: 010 Publishers, 24-34.

Brands, Bart/ Broekman, Marco (2010), "This is not a plan!", in: Provoost, Michelle (ed.), *New Towns for the 21st Century: The Planned Vs. The Unplanned City, The International New Town Institute (INTI)*, Amsterdam: SUN Architecture & Authors, 270-279.

Buitelaar, Edwin/ Schilder, Frans/ Bijlsma, Like/ Bellaard, Joeri (2014), *De waarde van stijl, een prijsanalyse van historiserende bouwstijlen*. Planbureau voor de Leefomgeving (PBL) and Amsterdam School of Real Estate (ASRE), Den Haag, http://www.pbl.nl/sites/default /files/cms/publicaties/PBL_2014_De_waarde_van_stijl_1422.pdf (Accessed August 8, 2014).

Černe, Andrej (2004), *Dispersed and decentralized settlement systems*, Ljubljana, 83-95, www.dlib.si/stream/URN:NBN:SI:doc-DF7JELZG/e7132 551.../PDF (Accessed August 6, 2014).

Faludi, Andreas/ van der Falk, Arnoud (1994), *Rule and Order, Dutch Planning Doctrine in the Twentieth Century*. Doetinchem: Kluwer Academic Publishers.

Hawthorne, Christopher (2004), "Design Dispatch; The Dutch Retouch Suburbia", *The New York Times online*, January 15, 2014, http://www.nytimes.com/2004/01/15/garden/design-dispatch-the-dutch-retouch-suburbia.html (Accessed August 12, 2014).

Jókövi, Margit/ Boon, Claudia/ Filius, Friedel (2006), *Woningproductie ten tijde van Vinex, een verkenning*, NAi Uitgevers, Rotterdam & Ruimtelijk Planbureau, Den Haag, http://www.pbl.nl/sites/default/files/cms/ publicaties/Woningproductie_ten_tijde_van_Vinex.pdf (Accessed August 6, 2014).

Korthals Altes, Willem (2008), "National Urban Planning, Dutch Planning Success or Failure?", in: Khakee, Abdul/ Hull, Angela/ Miller, Donald/

Woltjer, Johan (eds.), *New Principles in Planning Evaluation*, Aldershot: Ashgate Publishing, 221-238.

Lootsma, Bart (2002), "Super Dutch afterthoughts. Ein Blick in die Niederlande", in: Mausbach, Florian/ Kaltenbrunner, Robert/ Müller, André (eds.), Themenheft Baukultur-Planungskultur, Informationen zur Raumentwicklung 11/12.02, Berlin: Bundesamt für Bauwesen und Raumordnung, 683-691.

Lörzing, Han/ Klemm, Wiebke/ van Leeuwen, Miranda/ Soekimin, Suus (2006), *VINEX! Een morfologische verkenning,* NAi Uitgevers, Rotterdam & Ruimtelijk Planbureau, Den Haag, http://www.pbl.nl/sites/default/files/cms/publicaties/VINEX_Een_morfologische_verkenning.pdf (Accessed August 6, 2014).

Netsch, Stefan/ Kropman, Niels (2013), "Are the Netherlands Shrinking or Just Changing?", in: Schrenk, Manfred/ Popovich, Vasily/ Zeile, Peter/ Elisei, Pietro (eds.), *Proceedings REAL CORP 2013 Tagungsband - Planning Times - You better Keep Planning or You get in Deep Water, for the Cities they are A-Changin',* Papers of the 18th International Conference on Urban Planning, Regional Development and Information Society in Rome, 20.- 23.05.2013, Schwechat-Rannersdorf: CORP Publishers, 1089-1098. Reijndorp, Arnold/ Bijlsma, Like/ Nio, Ivan/ van der Wouden, Ries (2012), *Nieuwe steden in de Randstad, verstedelijking en suburbaniteit,* Den Haag: Planbureau voor de Leefomgeving (PBL), http://www.pbl.nl/sites/default/files/cms/publicaties/PBL_2012_Nieuwe-steden-in-de-Randstad_186_0.pdf (Accessed January 20, 2014).

Sleurink, Marijn (2012), *The Transformation of the Amsterdam Housing Market and How Young Adults Respond to Declined Access to Housing,* Master's Thesis Urban Geography, Graduate School of Social Sciences (GSSS) University of Amsterdam, http://dare.uva.nl/document/468292 (Accessed August 9, 2014).

Sloterdijk, Peter (2009), "Nur Verlierer kooperieren", *Die Tageszeitung (taz),* May 5, 2009, Berlin, http://www.taz.de/!34140/ (Accessed October 19, 2014).

van Dijk, Hans (1995), "800.000 huizen op zoek naar een plan", in: Bekaert, Geert (ed.), *Archis, June 1995,* Doetinchem: NAi in association with C. Misset Publishers, 9.

van Rossum, Hans/ van Wijk, Frank/ Baljon, Lodewijk (2001), *De stad in het uitersten, verkenningstocht naar Vinex-land,* Rotterdam: NAi uitgevers.

van't Hoff, Matthijs/ Jacobsen, Gladys/ Leroi, Martine (2006), *Via Vinex,* Rotterdam: Episode Publishers.

Wagenaar, Cor (2011), *Town Planning in the Netherlands since 1800,* Rotterdam: 010 Publishers.

Werkgroep Binnenstedelijk bouwen (2010), *Prachtig Compact NL, in opdracht van het College van Rijksadviseurs (commissioned by the Board of Government Advisors),* Den Haag: Atelier Rijksbouwmeester, 110-124.

The dynamics of the Eastern European suburbs. Kazan, Kyiv and Bucharest

Iana Korolova, Ion Alexandru Retegan and Iana Samakaeva

Introduction

The suburban phenomenon in Eastern Europe is strongly related to the collapse of the communist regime and the switch to more democratic forms of government. However, during the communist time, cities behind the Iron Curtain significantly expanded at their fringes, though in a different way from their Western counterparts. As a result of the centralized urbanization strategy, the suburbs of the communist cities were filled with residential districts of prefabricated blocks of flats, often encroaching former rural settlements or agricultural land.

The fall of communism and the transition to a free market economy brought the Eastern European suburbs into a new phase of development. Private small scale projects have replaced the state planned strategy of development. After 25 years, it is maybe the time to examine the patterns of urban sprawl that emerged and the driving forces behind them. Three case studies from three different countries have been selected to discuss the consistency of this phenomenon: two cities formerly part of the Soviet Union and currently part of two different states - Kazan (Russia) and Kyiv (Ukraine) -, and one city from the latest group of former communist countries that joined the European Union - Bucharest (Romania). What were the common features of the communist developments in the periphery of these cities and what individualized them during that time? Considering the different paths they followed after the fall of communism, what are the differences and the common issues of the contemporary suburban development?

The development of the eastern European cities during the communist time has been covered by the literature of that time as well as after 1990. However, the topic of the periphery has been discussed only partially. Kazan reflected the situation of the soviet city; therefore the main features of the communist periphery can be outlined from studies that focused on the Soviet Union as a whole. Concerning Kyiv, some information about its development strategy could be found in the documentation of the master plan of 1967, as well as in the planning documents that followed it. Bucharest's residential construction was analysed by Peter Derer (1985) and more recently by Giuseppe Cina (2010).

Regarding the post-communist suburbanization, Hirt and Stanilov (2009) present the overall picture of Eastern Europe with all the driving forces, features and typologies. Looking at the Russian context, one can say Moscow has monopolized all the research. However, comparing Golubchikov's, Phelp's and Makhrova's study "Moscow as a growth machine" (2010) with the case of Kazan, only insignificant differences can be noted, mostly regarding the scale of developments. In contrast to its Russian counterpart, the Ukrainian capital has not been given as much attention by researchers. Worth of mention are Kushnirenko's paper "Problems of reorganizing functional planning structures of Kyiv metropolitan area" (2012) and Brade and Savchuc's "A retrospective of the dacha-cottage development in the capital metropolitan region of Ukraine" (2012). Finally, the pioneering research "Suburbia: Beyond the City" (2013) offers some insight about the Romanian context, albeit less about Bucharest.

The general ideas of the above-mentioned literature have been verified with concrete information, through each case-study, such as local planning drawings, statistics data, interviews with local planners and conferences. Furthermore, empirical research played an important role, including site visits and discussions with local residents.

The paper starts with a brief overview about the developments that took place in the outskirts of each city during the communist time or even before. The second part focuses on the contemporary period, analysing the driving forces behind the suburban phenomenon and the subsequent land use typologies.

1. The socialist development

All three cities underwent substantial transformations during the communist time. The set-up of industrial clusters around the existing cities triggered massive waves of rural to urban migration, which generated an acute need of housing. As the existing cities were unable to absorb the inflow of population, the newcomers were housed in new sleeping districts of multi-storey prefabricated blocks of flats, located in the proximity of the industrial centres. Thus, large parts of agricultural land or even entire villages were replaced by

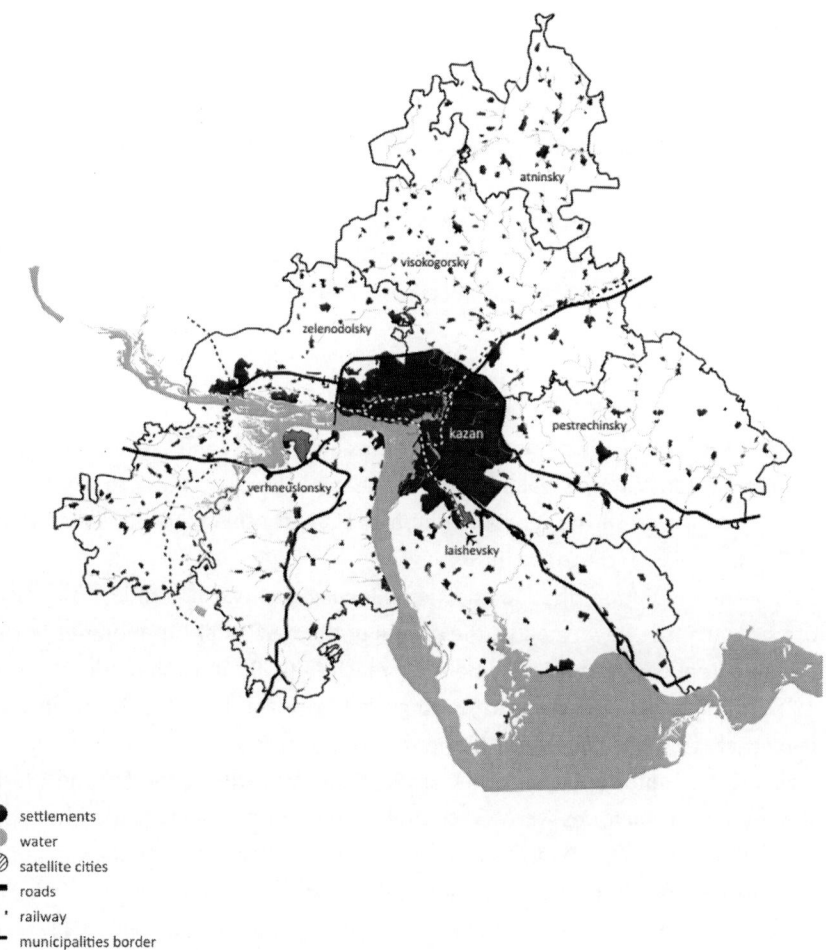

Figure 1: Kazan agglomeration area (Samakaeva 2014)

mono-functional high-density developments that significantly increased the area of the cities. However, when referring to Bucharest, there is also a history of suburban development happening before the communist period. After the First World War, the city experienced a significant increase of population and therefore expanded by adding low-density districts for either workers or well-off people. A large number of such projects were carried out by private developers, which was completely different from what was happening in Kazan and Kyiv at that time.

1.1 Kazan

1.1.2 General background

Kazan is the capital of the Republic of Tatarstan, one of the most economically developed and fast-growing regions of Russia. Six independent municipalities form the Kazan agglomeration area with a population of 1,560,000 spread on an area of 425.3 square kilometers. According to the census of 2010, 75% of Tatarstan's inhabitants live in urban areas, while 25% live in rural areas, respectively.

1.1.2 Historical development

Lying at the crossroads of major trade routes linking East and West, Kazan grew as an important commercial and political centre. The city started to expand after becoming part of the Russian Empire in 1552, reaching 200,000 inhabitants at the beginning of the 20th century.

During the revolution of 1918 and the following civil war, Kazan lost a quarter of its population. Nevertheless, the capital of the new Tatar Autonomous Soviet Socialist Republic recovered rapidly, to reach 400,000 inhabitants in 1939. In 1927 Joseph Stalin launched the strategy to transform the Soviet Union into an industrialized state; therefore numerous factories were built throughout the city, such as motor and helicopter production units. During the Second World War numerous factories were evacuated from other Soviet cities together with their labour force and relocated to the outskirts of Kazan, increasing the population even more. After the war, the severe housing shortage was addressed by Nikita Khrushchev's policy promoting the use of prefabricated panels. New ten-storey "sleeping districts" were built in the green fields, surrounding the industrial centres. They consisted of a large number of uniform urban blocks called "microrayon", separated by major roads and centred on cultural or educational amenities. Favouring quantity over quality, the living standards in these districts were rather low. Also, being planned as individual units in the vicinity of the workplace, public transportation connections with the city centre were not so good. To sum up, intensive urbanisation caused by high rates of rural to urban migration and industrialisation, pushed Kazan population over the threshold of one million inhabitants by 1970.

The communist period also introduced the "seasonal suburbanization" phenomenon (Golubchikov/Phelps/Makhrova 2010: 4). People were not allowed to build private houses, with some exceptions, such as Melnikov[1]'s house (Goldhoorn 2012: 14); however, the collective gardening programme introduced by the government in 1949 allowed the construction of small scale ground-floor summer houses, commonly known as "dacha". As in many parts of the country, large areas in Kazan's suburbs were divided into 600 square meter plots of land, which were then offered to the most prominent members of the working class by the trade union for agricultural and recreational uses.

1.2 Kyiv

1.2.1 General background

Kyiv is the capital and the largest city of Ukraine, counting 2.77 million inhabitants, according to the census in 2012, and covering 839 square kilometers of land (Institute of Master Plan of Kyiv 2011: 19). The largest cities of the Kyiv metropolitan area are Brovary (60,000 citizens), Boryspil (50,000 citizens) and Vasylkiv (40,000 citizens). The population of rural settlements and villages ranges between three and 20 thousand citizens. Overall, Kyiv's metropolitan area accounts five million people (Institute of Master Plan of Kyiv 2011: 12).

The city was founded in the 5th century. Situated on the biggest waterway of Ukraine, the Dnipro River, much of Kyiv's progress has derived from its advantageous geographical location: within its boundaries, there are about 448 bodies of water and an abundance of greenery. The right bank consists of woody hills, ravines and slopes, while the left bank is made up of sandy beaches and a rather flat surface. The latter has often experienced spills and floods; therefore this part was not as inhabited as the right bank.

1.2.2 Historical development

Kyiv started to grow from the right bank of the river. However, when talking about the first suburban areas of Kyiv we have to look on the left bank of the Dnipro River. In the beginning of the 16th century, these lands were donated to

---

[1] Konstantin Stepanovich Melnikov (1890 – 1974) was a Russian architect and painter of the avant-garde movement. As a sign of appreciation for his work, he was allowed to build a house for him and his familiy in the centre of Moscow.

or bought by Kyiv monasteries and churches for their household purposes. Peasants, who agreed to take care of the monastic lands and stay there, founded the settlements called "slobodka". After some time they were allowed to settle and use the land for their needs. Thus, the population of the "slobodka's" was growing and the settlements turned into villages. In the 18th century, workers participating in the construction of a connecting bridge set up another suburban settlement on the left bank, called "Predmostovaya".

In the 19th century, Kyiv became an administrative and cultural centre of the South-Western part of the Russian Empire. It was at this time that the city began its fast territorial expansion. With the development of the industry, the city's population grew. New worker settlements were established outside the city limits. The largest example was set up around the Kyiv military factory "Arsenal", on the left bank of the Dnipro. Later, another settlement - "Darnitsya" - was created for the workers of the new railways in 1870. In the beginning of 20th century, the left bank of the Dnipro was also the place where Kyiv elite built their summer houses ("dacha"). On the eve of the First World War, there were already more than half a million inhabitants in Kyiv.

The food crisis of the 1921-22, caused by the civil war and a bad harvest, determined the authorities to give plots of land for gardening to two thirds of the Kyiv population. The land was inside and outside the city limits, within a radius of 50 kilometers.

After the October Revolution in 1917, the city started growing again; therefore the administrative borders had to be reconsidered. Thus, in 1923, 20 settlements of the suburban area, including all the "slobodka's", were incorporated in the city limits. The territory of Kyiv increased more than two times. At the same time, the city was confronted with an acute housing shortage. Hence, starting from 1923, new housing units were built at the city borders, while in the center old buildings were reconstructed, and additional stories were added. During this time, the first worker settlements were set up in the western outskirts of the city.

In 1934, Kyiv became the capital of the new Ukrainian Soviet Socialist Republic (USSR), which contributed to the further development of the city. Starting from 1936, large industrial enterprises were reconstructed and built. New residential areas started to develop on the right bank of the Dnipro. They often included cultural and educational facilities such as cinemas, clubs and schools.

During the Second World War, the left bank area of Kyiv was severely destroyed by the German army. Almost all settlements were burned.

Right after the Second World War, thousands of families were living in the basements of the destroyed houses and ruins. There were only 1.5 square meters of living space per inhabitant. Therefore the authorities made the combating of the pressing housing crisis a priority. In 1949, new living districts started to be built in the western part of the city. In addition to the construction of apartment blocks, concessions were made for people who wanted to build a house out of their own funds, on free territories. Villages of the left bank of the Dnipro were expanded. Later, new large housing districts were built on areas previously threatened by floods, through land reclamation methods.

From 1956, the progress within construction industry offered the possibility to build large-panel houses and series of new standardized projects were implemented in the new districts of the city. In the 1960s, Kyiv inaugurated its first metro line.

As the city extended its area of influence, new urban development strategies were needed. In 1967, the project of a new Master Plan intended to increase the use of the left bank of the river. As a consequence, a lot of old settlements were demolished and new residential districts were built instead. It was the first time in USSR that hydraulic land fill technology was applied on a large scale. Due to the danger of floods, the first residential areas were allotted at a distance of three to five kilometers from the Dnipro River. The Master Plan of 1986 included the suburban areas in the overall development strategy of the city. Kyiv's population was planned to reach three million people. The most densely populated administrative districts were the districts located directly to the city limits, along the main transportation corridors (Kushnirenko 2012: 103).

1.3 Bucharest

1.3.1 General background

Bucharest is the capital of Romania and the sixth largest city in the European Union (eurostat 2014). However, since the fall of communism its population has been constantly shrinking, dropping from over two million in 1992 to approximately 1.9 million inhabitants in 2011. Nevertheless, if the surrounding Ilfov County is included, data shows a constant increase of population of around 20% in the last ten years. Adding to that, the migration from urban to rural areas in Ilfov County has overpassed the one from rural to urban since 2005. These facts might indicate the city is in fact growing, expanding beyond its administrative boundaries.

1.3.2 The allotted city (1911-1939)

Bucharest is a relatively young city in the European context. In 1859, it became the capital of the newly created state "The Romanian United Principalities" which triggered its development. However, the city started expanding after Romania's Union with Transylvania, Bessarabia and Bukovina in 1918. Between 1918 and 1939 the population registered a growth of 127%, the biggest ever recorded, reaching 870,000 before the outbreak of the Second World War (Giurăscu 1967: 189). As a consequence, the area increased by 39%, covering 7,800 hectares in 1939.

During this time, the outskirts of the city were the place where the main residential projects were carried out. Ranging from few hectares to entire neighbourhoods, these developments were a certain improvement for the city, structuring the organic urban fabric through planning regulations and adding infrastructures. However, the city was still far from the urban character of the Western metropolis. Even In 1954 86% of the built surface consisted of ground floor houses (Giurăscu 1967: 243).

1.3.3 The imposed urbanization (1948-1989)

Shortly after the Second World War, Romania became a communist country and followed the Soviet model of planned economic development. Intensive industrialization supported by accelerated urbanization changed the suburban landscape of many cities. Within 40 years, Bucharest doubled its population from 992,536 inhabitants, according to the census in 1941 (Giurăscu 1967: 232), to 2,211,460 in 1982 (Parusi 2007: 755). The surface also increased significantly from 7,800 hectares in 1939 (Giurăscu 1967: 254) to 25,596 hectares in 1978 (Parusi 2007: 745).

During the first years, the city was developed through small scale residential projects inside the perimeter of the city, filling available empty areas. It was in the 1960s when the focus shifted towards the outskirts, where large scale residential districts were laid out in the proximity of the industrial areas. Overall, they followed the modernist urban design principles of placing free-standing objects in vast green spaces. On a smaller scale, they respected the Soviet model of the "microrayon" with housing units disposed around commercial and educational facilities (Cina 2010: 222). Despite this influence, the use of prefabricated panels was not yet as widespread as in the Soviet Union. The most notable examples are "Drumul Taberei", and "Balta Albă-Titan", both designed for 100,000 inhabitants[2].

The last decade of the communist rule pushed the urbanisation strategy even further, prioritizing cost efficiency and fulfilling quotas. At the same time the new city development strategy focused on limiting its expansion to ensure a better use of the entire urban territory (Derer 1985: 137). Therefore, previous developments were densified by placing new buildings on green spaces or by closing the fronts of the main boulevards. The new, but less numerous developments, abandoned the isolated building typologies in favour of more intensive land use typologies, such as ten storey-high courtyards. Prefabricated panel technology grew more important once the first assembly lines were set up in Bucharest in 1975 (Derer 1985: 132). Overall, the living standard significantly depreciated as a consequence of the increasing density. The reduced sizes of the new apartments as well as the poor thermal and acoustic insulations of the panels contributed to this.

Summing up, it can be said that the periphery of the three cities was significantly transformed during the communist time. The flat lands available in the outskirts of each analysed city proved ideal for erecting replicable standardized structures. Their rapid expansion was facilitated by the development of the prefabricated panel industry which gradually spread from the Soviet Union to the other countries of the Eastern Bloc. The new apartment blocks were a certain improvement for the people coming from the rural areas, providing a decent home with all necessary utilities in a safe environment with public facilities within walking distance. Moreover, they were located in the proximity of the workplace which reduced the traffic in the city. However, in the constant search for efficiency, the stress was on quantity and not on quality. People were regarded as identical individuals with identical needs; therefore what these developments miss mostly is diversity. Nevertheless, people in Kazan or

---

[2] Over the following decades, they ended up housing around 400,000 inhabitants each through several densification processes.

Kyiv, as opposed to Bucharest, were offered an alternative, albeit not permanent, to this monotonous (sub)urban life: the "dacha". It is precisely here that the post-communist suburban phenomenon will start growing.

2. Suburbanization after 1990

The suburbs of the post-socialist eastern European cities have experienced an intensive growth over a relatively short period of approximately 25 years. The apparent chaotic morphology hides certain typologies that can be traced and decoded. Their emergence must be seen as an expression of certain driving forces that determined people to move into the suburbs. However, not all identified driving forces acted at the same time. Some were stronger in the beginning such as the privatization of agricultural land and the desire to escape from the communist apartments, while others were felt later, once the market economy grew from the transition phase, such as increasing land prices. As a consequence, the distribution of the suburban land use typologies must be related to a timeline. This chapter analyses the context of each city, highlighting the common and the particular typologies, as well as the driving forces behind them. Thus, a portrait of the post socialist eastern European suburbs can be sketched.

2.1 Kazan

2.1.1 The planning system

In order to better understand the context of the first case study, it is worth taking a look at the urban planning process in the Russian Federation and how it is applied in Kazan. Throughout the country, there are several planning regulations: the Federal Land and Town Planning Codes, the city master plan and other territorial planning documents. State owned land is divided into three categories: federal property, republican property, and municipal property, the latter being entitled to sell it to private individuals or companies.

In the case of Kazan, the main actors involved in the planning process are the Government (on federal, regional and municipal levels), the Ministry of Land and Property Relations of Tatarstan, the chief architect of Kazan, planning institutes, developers, investors and private owners. The city's recent suburban de

Figure 2: Single-family houses in Novaya Tura Kazan suburb - colour (Samakaeva 2014)

velopment falls between the authority of two planning documents, drafted by two different institutions: Kazan's master plan, by the Joint-Stock Company "Institute Kazgrazhdanproject" approved in 2007, and the Kazan agglomeration strategic plan, by State Unitary Enterprise "Tatinvestgrazhdanproject".

The deficiency of coordination between planners resulted in documents which are not consistent with each other, allowing random land distribution and countless suburban developments lacking appropriate infrastructure and transportation connections.

2.1.2 Driving forces of suburbanization

Like in all cities of the former Soviet Union, the main driving forces of suburbanization in Kazan were the decentralization of the planning system and the transition to the market economy. The suburbanization phenomenon grew to a larger dimension and became an important feature of the morphological transformation of the urban fabric. First, changes in Kazan's periphery were caused

- 16-17 century
- 1767-first grid plan
- 19 century
- 20 century
- present time
- water

Figure 3: Kazan's historical development (Samakaeva 2014)

by the weakened power of the authorities leading to illegal appropriation of land and corrupt transactions. However, the situation stabilized once the law of housing privatization was enforced in 1991 and the mortgage finance system was adopted in 1998. This was followed by the land privatization law in 2001. Thus, the urban development of post-communist cities stopped being a prerogative of the authorities (Hirt/Stanilov 2009: 2).

Another reason for suburbanization was the "Elimination of dilapidated housing" programme which started in 1996. During nine years, 33,372 families were resettled from their houses in the centre of Kazan to newly built low-cost "microrayons" in the outskirts. Despite the fact that people received new residences, this procedure followed the out-dated Soviet model of displacing people to the periphery without properly analysing the consequences and looking for alternative solutions. As a result, the transport network of Kazan was incapable to cope with the new pressure, leaving the new developments isolated from the rest of the city. Another negative consequence of the programme was the destruction of numerous historical buildings from the city centre, which were later replaced by elite multi-family apartment buildings without following any master plan (Kinosian 2003). In 2008, Kazan's municipality started a similar programme, relocating 2,425 families from dilapidated housing (Andreeva 2008).

After the breakdown of the Soviet Union, there were no restrictions on people's decisions about the city they wanted to live in. Kazan is known to be a magnet for people migrating from lower-income regions and rural areas; therefore, the demand on the housing market remains constantly high. In most cases new inhabitants have to settle in the suburbs due to the high prices of housing in the city centre. At the same time, higher-income people also choose to live in individual country houses located in the picturesque setting outside the city.

The vast majority of suburban residents commute daily for job or studies to the centre of Kazan. Although the settlements are usually developed around major highways, in most cases there is lack of public transportation connections to the city which results in a strong car-dependency.

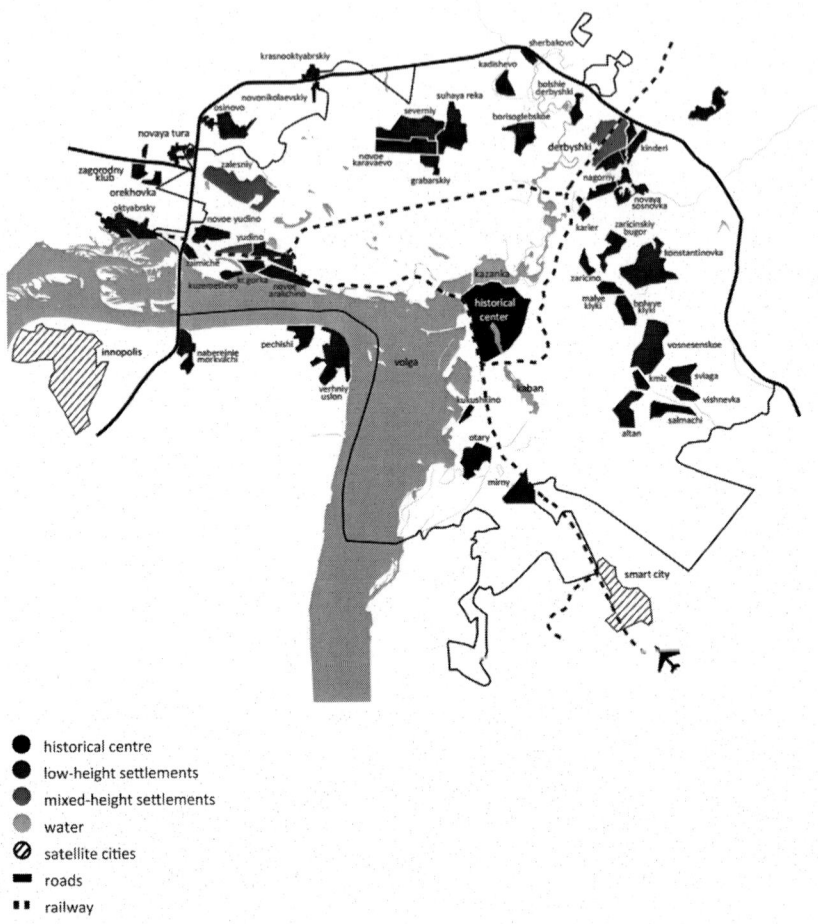

- historical centre
- low-height settlements
- mixed-height settlements
- water
- satellite cities
- roads
- railway
- city border

Figure 4: Kazan's periphery (Samakaeva 2014)

Currently, Kazan's suburban development is focused on the inclusion of the western areas within the city borders, building new settlements at the periphery, and moving the remaining centrally-located industries to the outskirts. Kzan agglomeration is expected to double its population by including two satellite cities, planned in the western and northern edges of the city.

2.1.3 Land use typologies

Unplanned suburban settlements with single-family houses

The most frequent land use typology can be seen in the myriad of chaotic unplanned developments with no single architectural style, caused by the absence of a master plan, regulations or design guidance. As a rule, after acquiring the land from the municipality, new owners build individual houses without coordination. These developments derived from the need for reasonably priced residences for people from the middle or lower-middle class.

The first type of unplanned developments emerged right after the fall of communism and involved the transformation of the "dacha" communities. Residents gradually replaced their tiny Soviet ground-floor wooden houses with permanent, individual two-storey brick houses. Frequently, families own both an inner-city apartment and a second home, constantly swapping from one to the other according to weather conditions or personal preferences. Similar transformations happened with some old wooden houses in villages. For example, in "Novaya Tura", a former "dacha" settlement in the Zelenodolsky municipal district, nearly 30% of the building stock already consists of new detached houses with gardens. The plots of land belong either to the municipality, or to private owners. The settlement is located 25 kilometers away from the city centre, to which it is connected via a motorway and a public transportation line. However, the bus stop is within considerable walking distance from the residential units, which determines the inhabitants to rely almost exclusively on their private cars. All utility works were carried out by the inhabitants themselves. "Novaya Tura" does not provide any public facilities; however, it has abundant green fields and a lake. Despite the trend of converting "dachas" into permanent residences, there are still many communities which have survived in their original form.

The second type of unplanned outskirts is the result of real estate transactions through which investors acquire former agricultural land, divide it into plots and sell it to private clients. Looking to maximize the profit, they often ignore the infrastructure works. For instance, "Emerald Valley" is a new development, located 15 kilometers away from the centre and bordered by forests on the

Figure 5: Single-family houses in Novaya Tura, Kazan's suburbs (Samakaeva 2014)

east. Several plots with detached houses of various styles are scattered throughout the rather empty area. The only facilities provided by the developers are gas and electricity; therefore the owners have to drill their own water wells and invest in building asphalt roads.

Planned gated communities of single-family houses

This new building trend emerged in Kazan over the last decade. Growing revenues and the spread of western lifestyle ideals took shape in prestige villa settlements, located in favourable geographical settings, mainly in the western outskirts of Kazan. As a rule, real estate companies offer several already built standard design houses, within a fenced compound where public access is limited by barriers and security checkpoints. Target groups are middle or upper-middle class people, in search for a safe and quiet environment.

"Orekhovka" and "Zagorodny klub" represent the most striking examples of gated communities. Located in "Zelenodolsky" municipal district, both settlements are highly car-oriented, since the only form of public transportation are rare regional busses. The developer considered the needs of people in the design stage and provided asphalt roads, street lighting and other necessary services. "Zagorodny klub" also includes a school, a kindergarten and sport facilities.

Despite the advantageous conditions for the residents, gated communities create even greater distance between the wealthy and poor strata of the society.

For instance, special facilities for the privileged society, such as private schools or kindergartens could also be useful for citizens of nearby villages.

Planned gated communities of row houses

This land use typology is a quite new phenomenon in Kazan. Targeted for the middle or lower-middle class, it is popular among relatively young families with children. Located in the south, only 15 minutes away from the city centre, "Lesnoy gorodok" consists of three-storey row houses and five-storey blocks of flats grouped around a courtyard. Available common facilities are recreation areas, playgrounds, a shopping mall, a kindergarten and a café. The complex has all necessary utilities, including water supply from its own source. Moreover, it is well connected with the rest of the city by public busses.

"Microrayons"

The basic unit of urban design in the Eastern Bloc, the "microrayon" is almost extinct from the toolbox of today's planners in post-communist Europe. Nevertheless, in Russia and in the countries of the former Soviet Union it is still in use, and Kazan is no exception. Housing shortage and inflated prices for apartments in the central districts led to the ongoing construction of low-cost high-density developments in the periphery.

"Radujniy" complex lies 20 kilometers from the city centre, close to the motorway in the north. It has been developed by the Limited Liability Company "Tatstroyinvest" and consists of prefabricated ten-storey apartment blocks, which serve the needs of the lower-middle class. Despite the low-budget investment, the development includes playgrounds, a kindergarten and sport grounds. "Radujniy" is accessible by car or public bus.

Post-Soviet autonomous districts

Former industrial autonomous districts were included within the boundaries of Kazan 30 years ago, but are still considered as periphery.

The most famous example is "Derbyshki", situated close to the north-east motorway, 22 kilometers from the city centre. During the Second World War, several industrial enterprises were relocated there from the besieged Saint Petersburg (formerly Leningrad), causing a massive inflow of population and the fast development of the area. Nowadays, two factories are still functioning and public facilities are growing. Therefore, the population of 80,000 inhabitants has remained relatively stable. However, it is an ageing population, with 60% aged between 45 and 70 years. Most of the young individuals, between 16 and 25, prefer to move to the centre of Kazan. Nevertheless there are young couples moving in, attracted by the affordable prices of accommodation and the nearby forests and lake. "Derbyshki" is quite a dense settlement with a limited amount of open space. The housing stock is mixed, consisting of prefabricated high-rise communist blocks of flats, permanent single-family low-storey houses and seasonal "dachas". The main disadvantage of "Derbyshki" is public transportation deficiency and, as a result, high car-dependence.

Satellite cities

These structures continue the tradition of the post-Soviet autonomous districts formed around the main industry hubs. Planned on federal and regional levels, "Innopolis" and "Smart City" are giant autonomous developments, which aim to attract new investors, reinforcing Kazan's role as a regional economic centre. Located 30 kilometers west from the centre of Kazan, close to the Volga River and Moscow motorway, Innopolis is part of the "Verhneuslonsky" municipal district. The new city will host a large IT park, the first IT University in Russia and a Special Economic Zone. 150,000 short-term and permanent residents will be accommodated in various types of housing, ranging from six- to nine-storey multi-family houses to individual and row houses. The entire infrastructure is provided by developers. The project is based on a public-private partnership.

"Smart City" is being built close to Kazan International Airport, in the South-East suburbs. The project will become a new business hub with a Special Economic Zone which will accommodate approximately 60,000 people.

2.2 Kyiv

2.2.1 Driving forces of the suburbanization

Similarly to Kazan, the post-communist suburban phenomenon in Kyiv was firstly driven by the privatization of land, granted by the land reform adopted in Ukraine in 1992. As a result, municipal control over the development of Kyiv weakened and a large number of single family houses settlements appeared at the outskirts. In general, these developments do not offer any working oppor

The dynamics of the Eastern European suburbs 199

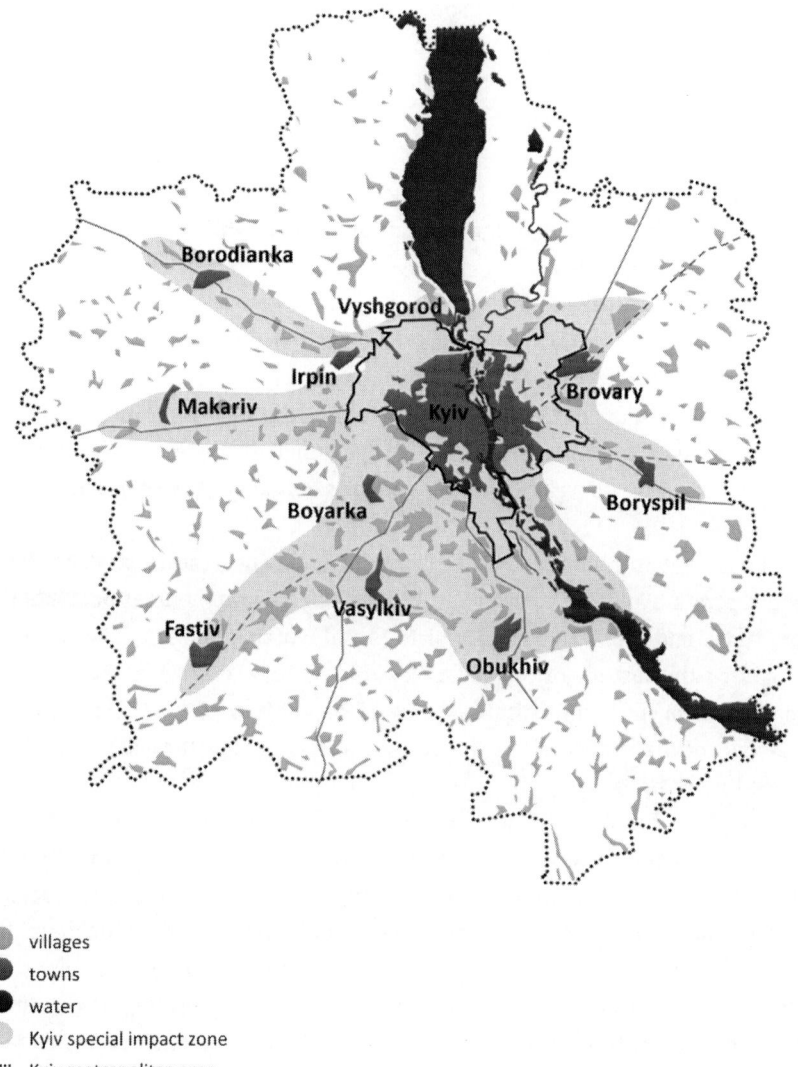

- villages
- towns
- water
- Kyiv special impact zone
- Kyiv metropolitan area

Figure 6: Areas of spatial influence of the city of Kyiv (Korolova 2014, based on http://kyiv.me/general-plan-of-kyiv-city/1-basic-lines-of-social-and-economic-development/)

tunities; therefore the inhabitants have to commute to the city on a daily basis. After the collapse of the Soviet Union, investments in public transportation have been drastically reduced, propelling massive increases in private automobile ownership. On one hand this allowed people more freedom when choosing the location of their house, but on the other, it generated severe congestion on the existing road infrastructure. Another driving factor for suburbanization are commercial centres, located along important roads, which act like a seed for new suburban settlements.

The "seasonal suburbanisation" that started in the communist time is strong to this day. Hundreds of "dacha" owners move to their summer house during the summer week-ends. Thus, Kyiv's permanent population of 2.77 million people temporarily expands to 3.5 million (Executive Body of Kyiv City Council 2011: 7). The recent suburban development of Kyiv follows the main international transport corridors as well the north-south axis defined by the Dnipro River.

It is important to mention that a significant imbalance can be noticed when looking at the two banks of the river. The left bank accommodates 36.2% of the population and offers only 19.7% of the total working places, while the right bank hosts the vast majority of 63.8% of inhabitants and provides 81.3% of the work places in the city (Institute of Master Plan of Kyiv 2011: 7). As a result, a large part of the traffic follows the east-west direction, increasing the pressure on the Dnipro bridges.

Regarding the future developments of the city, the master plan from 2011 intended to expand municipality control over the suburbs, increasing the administrative area from 83,600 to 143,400 hectares, and at the same time focused on increasing density. However, it was not approved due to disagreements between the parties involved: neighbouring town administrations, regional state administrations, Kyiv Regional State Administration and Kyiv Regional Council. In the meantime, territories foreseen for the urban development have already been built-up with single-family house settlements and "dachas" (Institute of Master Plan of Kyiv 2011: 10).

Figure 7: "Dachas" Osokorky (Korolova 2014)

2.2.2 Land use typologies

Summer houses ("dacha")

Like elsewhere in the former Soviet Union, during the communist time, people with exceptional contributions in their field of work were offered plots of land outside the city to grow vegetables and build "dachas". In Ukraine, this practice is still being used, for example to reward soldiers fighting against the insurgents in the east of the country. Besides its recreational function, the "dacha" and its garden have also served as a means of surviving during the hard times Kyiv often experienced throughout its history, such as the famine of the 1920s. One of the first notes about Kyiv's "dachas" was given by G.I. Velychko (1930): "During the summer the prosperous part of Kyiv's population went to the suburbs." According to Encyclopaedia Handbook "Kyiv" (1986), "dachas" outside the Kyiv region were used by about 50,000 citizens, out of a total population of 595,000 at the beginning of the 20th century. After the collective gardening programme introduced by the Soviet government in 1949, the number of "dacha" users

Figure 8: "Microrayon" Osokorky (Korolova 2014)

rose to 100,000 people in the 1970s. The most sought-after settlements inside the city were "Rusanovsky", "Osokorky" and "Berkovtsy". Initially, "dacha" settlements did not have any kind of infrastructure. Thus, people built roads, dag wells and brought electricity generators, and sometimes gas cylinders, at their own expense. Each "dacha" settlement has its own leader and administration, which organise meetings to discuss community issues. Nowadays, more and more "dacha" owners renovate their houses for permanent living or they sell their plots of land. According to the Constitution of Ukraine, each person has a right to have 0.1 hectare of land for individual "dacha" construction. Nevertheless, by paying large bribes to the authorities larger plots can be acquired.

Suburban single family house settlements

Like in Kazan, the suburban single-family house has become very popular among the upper middle class. Every year, several new settlements spring up around Kyiv. Most of them are poorly connected to the city in terms of public transportation and technical infrastructure. Work places and public facilities such as schools, kindergartens, hospitals or cinemas are also absent. As a consequence, more than 350,000 people commute to the city on a daily basis, increasing traffic-jams. As it has been mentioned before, this is the result of the miscommunication between Kyiv's administration and the regional power.

"Microrayons"

Like in the case of Kazan, new high-rise neighbourhoods according to the model of the "microrayon" are still being built in the outskirts of Kyiv, this time by private investors. They are often located in areas surrounded by greenery, inside the city limits or within short driving distance from the city. However, in most cases, developers try to save money by not providing any public facilities, thus creating mono-functional sleeping districts.

The residents also struggle with poor quality public spaces. "Osokorky", situated inside the city limits, on the left bank, can be cited as a relevant example.

2.3 Bucharest

2.3.1 Driving forces of suburbanization

Restitution of property

Once the land reform law was voted in February 1991, people started to reclaim their plots of agricultural land according to the situation prior the collectivisation. Thus, the formerly state-owned agricultural land was divided in parcels of all sizes and shapes. In many cases the new owners did not use the land for any agricultural activity but built a secondary home instead.

Low quality housing

The census of 1992 showed that apartment blocks accounted for 77% of the total housing units, out of which 91% were built after 1945. Even though the supply was enough to meet the demand, it was the living quality that didn't prove satisfactory anymore. The average number of rooms in the apartment blocks was 2.35, whereas the average surface was 34.23 square meters (National Institute of Statistics 2014). Thus, the "nouveau riche" class began to look for options to escape this situation by moving "back to nature" (Ghenciulescu 2013: 179).

Geographical setting

The geographical setting around the capital provided the ideal environment for suburban sprawl. Bucharest is situated on a relatively flat area. It is crossed by the river Dâmbovița and bordered by forests and a string of lakes, formed by the river Colentina, in the North. After 1989, this former natural limit of expansion turned into a magnet attracting the wealthy class. The middle class could only afford to accomplish their suburban dream in the plains of the West and South. In all cases the flat land kept building costs affordable, for both individual entrepreneurs and real estate companies.

Land price

Increasing prices for rents and purchase of housing units inside the city limits determined many people to look for an alternative in the outskirts. However, land prices in the suburbs soon started to rise too, as a consequence of the suburban "villa frenzy" of the 1990's. Therefore, developers turned to more profitable solutions, such as apartment buildings construction. Paradoxically, the suburbanites were caught up by the same image of the collective housing that they were running from (Ghenciulescu 2013: 180).

Administrative issues

The administrative area of Bucharest has remained almost unchanged since 1989, even though the city has expanded beyond these limits. This is reflected in the growth of the built-up areas of the surrounding villages and towns. Between 1993 and 2008 the total built-up area of neighbouring Ilfov county grew 50 times, from approximately 400 hectares to around 20,000 hectares, overpassing the one of Bucharest, which measures 16,000 hectares.

Considering land prices and the possibility of avoiding the bureaucratic procedures of obtaining the building permit in Bucharest, many developers looked for sites in the jurisdiction of the surrounding councils (Ioan 2010). Therefore the majority of the suburban development of Bucharest happened in fact outside its administrative territory.

2.3.2 Land use typologies

Suburban single family houses

In the 1990's, one-storey detached houses of various architectural styles were built on the recently reclaimed plots of agricultural land. They were the expression of a "good life" standard shaped by the media (Vöckler 2008: 50). However, public infrastructure was absent from these "ideal" oases, and owners had to rely almost exclusively on private initiatives. Electricity and water were provided according to individual contracts with the distribution companies, whereas waste water was collected in septic tanks and garbage dumped in the surrounding fields. Accessibility was a challenge even for cars, considering dirt roads were the only connections.

The first examples of this typology were built in the northern part of the city and, as they gradually filled almost all available land, they later "migrated" to the western and southern outskirts. Thus, it can be asserted that this typology is the beginning of a life cycle of the suburbs. Moreover, considering the young age of the suburbs in Bucharest it is not surprising that this is the land use typology, which is found most often.

Gated communities

After 2000, the raise of domestic expenditure and the prospect of joining the European Union created an economic boom that activated the real estate market. Land became more expensive and other profitable solutions were sought. Therefore larger estates were cut from the agricultural land and developed as districts of individual houses for sale or rent, targeting the upper middle class and the expatriate community. Being often located in the proximity of existing villages, the developers foresaw a potential discomfort in interacting with the indigenous less well-off population and restricted public access to the properties with fences and guarded gates, creating areas commonly known as gated communities. The first example is considered the "French village" built by the Bucharest city hall in partnership with Bouygues for the expatriate community in Pipera village as early as 1993 (Nae/Turnock 2011). It covers seven hectares and has 30 fully equipped houses for rent, as well as common facilities such as a spa area, swimming pool, tennis court and kindergarten (Benezic/Ciurcanu 2008). Similar examples of this typology were built mainly in the North.

Condominiums

As land prices rose even further, high density projects started to be preferred by the developers. Thus, the most recent typology emerged. Slightly smaller plots than in the previous example were selected or assembled for residential blocks of up to ten floors, trying to combine the features of urban life with the benefits of nature. Luxurious developments in the North included facilities like swimming pools, supermarkets, kindergartens, sports fields or playgrounds, used exclusively by the residents of the complexes; whereas low-cost developments located mostly in the western part of Bucharest did not provide any communal facilities. In the case of the latter the use of the ground-floor has been informally changed from housing to commercial activities, similarly to the situation in former communist blocks. Shopping facilities, Office parks, Industrial hubs This land-use typology includes all large scale developments of various uses, usually located next to the main traffic corridors. Commercial centres were in many cases the magnet for the residential developments. International chain retailers were among the first "settlers" in the suburbs of Bucharest. The largest shopping areas were located along the DN1 road in the North and A1 highway in the West. Few office buildings were constructed along the DN1 road, while industrial buildings, warehouses and logistics centres were built along the outer ring or the A1 highway.

2.3.3. "Henri Coandă" project

When looking at the above-mentioned typologies the "Henri Coandă" pops out as a striking exception, not only because of its scale but also because it was a state driven project. Developed by the National Dwelling Agency (ANL) on a 115.9-hectar plot of land, of which 60.5 hectares were owned by Bucharest's municipality and 55.4 hectares by the municipality of Voluntari, it was the first example of cooperation between the capital and a neighbouring municipality. The land became available for construction once the nearby airport restricted its activity in 2009.

1,108 mortgage financed social housing units were planned, 521 in Bucharest and 587 in Voluntari, as well as eleven condominiums, five in Bucharest and six in Voluntari. Public facilities were also provided in the construction plan.

The construction started in 2005 and two years later most of the houses were erected. However, no work has been carried out for any kind of infrastructure

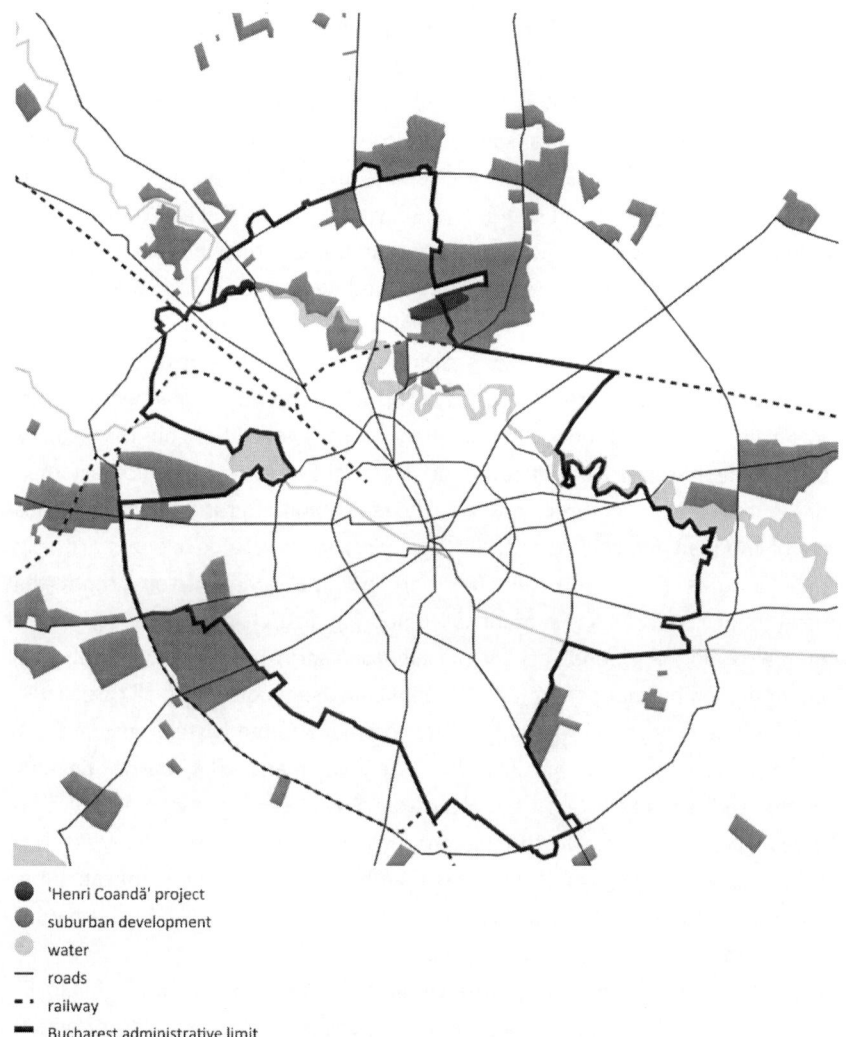

- 'Henri Coandă' project
- suburban development
- water
- roads
- railway
- Bucharest administrative limit

Figure 9: Bucharest's suburban development after 1989 (Retegan 2014)

by neither of the two municipalities. The few people who adventured to move in had to manage all the facilities on their own: connecting individually to the electricity grid, digging wells for the water supply or using individual heating systems. Garbage has been collected only in the part controlled by Bucharest city hall, as there is no public waste collecting service in Voluntari. Moreover, no roads have been paved (Pavalasc 2013). The site is accessible almost exclusively by car but even that proves to be a challenge, unless 4x4 vehicles are used. The closest public transportation connections are the metro terminal Pipera, within 40 minutes walking distance, and a bus stop for two lines, 16 minutes away by foot. Out of the two, only one goes to the city centre. So far only 20 families have moved in and another 100 use their houses only during the week-end. The rest have abandoned the buildings for which they paid between 50,000 and 120,000 euros (Pavalasc 2013). In this surreal landscape where human life struggles, ever growing packs of straying dogs have become the new rulers. In all three cities, the switch from a centrally planned economy to a free market economy was the spark that triggered the suburban sprawl. Looking deeper, one can notice the driving forces of suburbanization are more or less the same in all three contexts. The restitution of property and the transfer of the planning role from the municipality to private developers are common features in all three cities. Furthermore, the same flat topography that used to facilitate building prefabricated housing districts during the communist time also laid the groundwork for the suburban sprawl. However, the suburban phenomenon has not generated the same land use typologies in all three cities. The high density residential unit of the communist time is still in use in Kazan and Kyiv, being now the product of private investments. The "dacha" developments, that set apart Kazan and Kyiv from Bucharest in the communist time, are still present and slowly turning into semi-permanent residential areas. Nevertheless, what brings all three cities together is the prevalence of the suburban single family house, which accounts for the large part of the suburban development.

Regarding the challenges the three cities face today, one should highlight the unsustainable character of the suburban development. Large parts of agricultural land are constantly turned into housing estates, reducing the percentage of green areas around the city. The uncontrolled expansion also puts pressure on the existing infrastructure of the city. Public transportation does not reach the new developments and the suburbanites rely on their private cars to commute to the city, causing severe traffic congestion. The extension of the water supply, sewerage, electricity and heating networks is too expensive for the municipality; therefore this task is left for private initiatives. Private developers often disregard these facilities and it is up to the individuals to find solutions.

The dynamics of the Eastern European suburbs 209

Figure 10: "Henri Coandă" development (Adrian Timaru 2014)

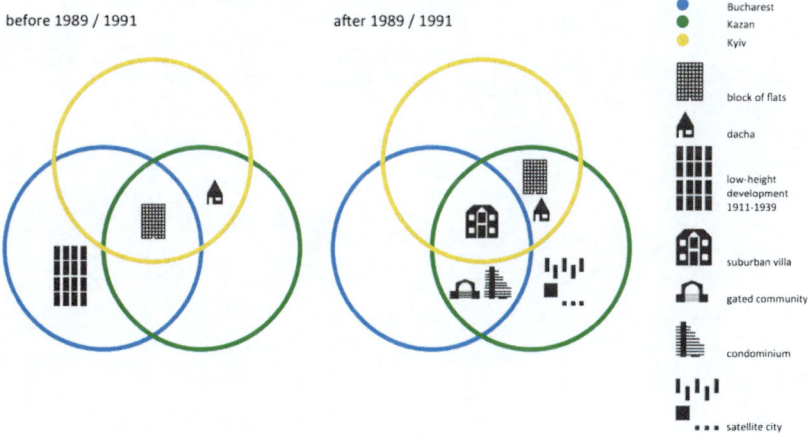

Figure 11: Suburban land use typologies in Bucharest, Kazan and Kyiv (Retegan 2014)

What is more, the suburbs of Kazan, Kyiv and Bucharest suffer from the reduced number of public facilities and working opportunities, forcing their inhabitants to commute to the city either for work, school or leisure.

Looking from a social perspective, one can distinguish the "nouveau riches" among the first settlers of the post-socialist suburbs. They afforded the priviledge to build new residences in the picturesque settings located in the outskirts of Kazan, Kyiv or Bucharest. In order to avoid unwanted interaction with local rural populations, they preferred to segregate themselves either individually, through opaque fenced properties, or collectively through gated communities. Less-scenic areas in the outskirts were left for less well-off people who were planning to start a family and did not want to invest in a depreciated socialist apartment. In some cases this meant a poor quality house further away from the city or high-density developments such as in Kazan and Kyiv.

In the end, the eastern European suburban leap is best described by this ad for a residential complex:

> "*The city is not for you. Too many people in such a small place. Too many cars crowded in traffic. Even the air tells you to find a better place. Fortunately, you don't have to go far.*" *(Green Vista Residence 2014)*

References

Andreeva, Ludmila (2008), *Municipal program. The relocation of citizens from dilapidated housing stock in Kazan in 2008-2015*, Kazan: Municipality of Kazan.

Axenov, Konstantin/ Brade, Isolde/ Bondarchuk, Evgenij (2006), *The Transformation of Urban Space in Post-Soviet Russia*, London: Routledge.

Benezic, Dollores/ Ciurcanu, Andrei (2008), "*Satul Francez își schimbă stăpânul*", evz.ro, http://www.evz.ro/detalii/stiri/satul-francez-isi-schimba-stapanul-3164.html (Accessed March 01, 2014).

Blinnikov, Mikhail S. (2010), *A Geography of Russia and Its Neighbors*, New York: Guilford Press.

Brade, Isolde/ Savchuk, Ivan (2012), "Retrospektiva razvitiya dachno-kottedgnoy zastroiki v stolichnom regione Ukrainu (A retrospective of the dacha-cottage development in the capital metropolitan area of Ukraine)", *Vestnik Argo (Messenger Argo)*, 145-179.

Cina', Giuseppe (2010), *Bucharest: from village to metropolis: urban identity and new trends*, Bucharest: Capitel.

Derer, Peter (1985), *Locuirea urbană: Schiță pentru o abordare evolutivă*, Bucharest: Editura Tehnică.

Encuclopeditchesky spravochnik 'Kyiv' (Encyclopedic catalogue 'Kyiv') (1986), "Kyiv", in: Kudritsky, Anatoliy (ed.), *Kyiv: Ukrainskaya Sovetskaya Encuclopediya* (Ukrainian Soviet Encyclopedy), 768.

Eurostat (2014), "Population on 1 January by age groups and sex - cities and greater cities", http://appsso.eurostat.ec.europa.eu/nui/ submitViewTableAction.do?dvsc=8 (Accessed March 01, 2014).

Executive Body of Kyiv City Council (2011), *General plan of Kyiv City 2011*, http://kyiv.me/ (Accessed January 15, 2014).

Federal State Statistics (2014), "Demography of Russia", http://www.gks.ru /wps/wcm/connect/rosstat_main/rosstat/ru/statistics/population/demo graphy/ (Accessed November 10, 2013).

Ghenciulescu, Ștefan (2013), "Suburbia", in: Goagea, Cosima/ Goagea, Constantin/ Ghenciulescu, Ștefan/ Caciuc, Cosmin (eds.), *Beyond the City*, Bucharest: Editura Universitară "Ion Mincu", 179-187.

Giurăscu, Constantin C. (1967), *Istoria Bucureștilor*, Bucharest: Editura pentru literatură.

Glazychev, Viacheslav L. (2011), *Gorod bez granits (City without borders*, Moscow: Territoriya budushego (The territory of the future).

Goldhoorn, Bart (2012), "The Libertarian Revolution", *Volume #30:Privatize!*, 12-14.

Golubchikov, Oleg/ Phelps, Nicholas/ Makhrova, Alla (2010), "Post-Socialist Post-Suburbia: Growth Machine and the Emergence of «Edge City» in the Metropolitan Context of Moscow", *Geography, environment, sustainability, 1*, 3, 44-55.

Green Vista Residence (2014), *Green Vista Residence,* http://www.greenvista.ro /PDF/brosura_GV2_lowres.pdf (Accessed March 01, 2014).

Hirt, Sonia/ Stanilov, Kiril (2009), "Twenty years of transition: The evolution of urban planning in Eastern Europe and the Former Soviet Union, 1989-2009", *Human settlements global dialogue series 5*, Nairobi: U.N. HABITAT.

Institute of Master Plan of Kyiv (2011), *Master Plan of Kyiv,* http://kievgenplan.grad.gov.ua/ (Accessed September 15, 2014).

Ioan, Augustin (2010), "Bucharest as a Battle-ground, 1998-2009", in: Dimitrieva, Marina/ Kliems, Alfrun (eds.), *The Post-socialist City. Continuity and change in urban space and imagery*, Berlin: Jovis, 196-207.

Kahrik, Anneli/ Leetmaa, Kadri (2009), "Residential preferences towards suburban living in post-socialist metropolis", http://www.soc.cas.cz/ (Accessed September 10, 2014).

Kazan Urban Forum (2014), "The lecture series: 'Kazan agglomeration', 'Reorganization of industrial areas'", https://www.youtube.com /watch?v=P4fqkqprH54 (Accessed September 02, 2014).

Kinosian, Nadir (2003), "Problemi rekonstrukcii centra Kazani (Problems of reconstruction of the Kazan center)", *Tartaria,* http://tartaria.ru /press23.html (Accessed September 02, 2014).

Kirillov, Pavel & Makhrova, Anna (2009), "Suburbanizatsiya v Moskovskom Stolichnom Regione: Sovremennoe i Perspektivnoe Sostoyanie (Suburbanization in the Moscow Capital Region: The Current and Prospective Situation)", *Regional'nie Issledovaniya (Regional Studies)*, 25, 4, 42-54.

Kushnirenko, Mariya (2012), "Problemu reorganizacui funkcuonalno-planirovochnoy strukturu kievskoy aglomeracui (Problems of reorganizing functional planning structures of Kyiv metropolitan area)", http://irbis-nbuv.gov.ua/ (Accessed August 28, 2014), 101-106.

Lentz, Sebastian (2006), "More gates, less community? Guarded housing in Russia", in: *Private cities: global and local perspectives*, London: Routledge, Taylor and Francis, 206-221.

Marozas, Martynas (2009), "Post socialist city. Adaptation of USSR-made urban structure in Lithuania", *Delft: Delft University of Technology*.

Ministry of Construction of Tatarstan (2013), "Territorial Planning Documents of Tatarstan", http://maps.tigp.ru/graddoc/pages.php?id=stp_rt_izmen (Accessed September 02, 2014).

Municipality of Kazan (2014), *Kazan Master plan*, http://www.kzn.ru/ (Accessed October 15, 2013).

Nae, Mariana/ Turnock, David (2011), "The new Bucharest: Two decades of restructuring", *Cities, 28*, 2, 206-219.

National Institute of Statistics (2014), "Recensământul Populației și al Locuințelor 1992", http://colectaredate.insse.ro/phc/aggregated Data.html (Accessed March 01, 2014).

Nefedova, Tatyana/ Treivisch, Andrey (2002), "Mejdu gorodom i derevney (Between urban and rural)", *Mir Rossii (The Russian World), 4*, 61-82.

Oreshina, Ekaterina (2013), "*Prygorod kak stil jizni (Suburbia as a style of life)* ", *Kazan First*, http://kazanfirst.ru/feed/5495 (Accessed December 06, 2013).

Parusi, Gheorghe (2007), *Cronologia Bucureștilor,* Bucharest: Editura Compania.

Pavalasc, Marian (2013), "UPDATE. Vezi pe cine dă vina Agenția Națională pentru Locuințe! Din cel mai luxos cartier nu se poate comanda nici pizza", *evz.ro*, http://www.evz.ro/din-cel-mai-luxos-cartier-nu-se-poate-comanda-nici-pizza-1072422.html (Accessed 01 March, 2014).

Reiner, Thomas/ Wilson, Robert (1979), "Planning and Decision-Making in the Soviet City: Rent, Land, and Urban Form", in: French, Richard A. / Hamilton, F. E. Ian (eds.), *The socialist city: Spacial structure and urban policy*, New York: John Wiley & Sons.

Stanilov, Kiril (2007), "Urban development policies in Central and Eastern Europe during the transition period and their impact on urban form", in: Stanilov, Kiril (ed.), *The Post-Socialist City*, Cincinnati: Springer, 347-359.

Tatarstan Statistics (2014), "Population of Tatarstan", http://tatstat.gks.ru/wps/wcm/connect/rosstat_ts/tatstat/ru/statistics/population/ (Accessed September 02, 2014).

Tesler, Semen (1975), "Novue gulue rayonu Kieva Geleznodorohgnuy, Uritskogo, Prospect 40-letiya Oktiabria, Vasilkovskaya, Teremki I, Teremki II (New residential district of Kyiv Geleznodorohgnuy, Uritskogo, Prospect 40-letiya Oktiabria, Vasilkovskaya, Teremki I, Teremki II)", Kyiv: Reklama (Advertisement), http://archunion.com.ua/history/history_012_01.html (Accessed September 14, 2014).

Tosics, Ivan (2005), "Transformation of cities in central and Eastern Europe: Towards globalization", in: Hamilton, Ian/ Dimitrovska-Andrews, Kaliopa (eds.), *City development in Central and Eastern Europe since 1990: The impacts of internal forces*, New York: United Nations University Press, 44-79.

Vöckler, Kai (2008), *Prishtina is Everywhere. Turbo Urbanism: the Aftremath of a Crisis*, Amsterdam: Archis.

Yudkevich, Maria (2011), "Ot arhitectury vi nikuda ne denetes (You will not get rid of architecture)", *tatpressa*, http://www.tatpressa.ru/news/3087.html (Accessed January 06, 2014).

Suburban development in Argentina: a historical overview and the current trends. The case of Cordoba

Carlos Grezzi, Monica Ramé, Christian Terreno and Regina Vidosa

1. Historical Approach to Urban Development in Argentina

Argentina is the second largest country in South America, located at the southernmost end of the continent. The current territorial configuration of the country started to develop in the 16th century, after the arrival of Spanish colonizers and their implementation of a particular economic and political organization. This process resulted in a large-scale territorial transformation, which consolidated during the 19th century after the country's independence.

At the same time, the urban configuration of the cities has depended on their geographical regions, not only due to their relation to the environment, but also to the cultural influences of natives and immigrants.

Nowadays Argentina has one of the highest urban population rates in the world, nearly 90% of its 40 million inhabitants live in urban settlements (United Nations Population Fund 2007). Moreover, the concentration of population is another distinctive feature of the territorial configuration, given that almost half of the population lives in the five largest metropolitan areas of the country: Buenos Aires, Córdoba, Rosario, Mendoza and Tucumán (Instituto Nacional de Estadísticas y Censos 2013). This concentration process accelerated during the 20th century, mainly as a result of the industrialization of the country.

Because of the diverse problems inherent to this situation, the current planning strategies attempt at balancing this process, boosting the potential development of each region. Indeed, the ongoing Territorial Strategic Plan (PET after its name in Spanish), called "Argentina of the Bicentennial 1816-2016", (Ministerio de Planificación Federal, Inversión Pública y Servicios 2008) seeks to achieve a more balanced territorial configuration. Nevertheless, this latest plan does not represent a recent challenge. Many successive models of territorial organization can be observed over time.

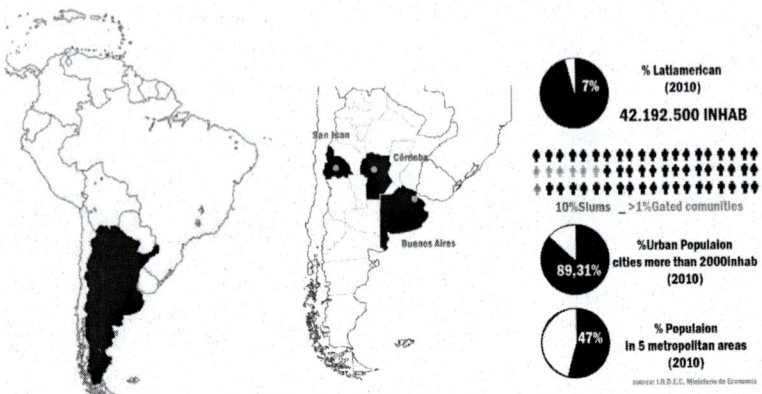

Figure 1: Argentina, location and population (Grezzi/Rame/Terreno/Vidosa based on Ministerio de Planificación Federal, Inversión Pública y Servicios 2008)

According to the PET, the historical evolution of the territorial development can be interpreted in five periods. This periodization of the development of urban structure in Latin America has also been described by Borsdorf et al. (2002); actually, the authors specifically concentrate on the development in the Argentinean cities.

1.1 Spanish Colony (1500-1816)

The foundation of the most important cities of Argentina started in the early 16th century, with the arrival of the Spanish colonizers. Along the colonization process, cities played the main roles as centers of territorial expansion, and as organizers for the extraction of resources. Accordingly, they were founded on strategic locations and connected by routes all of them leading to the port of Buenos Aires. As a result, a city hierarchy was established, since port cities and cities in nodes of the roads were more developed than the remaining cities.

The majority displays the following urban structure pattern: an orthogonal urban grid that was repeated with slight differences in each new city. Each characteristic urban element had not only physical but also symbolic functions. The most important one was the main square, which represented the physical, commercial, religious, and administrative center of the city and also the hubs of social activities. In this way, this urban structure shows a clear differentiation between center and periphery, taking a monocentric shape with urban belts around the center, which determines a hierarchical social location.

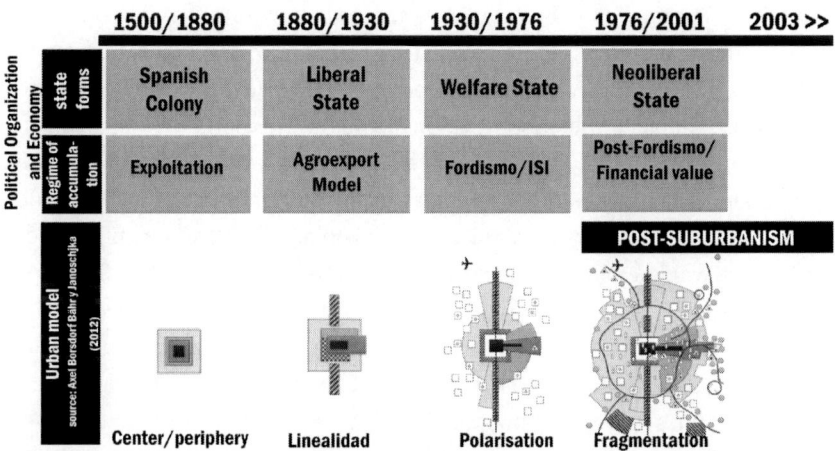

Figure 2: Periods of historical urban development. (Grezzi/Rame/Terreno/Vidosa based on Ministerio de Planificación Federal, Inversión Pública y Servicios 2008; Borsdorf et al. 2002).

1.2 Liberal State: Formation of the Argentinian State (1816-1930)

The independent state was organized following the ideas of the French Revolution, and was led up to a modernization process with a deep economic dependency on the British Empire. During this process Argentina became one of the most important agricultural exporting countries in the world, organized around the tempered plain region Pampa, and centralized in the port of Buenos Aires as political, economic and cultural capital. The development of an extensive railway network began in 1855 and organized the territory in order to export the production from Buenos Aires, thus integrating existing cities that produced something exportable and establishing new ones to that end. This applied, for example, to the city of Córdoba which is located in the middle of a productive area, and also to the cities of Tucumán and San Juan as centers of regions where sugarcane and wine production predominated.

Out of the high number of immigrants (mostly European) that arrived to populate the rural territory from 1870 on, the major part finally settled in Buenos Aires and in the main cities. As a result, few cities, mainly Buenos Aires [1], started to concentrate population and to improve their technological and commercial potential.

---

[1] With a million inhabitants at the beginning of the 20th century, Buenos Aires was the largest city in Latin America.

In order to liberate from the colonial image, to incorporate the new inhabitants and to supply the necessary infrastructure to adapt to the population growth, the cores of the cities were reorganized. As a consequence, new streets were laid out, overlapping the existent colonial grid. In the capital city, an expansive physical transformation process started following the design patterns that Haussmann applied in Paris. Many cities of the country replicated this modern urban design, and a tendency towards developing plans and creating building codes that would embellish the growth process of cities began. The first expansion process in the main Argentinean cites developed along new avenues. Through this process, the first suburbs emerged as a result of the need for housing, in an attempt to create clusters of productive facilities, and also to provide leisure areas for the bourgeoisie.

Meanwhile, small cities linked to the production of raw material developed along the railway tracks, consolidating a linear urban structure.

1.3 Welfare State (1930-1976)

The Welfare State of Argentina started with the intention of transferring benefits from the agricultural exporting model to the urban industry. This economic strategy was aimed at generating full and productive employment, ensuring demand with high salaries to stimulate expenditure. During the 20th century there was a permanent tension between the existent external dependency and the sake for greater autonomy of the country. This tension had an impact on the development of the country, and particularly on its urban structure. There was a strong tendency towards urban concentration in big cities, given that the State directed the planning processes within the policies of industrialization for import substitution, since 1945. This meant an increased need for manpower, which translated into an important internal migration process, from rural to urban areas.

The new population had to be located near their workplaces and the State took that responsibility. The national administration promoted not only the industrial clusters, but also the housing for working classes in the surrounding areas and the necessary infrastructure to complete these neighborhoods: schools, hospitals and sports centers among other public institutions and services. The location of these new urban extensions was peripheral to the city core and showed weak connection to the center and between each other. The most representative example of the Welfare State policies, not only in terms of urban structure and architectural design but also regarding the symbolic aspect, is the public housing "Ciudad Evita" in the district La Matanza in Buenos Aires. It was a project of 15,000 houses including all necessary public facilities and services, addressed to the new working class. In this venture the cult of Eva Perón's personality was reflected through an urban layout that represents her iconic facial profile.

While workers were housed in large modern but peripheral housing estates, rural migrants who arrived in the city without appropriate knowledge for industry related jobs had difficulties to be incorporated in the formal economy and labour system. They settled at the interstices or at the edges of the urban areas, conforming growing slums. Alongside, an enriched middleclass migrated from the core of the city to the wealthy suburbs. This led to a social and spatial division of the city, known as polarization. Until today the tendency to segregate the rich and the poor within the city and the city region continues up to day (Bähr 1976; Borsdorf 1982).

1.4 Neoliberal State (1976-2001)

From the mid-1970s, the model of import substitution starts to lose hegemony. In this context, a new model of accumulation around financial capital emerges in detriment of the industry.[2] Once the change of the socio-economic paradigm - made by the national administration - was established, i.e. from a Welfare State to a Neoliberal model, several responsibilities relied on private stakeholders. According to the global trend, Argentinean cities and metropolitan areas were strongly influenced by globalization. As a result of the retreat of the State, of privatization and of deregulation, investors, planners and citizens had greater liberties (Borsdorf 2003).

The real estate market took over the urban planning in order to obtain maximum profit, while State supervision was significantly weakened. Since the beginning of the 1990s, the typical North American urban sprawl process was re-

---

[2] By this we mean: placement of surplus, by large enterprises in different financial assets in both, the domestic and the international market. This process expands due to the following reasons: a) interest rates or the link between, them exceeds the profitability of the various economic activities, b) the rapid growth of external debt, of public and private sectors, enabling the transfer of local capital abroad and operating as a mass of recoverable surplus and/ or to release earnings for these purposes (Catellani/Schorr 2004).

produced in Latin America. Many residential projects focused on the middle and high social classes according to private developers, while the importance of social housing policies diminished. In Buenos Aires, the district of Pilar, which concentrates more than 180 gated neighborhoods, is a paradigmatic example of these urban trends. This area was created as a place for recreation and sports clubs in the mid-20th century, but after the 1990s single family houses for the clubs' members began to be built. Nowadays, 25% of the district population lives in gated communities.

This urban growth process, which affected most of the major Argentinean cities, resulted in an increasingly enclosed urban landscape, a loss of real public spheres and a change in citizens' habits as Janoschka (2002) shows in his case study of Nordelta, the largest private real estate development in Argentina.[3]

The polarization tendencies in the cities, i.e. the differences between the rich and the poor, were reflected in material terms through spatial fragmentation. This new type of separation of urban uses/functions and socio-spatial elements changed the scale from large dimensions (rich city, poor city, residential zone, industrial zone) to small ones (Borsdorf 2003). Gated neighborhoods, slums, shopping centers and industries are now spread over the metropolitan areas, one next to the other; surrounded by walls, both in physical and in symbolic terms. This means that social connections lost strength and the metropolitan areas tended to be configured as islands. The original urban structure of center and periphery was replaced progressively with a more complex urban polycentric scheme, where fragmentation and social composition tend to go hand in hand (Gorelik 2011).

1.5 The Last Decade (2003-2013)

On December 20th 2001, Argentina plunged into a deep economic crisis which marked the end of the accumulation model. The end of the crisis was induced with the definition of a new model of economic growth, which between 2002 and 2010 achieved one of the highest annual growth rates in the history of the country (7.6%) (CIFRA 2012).

---

[3] For Janoschka (2002), Nordelta represents the decadence of the Argentine State, being a good example of an urban development guided by a maximum economic return to the detriment of the social interest of urban projects.

In this context, the government launched the "Plan Argentina 2016" in order to achieve a more balanced, integrated and sustainable development. For this purpose, the Secretary of Housing and Urban Development has addressed efforts towards the provision of technical support and methodological guidance to provincial and municipal planning agencies. In spite of this, it is difficult to recognize significant changes in comparison with the urban trends that took place during the 1990s.

The aim of improving the competitiveness of cities and their location factor by attracting visitors and investors, led to what David Harvey (1989) calls the "entrepreneurial city", defining new patterns of territorial configuration (Pradilla Cobos 2009). The decentralization process that came along with this aim was constitutionalized in 1994 and local governments were granted responsibilities for improving their own social, economic and institutional basis (Compans 2004).

The projects conceived under the so called "new urban policy" have produced urban transformations of two different scales: On the one hand, there are Large-Scale Urban Projects (in Spanisch Grandes Projectos Urbanos GPU) which have profound effects on the aesthetics of the city, and whose essential point is "rebuilding the city" (Swyngedouw et al. 2002). These projects include spacious buildings in port areas, such as Puerto Madero in Buenos Aires, or the revitalization of the very common historic districts in the oldest areas of the major Latin American and North American cities (Carrión 2001; Cuenya 2012; Garay 2001; i.a.). On the other hand, there are smaller projects, which probably have greater impacts than the first ones, such as the consolidation of new centers in the urban periphery through urban planning policies designed to improve the functional distribution and the building density, in order to reach a more compact city (Borja 2011).

At the territorial level, it is important to mention that the growth process of intermediate cities such as Córdoba or Rosario has been more substantial than the larger ones in the last twenty years. These cities have experienced a faster growth of population and of urbanized metropolitan areas, mainly as a result of productive restructuring and redistribution of trade and services such as banking, health, education, etc. This recent process has offered the opportunity to define new regional policies, in order to empower the regional production,

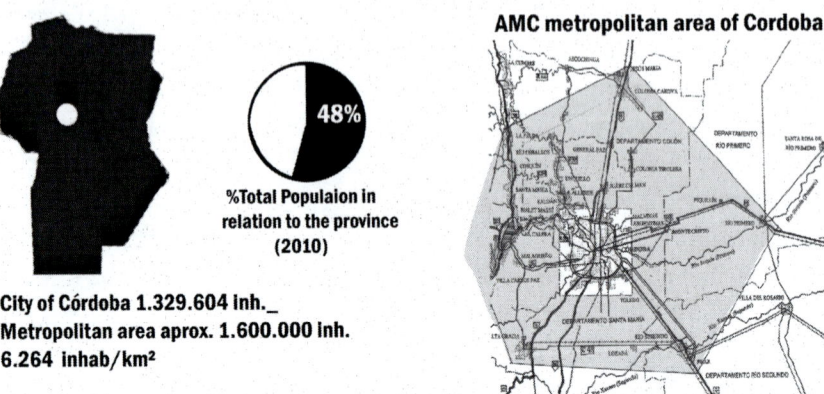

Figure 3: Córdoba, location, population and metropolitan area (Grezzi/Rame/Terreno/Vidosa based on Municipalidad de Córdoba 2012)

based on technology, and interconnect them within the country as a whole, without the historical high dependency on Buenos Aires (Seassone 2000).

In short, changes linked to socioeconomic restructuring processes historically led to new urban organizations and to different planning strategies. In this regard, the following section analyzes the complexity of Argentinean urban development through the study of a particular case, the Metropolitan City of Córdoba.

2. The Metropolitan City of Córdoba

Córdoba´s city, the capital of the homonymous province, has the second largest metropolitan area of Argentina, known as "El gran Córdoba", "The Greater Córdoba". The city has historically taken advantage of its central and strategic location. Córdoba was founded by Spanish conquerors in 1573 and was one of the midpoints of the Bolivian silver route to the port of Buenos Aires as a supplier of goods (Bischoff 1979). In the Liberal State (since 1880) Córdoba continued to profit from its location: the Pampa, between the Northwest region and the plain land, newly opened to production with the assistance of British financial and infrastructural resources (Luna 1994). Since the first decades of the 20th century, and particularly in the Welfare State period, the city became an industrial node in the process of import substitution; particularly in relation to the mechanical industries with the highest growth rate in its whole historical development, associated with deep changes in terms of social-economical and spatial structure (Rettaroli 1996). In recent decades, the city has been struggling with global market trends, with the integration to Mercosur, and with Argentina's internal problems associated with developmental cycles of economic crisis and social inequality (Tecco 2006).

2.1 Urban and Population Growth

In Colonial times population grew very slowly, so the real occupation of the original layout of 70 blocks happened 200 hundred years after the foundation of the city. However, it should be mentioned that the Native Americans, "indios", were not allowed to live in the city, so they built their own neighborhood named Pueblo de Indios in the periphery of the Spaniard's city. Furthermore, many activities took place outside the foundational layout because they were against the church rules (drinking, gambling, prostitution, etc.) or had health-impairing consequences (slaughterhouses, etc.) (Page 2007).

During the formation of the Argentinean State (1880-1930) immigration had a strong impact on the population structure and it was necessary to build new neighborhoods around the foundational grid as a continuation of the original one. The creation of these neighborhoods also responded to the location of roads, new railway lines, the main river and the topography. At the same time, the state undertook a big venture: a water channel network was built for agricultural uses, which transformed the dry area around the city into a productive green belt (Bischoff 1979).

In the Welfare State period, particularly after 1945, two big automotive manufacturing plants were set up in Córdoba, additionally to the already existing aircraft factory. Immigration from rural areas to the city in search for paid employment caused the city population to duplicate every ten years for over three decades (Bischoff 1979). This resulted in an explosive urban growth, and a wide range of new neighborhoods were offered from private owners and real estate agents to the new inhabitants. Within this context, new neighborhoods lacking infrastructure were built far away from downtown; while the creation of wealthy suburbs located in the best natural environment with a neat garden city design took place (Foglia 1990). The State also started to build social housing, however, it wasn't enough to address the social inequity.[4] For those who could not be integrated into the "formal city"[5] (Cravino 2013) the remaining option was to settle in the slums called "villas miserias"[6] (Cravino 2013). These slums are normally located close to the city core but in environmentally hazardous places and degraded areas, consisting of low quality, self-built houses.

The last three decades show new trends in urban population growth: there is very low rural to urban migration, a decline in the urban growth rate of the core city of Córdoba and, conversely, high growth rates in the small cities of the metropolitan area. These intra urban population movements have different driving forces: a) high land prices in the city core where regulations are tighter, but services and infrastructures are better; b) impoverishment of a great part of the middle class, which looks for cheaper options in the cities of the surrounding metropolitan area; c) new models of family life for middle and high classes partly associated with the globalization process; d) changes in national and global economy resulting in high prices for Argentinean produced commodities and the investment of these earnings in the real estate market, i.a.[7]

The outcome of the process is a "fragmentary occupation"[8] (Prévôt et al. 2002) of the metropolitan area. On one hand, the development of infrastructure and improvement of environmental qualities in areas occupied by high-income groups is observed. On the other hand, the lower-income group which is generally located in isolated areas with significant environmental problems. This spatial distribution reflects the social inequity developed in Argentina, which has deepened in the last three decades.

---

[4] In addition, the State started to build social housing though not enough to address the social inequitiy. The difference in access to housing, sanitation, basic education and the minimum income (Maguid 2000).

[5] The formal concept refers to the legal regularity in subdivisions and private ownership of land (Cravino 2013).

[6] Unplanned settlements, appearing after groups of citizens illegally take over vacant land and construct their houses there on their own. These places often lack the most basic infrastructure and services (water, electricity, sanitation, garbage collection, etc.). The result is an informal city, with high density, growing as there is space to do so (Cravino 2013).

[7] Agricultural production in Argentina has traditionally been a source of income, but since soybean prices rose at the end of the 1990s, the agricultural sector has devoted to produce this oilseed generating high return which does not flow to the capital market but rather to real estate investment due to frequent crisis in the local financial market.

[8] In terms of space, it is clear in the emergence of strategic spaces restructured due to a high concentration of capital investments, as well as large residuals, abandoned areas (Prévôt et al. 2002).

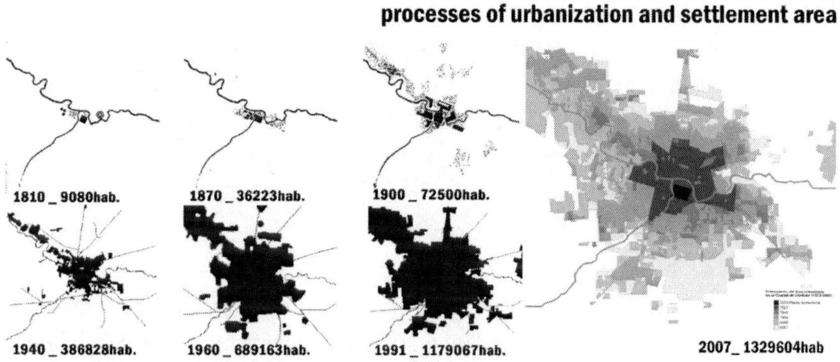

processes of urbanization and settlement area

1810 _ 9080hab.   1870 _ 36223hab.   1900 _ 72500hab.

1940 _ 386828hab.   1960 _ 689163hab.   1991 _ 1179067hab.   2007_ 1329604hab

Figure 4: Córdoba: Process of urban growth (Grezzi/Rame/Terreno/Vidosa based on Municipalidad de Córdoba 2012)

2.2 Urban Planning

The origin of the city corresponds to the common Renaissance plan for the new Spaniard cities in America, with a clear and simple layout, but without the possibility of being adapted to the particular geographical conditions. In Córdoba there is a small stream going through the city called La Cañada. It periodically floods the city, because of the heavy summer rain. This feature was not taken into account. Moreover, this planned city coexisted with an informal periphery of marginal inhabitants (Rettaroli 1997).

The guidelines for the formation of the Argentinean State were based on liberal ideas, therefore, the entrepreneurs' proposal for new neighborhoods started the urban developments and, after that, the State contributed with infrastructure and services. Here started a tradition of "good business" for those private groups who are closely connected with the current government (Foglia 1990).

During the Welfare State period, particularly between 1945 and 1955, there were strategies for economic development and social empowerment. However, there were no planning strategies for cities. This activity was delegated to the interests of private agents. The explosive growth boosted land prices and the leapfrog strategy configured the periphery as a mosaic of neighborhoods in-between vacant land. This caused high environmental impacts because this land was part of the productive green belt, built in the late 19th century. Only at the end of the 1950s a planning proposal was developed following functional and zoning ideas (Diaz 2001).[9] However, this proposal was a typical feature of urban planning. It was used not as a tool for long-term planning but rather as a means of solving present urgent needs (Foglia 1990).

When democracy was restored in the country (1983), Córdoba's local government started a strong planning strategy for its administrative area, but this one had no relation to the metropolitan one that had started to grow. In the 1990s the country opened to globalization and neoliberal ideas, so cities started to compete against each other to attract global capitals. In this way Córdoba has developed several strategic plans for the core city and its administrative area, however, the reorganization basis of the metropolitan phenomena remained unconsidered for the most part. Since 2007 a provincial metropolitan planning office has been created (IPLAM) but the implementation of its proposals depends on each municipality. The municipality has the authority to ratify or not what was planned in its boundary. So the challenge would be to achieve effective metropolitan governance.

At regional level, Córdoba has historically been an important regional node in economic, political and cultural terms and has therefore attracted resources, activities and inhabitants. In the current context it is more difficult to integrate in the competitive global world and the regional Mercosur market for different reasons (localization outside the most important roads with Brazil and Chile, changes in local political guidelines, changes in the economic dynamics of the whole region, i.a.). At local level, the regional structure is reflected on the urban structure, centralized around the original layout and the extension in relation to old routes in colonial times, to railways in the 19th century and to highways from the second half of the 20th century until today. Public transport investment has been reduced in the last decades associated to liberal privatization criteria. Furthermore, the service offered has low quality, thus it is used only by people without another option. So most of the new urban extensions (residential, commercial-entertainment and industrial) are car oriented. The resulting traffic congestion should be solved by government investment in new or wider roads, but mainly by the improvement of the public transport system.

Something similar happened in relation to infrastructure and facilities: private investors or social housing agencies allocate new urban extensions in places

---

[9] Following the precepts of the Charter of Athens of 1933 (zoning, traffic organization, industrial location, etc.)

without or with poor infrastructure and demand a provision of infrastructure by the local government afterwards. One of the reasons for this is a non-effective metropolitan planning policy. Most cases of new urban extensions are highly dependent on the city core. The long distance, the traffic congestion, and the poor public transportation system stimulate the emergence of new urban centralities along the most important axis, showing a tendency to a multi-core urban system.

2.3 Patterns

The results of the historical and ongoing process show a metropolitan territory that is getting gradually more complex, where allocation is defined by different driving forces which have been mentioned above. The spatial fragmentation and the high level of autonomy of each urban extension could be represented with the figure of a mosaic, in which the pieces are the urban extensions and the background is the rural territory having a complex network of relations among them. Some cases in this network are listed here:
- gated neighborhoods developed for high-income class, close to the hills landscape and connected to expressways for fast accessibility to core city or a sector centrality;
- near these gated neighborhoods there are low income ones located in relation to public transport routes. These neighborhoods are inhabited by people who are in charge of domestic chores, children care and home maintenance of wealthy households;
- Industries located in metropolitan municipal boundaries with low level of regulation and good accessibility;
- low-income residential areas surrounded by fumigated fields devoted to agriculture;
- a private cemetery in an idyllic landscape is next to a logistic center and a gated community;
- or some other more conventional locations: shopping centers or office towers connected to express highway.

These are only some examples of this complex network and its resulting environmental problems (social and physical).

Below, some examples will be presented in more detail to show their use, urban design, morphology, typologies and open space.

Figure 5: Gated Community "Las Delicias" (Grezzi/Rame/Terreno/Vidosa based on a real estate brochure and Municipalidad de Córdoba 2012)

2.4 Some examples

In this section some examples of the urban patterns described are presented and analyzed.

Gated Community "Las Delicias"

This is the first example of a gated community in Córdoba, developed in 1989. This kind of neighborhood has been called in Spanish with the English word "Country", expressing a different way of life in deep relation to the countryside. The name "Las Delicias" suggests what will be found inside: "Delights". There is a nice view to the hills and the center of the layout is a big 18 holes golf course. It is twelve kilometers from Córdoba downtown and seven kilometers of La Calera (a small metropolitan city), and it is connected to both via expressway. In its surroundings there are other gated communities, one of the city's water treatment plants, a natural reserve, construction materials factories and storehouses as well as a popular neighborhood called La Loma Colorada. The enterprise is 158 hectares with 400 lots for individual houses. The layout follows some ideas of the Garden Cities: detached houses, no material boundaries, low level plot occupation, no straight roads and cul-de-sacs. The prices are the highest in the market and living there represents a clear social distinction. The investors are from Argentina (from San Juan province) associated with an old local real estate company (Valdes 2001). Access is controlled; there are two gateways and a perimeter fence with cameras and security controllers working 24 hours. Public transport is not allowed inside.

Gated Neighborhood "Valle Escondido"

Created in 1996, it is divided in 16 units, the latest opened in 2013. This is one of biggest real estate developments in the metropolitan area of Córdoba: 300 hectares with plots from 350 square meters to 1200 square meters for individual houses and townhouses. The name "Valle Escondido" meaning "Hidden Valley" refers to its isolated natural location, only eight km from Córdoba downtown and one kilometer of a highway. This is an example of the lack of a comprehensive planning strategy because the connection to the highway was neither designed nor built, and the valley is part of a drainage basin so nowadays there are problems in the basin's surroundings due to floods caused by rainfall. In the coming years the local government should invest public budget for road junctions and a complex drainage system.

Although the idea is a green neighborhood following the morphological criteria of the Garden City model (detached houses, no material boundaries, no straight roads), the small size of the plots in relation to the buildings results in scarcity of green in the landscape perception. There are no big green areas, only the central green surface in the cul-de-sacs and boulevards, and some small squares in each area. Originally it was created as an open neighborhood with one gate with "internal" control and a perimeter fence. So the inhabitants do not pay the extra taxes as a gated community. Today it belongs to an intermediate category named Barrio Cerrado or "Gated Neighborhood". This category is different from countries that are at the top of the range of this kind of urban extensions and pay an extra tax to be separated from the rest. There is a private collective transport that runs at rush hours, going downtown and coming back (used to commute by those who live in the neighborhood but work downtown, and the ones who live in the city and work in the neighborhood as domestic service workers).

Figure 6: Gated Neighborhood "Valle Escondido" (Grezzi/Rame/Terreno/Vidosa based on real estate brochure and Municipalidad de Córdoba 2012)

In its surroundings there are big commercial surfaces, a religious education center, vacant land, a military basis and a big public green area. It is financed by global capital investors associated with a Chilean real estate company. The prices per square meter are high, but the parcels are small, so many middle class families with children choose this option as a safe and green option.

Public Housing "Barrios Ciudad"

This neighborhood is part of a program carried out by the provincial government with funds of the Inter-American Development Bank (IDB-BID). The aim of the program is to relocate the population living in risk areas, in the case of Córdoba, in Villas Miserias along the river and channel banks. The reason why impoverished groups settle in this hazardous areas is that they have a central position in the city or are close to labor sources (middle and high income households, buildings under construction, places where recyclable waste accumulates, i.a.) and they also have easy access to public facilities (health, education, entertainment, etc.). The program develops the relocation of the inhabitants of the slums in new neighborhoods in the suburban area (Boito 2009). In the last years, land prices have risen in Argentina´s cities, so the government chooses inexpensive places in low occupied surroundings far away from downtown.

Figure 7: Public Housing "Barrios Ciudad" (Grezzi/Rame/Terreno/Vidosa based on real estate brochure and Municipalidad de Córdoba (2012)

Most of the new neighborhoods border with agriculture fields with intensive production. The name proposed was "Barrios Ciudad", which could be translated as "a neighborhood as a city", to reflect that they would be relatively autonomous; they have many facilities and each has developed their own cultural identity. They are organized like a gated community: a big gateway without inner control (many times the police car is parked outside) is present and in many cases a perimeter fence delimits the neighborhood, as there is no urban continuity. A school is the only public facility. All these elements emphasize the isolation of the neighborhood. The distances to the city center and to work places as well as the weak public transport system display the functional side of the isolation. To decrease the production cost, only one type of houses was built. The house enables the construction of bedrooms in the backyard but it cant't grow in high because of the pitched roofs. Only the change in the position of the blocks and the use of a varied range of colors attempts to achieve urban space diversity.

Figure 8: Gated Condominium "*Milenica V*" (Grezzi/Rame/Terreno/Vidosa based on real estate brochure and Municipalidad de Córdoba 2012)

Gated Condominium "Milenica V"

This is a small size development: 15 hectares with two towers, 86 apartments and amenities (swimming pool, a meeting room, a gym, i.a.) but 20 kilometers far away from downtown and 15 km from the metropolitan city Carlos Paz. It is well connected through a highway, but there are no urban centers around, as the boundaries are a military basis, a natural area and extensive cattle raising fields. On the other side of the highway there are two gated communities. There are no formal public transport stops nearby. The typology is brand new in the suburb because in Argentina, and particularly in Córdoba, apartments in high-rise buildings are associated with downtown or central areas in the metropolitan region. It is financed by local capital investors who manage a supermarket chain and an entertainment center, and own many real estate enterprises in the city and its metropolitan area.

3. Final Inferences

At the beginning of this article, it has been explained that the analysis of the case study of Argentina would be addressed by the question of whether the current metropolitan urban growth process could be understood as an imminent post-suburbanization process or if there is still a continuity of the historical suburbanization process. In this respect, it is necessary to take into account that according to Sieverts (Sieverts in: Keil 2013) the post-suburbanization pro-

cess would be associated with some growth patterns, such as a more complex changes in scale and functionality, a mix of socio economic structures, and a new relation between urban and natural environments, increasingly recognizable in the cities. Nevertheless, these patterns can be taken into account only as first signs of a new process which may be nuanced
by the historical, geographical, cultural, or even political features that each city boasts.

The analysis of the urban development in Argentina based on the case of the Metropolitan City of Córdoba has revealed something interesting regarding the growth patterns. Along with previous studies of other metropolitan cities (e.g. Buenos Aires as an example for a mega-city explored by Janoschka (2002), or San Juan as an example for a medium-sized city described by Papparelli (2007)), it is possible to establish at least four patterns of growth in Argentina's case study, beyond the nuances of their scales: First, it can be claimed that there is a step towards a complex and polycentric structure of the metropolitan areas and that there exist different degrees in every city. Second, symptoms of a new social and spatial interrelationship perceived in the studied areas can be recognized. Third, it may be stated that there is an increasing functional complexity of the system. And fourth, a relationship between the surrounding cities and the natural environment can be identified.

Urban structure

The traditional urban structure characterized by the suburban growth is definitively changing or has already changed in most of the cities. The metropolitan expansion crossed the jurisdictional boundaries incorporating new urban centers to a new whole. The "satellite towns", initially created as providers of urban services to the rural activity and as mediators between the rural area and the city, formed part of the metropolis after a suburbanization process. However, the new role of these former towns' centers was uncertain until they began assuming an own character. Nowadays they are recognized as new centralities, essential pieces in the global scheme, where a multi-core urban configuration is needed to achieve a better flow of information and capital. It is evident, however, that even when the post-suburbia phenomena could be affecting every city, no matter their scale, the political and economic situations affect their rate of growth.

Spatial and Social Interrelationship

The suburban growth in Argentina has had many faces in the last decades: high-income groups decided to move outside the city looking for a new way of life in relation to a safer and more natural environment; low incomes groups are looking for a cheap solution for housing in the metropolitan area; industrial undertakings are looking for accessibility and low controls by local authorities; commercial enterprises are looking for a strategic point to attract as many potential customers as possible and of course there are inhabitants and activities which cannot be inside of the city. As a result, one can observe a high variety of activities and patterns on the territory. In a first spatial approach, homogeneous "islands" with clear boundaries can be distinguished. But when analyzing the activities and the level of interaction between them, it appears a very complex network of relations as explained in this paper. However, to draw conclusions about it, a deep interdisciplinary approach is paramount.

Increasing Functional Complexity

The new relevance of some elements of the urban structure, together with a new social distribution characterized by being highly fragmented in spatial terms, has led to a superposition of different functional layers. In the new functional configuration it is possible to identify overlapping circuits; some of them highly exclusive, as it happens between the gated communities and the shopping centers and malls; some more dispersed and open, as a continuity of use of the traditional spaces of the city, such as squares and the foundational urban core; and some atomized in strategic and less controlled places, related to informal trade. This mixture of functional circuits takes place in the whole metropolitan area, but concentrates or tends to converge in the multiple urban centers. This is creating a complex urban environment, a multiple and diverse functional fabric, used in a different manner by the different socio economic groups of the metropolis.

Relation between Urban and Natural Environment:

Regarding the relationship urban-nature, it is important to recognize, on one hand, the permanent tension between them. The country's historical development left many unused or empty areas that remain natural or in the wild, while, at the same time, the idea of urban is associated with progress. In some cases the interrelation between urban and rural areas seems to develop in an environmentally friendly way, striking a balance (i.e. gated community "Las Delicias"). But in other cases, the interaction shows a wide variety of environmental problems (i.e. gated neighborhood "Valle Escondido" or public housing "Barrios Ciudad"). On the other hand, it is important to mention the role that these natural areas play according with the different actors' interests. While there is an appropriation of natural values (views, rivers, forest, etc.) by private actors and high-income groups, the location of low-income groups tends to take place precisely in the same areas, given that these places are perceived as an opportunity to settle, even when they represent a permanent environmental risk among other conflicts.

Finally, it is important to highlight the weak urban planning tradition in the country, generally more concerned with solving specific and relevant urban problems than to define medium and long term strategies. Additionally, it is possible to identify the dominance of private actors in decision-making regarding how the city should grow. This has been definitively affected the public interest in the urban growth process. Moreover, in the context of globalization and neoliberal ideas the modus operandi, used by private actors to influence the urban policies and the city transformations, has strengthened through new and more complex strategies. Only in recent years, an emergent debate has taken place about the planning issue, with renovated discussions about the importance of the public space development or the recovery of the added value of land.

Though it is possible, following the aforementioned signs, to identify this process as a post-suburbanism, a deep analysis of others Argentine cases would be necessary to confirm so, and to define the specific characteristics of the phenomena in the region.

References

Bähr, Jürgen (1976), "Neuere Entwicklungstendenzen lateinamerikanischer Großstädte", *Geographische Rundschau*, 28, 4, 125-133.

Bischoff, Efraín U. (1979), *Historia de Córdoba*, Córdoba: Plus Ultra Editores.

Boito, M. Eugenia et al. (2009), "La gestión habitacional de la pobreza en Córdoba: el antes y después de las Ciudades-Barrio", *Boletín Onteaiken*, CEA-UNC, Año 4, N°7, http://www.accioncolectiva.com.ar/revista/www/-sitio/boletines/boletin7/2-4.pdf (Accessed August 16, 2014).

Borja, Jordi (2011), *Revolución urbana y derecho a la ciudad*, Quito: OLACCHI.

Borsdorf, Axel (1982), "Die lateinamerikanische Großstadt. Zwischenbericht zur Diskussion um ein Modell", *Geographische Rundschau*, 34, 11.

Borsdorf, Axel (2003), "Cómo modelar el desarrollo y la dinámica de la ciudad latinoamericana", *Eure*, 29, 86, 37-49, http://www.eure.cl/numero/como-modelar-el-desarrollo-y-la-dinamica-de-la-ciudad latinoamericana/ (Accessed August 16, 2014).

Borsdorf, Axel/ Bähr, Jürgen/ Michael, Janoschka (2002), "Die Dynamik stadtstrukturellen Wandels im Modell der lateinamerikanischen Stadt", *Geographica Helvetica*, 4, 300-310.

Carrión, Fernando (2001) (ed.), *Centros Históricos de América Latina y el Caribe*, Quito: FLACSO - Sede Ecuador.

Compans, Rose (2004), *Empreendedorismo urbano: entre o discurso e a prática*, São Paulo: Editorial UNESP.

Cravino, María Cristina (2013), "Repensando la ciudad informal en América Latina", *Colección Cuestiones metropolitanas*, N° 11, Los Polvorines-Prov. Buenos Aires: Universidad Nacional de General Sarmiento.

Cuenya, Beatriz (2012), "Grandes proyectos urbanos, cambios en la centralidad urbana y conflictos de intereses. Notas sobre la experiencia argentina", in: Cuenya, Beatriz/ Novais, Pedro/ Vainer, Carlos (eds.), *Grandes proyectos urbanos: miradas críticas sobre la experiencia argentina y brasileña*, Buenos Aires: Café de las Ciudades.

Díaz Terreno, Fernando (2011), "Los territorios periurbanos de Córdoba: entre lo genérico y lo específico", *Revista Iberoamericana de Urbanismo*, N°5, 65-84, http://upcommons.upc.edu/revistes/bitstream/2099/ 12500/1/ 05_05_FernandoDiazTerreno.pdf (Accessed January 27, 2015).

Ekers, Michael/ Hamel, Pierre/ Roger, Keil (2012), "Governing Suburbia: Modalities and Mechanisms of Suburban Governance", *Regional Studies*, 46, 3,

405-422, http://dx.doi.org/10.1080/00343404.2012.658036 (Accessed August 16, 2014).

Foglia, M. Elena (1990), "Los procesos de modernización en la estructura urbana de Córdoba y su significado actual", in: Foglia, M. Elena/ Goytia, Noemi, *Los procesos de modernización en Córdoba*, Córdoba: FAUD- Universidad nacional de Còrdoba.

Gorelik, Adrian (2011), *Correspondencias: arquitectura, ciudad y cultura*, Buenos Aires: Nobuko.

Harvey, David (1989), "From Managerialism to Entrepreneurialism: The Transformation in Urban Governance in Late Capitalism", Geografiska Annaler, Series B, *Human Geography*, 71, 1, 3-17.

INDEC: Instituto Nacional de Estadísticas y Censos (2013), *Resultados Definitivos: Censo 2010*, Buenos Aires: INDEC, http://www.censo2010.indec.gov.ar/ (Accessed August 20, 2014).

Janoschka, Michael (2002), "El nuevo modelo de la ciudad latinoamericana: fragmentación y privatización", *Eure*, 28, 85, 11-20, http://www.eure.cl/numero/el-nuevo-modelo-de-la-ciudad-latinoamericana-fragmentacion-y-privatizacion/ (Accessed August 16, 2014).

Keil, Roger (2013) (ed.), *Suburban constellations: Governance, Land and Infrastructure in the 21st Century*, Berlin: Jovis Verlag GmbH.

Luna, Félix (1994), *Breve historia de los argentinos*, Buenos Aires: Planeta.

Maguid, Alicia (2000), "El sistema de indicadores sociales en Argentina", *Documentos del 6º Taller regional del MECOVI*, Buenos Aires: INDEC- CEPAL.

Ministerio de Planificación Federal, Inversión Pública y Servicios (2008), *1816-2016. Plan Estratégico Territorial del Bicentenario*, Buenos Aires: MPFIPS, http://scripts.minplan.gob.ar/octopus/archivos.php?file=400 (Accessed January 27, 2015).

Municipalidad de Córdoba (2012), *Córdoba una Ciudad en Cifras. Guía estadística de la ciudad de Córdoba*, Julio 2012, http://ww2.cordoba.gov.ar/portal/wb-content/uploads/2010/10/Cordoba-una-ciudad-en-cifras-2012.pdf (Accessed August 16, 2014).

Page, Carlos A. (2007), "El pueblo de Indios de la Toma en las inmediaciones de Córdoba del Tucumàn. Un ejemplo de asentamiento periférico. Siglos XVII al XIX", *Cuadernos de Historia*, Serie Ec. Y Soc, Nº 9, Córdoba: CIFFyH- Universidad nacional de Córdoba.

Papparelli, Alberto et al. (2007), *Características de la distribución espacial en el Gran San Juan - Estadística Urbana Año 2005*, Buenos Aires: Editorial Klickzowski/NOBUKO.

Pradilla Cobos, Emilio (2009), *Los territorios del neoliberalismo en América Latina*, México DF: Editorial Miguel Ángel Porrúa y UAM-X.

Prévôt-Schapira, Marie-France. (2002), "Fragmentación espacial y social: conceptos y realidades", *Perfiles Latinoamericanos*, Diciembre, 33-56.

Rettaroli, José/ Eguiguren, J. Álvarez, Teresa/ Cohen Arazi, Alejandro/ Rubioli, José (1997), *Los barrios pueblos de la Ciudad de Córdoba: la ciudad objeto didáctico*, Córdoba: Ediciones Eudecor.

Sassone, Susana María (2000), "Reestructuración territorial y ciudades intermedias en la Argentina", *Ciudad y Territorio: Estudios Territoriales, 2000 PRIMAVERA; XXXII (123)*, Madrid: Ministerio de Fomento. Centro de Publicaciones, 57-92.

Swyngedouw, Erik/ Moulaert, Frank/ Rodriguez, Arantxa (2002), "Neoliberal Urbanization in Europe: Large-Scale Urban Development Projects and the New Urban Policy", *Antipode*, 34, 3, 542-577.

Tecco, Claudio/ Valdes, Estela (2006), "Segregación residencial socioeconómica e intervenciones para contrarrestar sus efectos negativos. Reflexiones a partir de un estudio en la ciudad de Córdoba, Argentina", *Cuadernos de Geografía*, 15, http://dialnet.unirioja.es/servlet/articulo?codigo=4014164 (Accessed January 27, 2015).

UN-Habitat United Nations Human Settlements Programe (2012), *The state of Latin American and Caribean Cities 2012: Towards a new transition*, Kenia: Nairobi.

Valdès, Estela (2001), "Los guetos urbanos residenciales. El caso del Country Las Delicias", *Anuario de la Escuela de Historia*. Año 1, Nº 1, Córdoba: Ferreira.

Geographies of suburban transformation: the case of Amman, Jordan

Mazen Alazazmeh

Introduction

Jordan is a small country in the Middle East that borders Syria, Iraq, Saudia Arabia, Palestine and Israel. It is a country of great historical and geographical significance. Its population is mainly concentrated along the Mediterranean climate where its major cities Amman, Zarqa, Madaba, Salt and Irbid are located. The population of these cities and their immediate hinterland amounts to 75% of the country's residents (Makhamreha 2011). In the 1920's, Jordan's capital Amman was a small town with a little more than 2000 residents. Today it is a major regional city with a population of over two million inhabitants (Municipality, 2008).

One of the main reasons for the continuous growth of residents in the Amman region has been warfare. Immigrants at various phases from many surrounding countries sought shelter in Jordan, and primarily in Amman. It thus became known as the city of refugees. It is the city's political stability, security, and job opportunities that attracted people from the region. Since the second half of the 20th century Amman's growth has been phenomenal in terms of its population due to the unexpected political events in the Middle East, particularly those of Palestine. As a result, persistent city planning was almost impossible. The city was numerously compelled to adapt to the sudden demographic changes brought upon by the region's political instability. This incredible growth of the urban area in both size and significance has occurred in "drastic growth spurts that have transformed the look and feel of the city" (Al-Asad 2005 in: Potter 2009: 81).

The fate of the suburbs of Amman has never been predictable. This is due to the rapid growth and numerous transformations that have been developing in the city. To understand suburbanism in Amman, one must look at the city's historical development as well as its political context. This paper aims to explain suburbanism in Amman throughout the city's growth pattern and structural evolution, with reference to the political and economic discourse of the period. The paper will go further by describing case studies that support the theories and arguments proposed.

1. Amman's Growth and Development

1.1 Segregation in Amman

In the 1960s and 1970s, the economic situation of Jordan was relatively poor, thus many migrated to oil-rich countries in the region (Municipality, The Story of Amman, 2009). After the oil crisis of 1973, Amman flourished economically due to the return of the wealthy migrated Ammanis. Further on in the 1990's, more expatriate Jordanians returned due to the 1991 Gulf War, raising the total population of the capital from 1,013,000 to 1,800,000 (Municipality, Urban Strip Charette, 2003).

The homecoming of the prosperous migrants highly contributed in the growth of Amman in the last fifty years. This growth has been mostly concentrated in the "respectable and upmarket West Amman" (Teller 2002 in: Potter 2009: 85). Other districts have a higher population which is relatively poor. This pattern can be originated from the early growth of Jabal Amman as being one of the wealthiest quarters of the city towards the west of downtown. This trend continued as the city developed and the high social status sector extended westwards from the city center. This resulted in the city of Amman of today that contains relatively low population densities in the western part of the city with a contrast of high densities in the east.

The residential quarters of contemporary Amman enlighten the social division that has resulted from its history of rapid growth. Present-day guides to Jordan are also aware of this social segregation that seems to differentiate urban space within the city.

> "Residents talk openly of two Ammans, although in truth there are many. Eastern Amman (which includes Downtown) is home to the urbanised poor: it's conservative, more Islamic in its sympathies, and has vast Palestinian refugee camps on its fringe. Western Amman is a world apart, with leafy residential districts, trendy cafes and bars, impressive art galleries, and young men and women walking openly arm in arm." (Ham/Greenway 2003: 98)

Geographies of suburban transformation: the case of Amman, Jordan   241

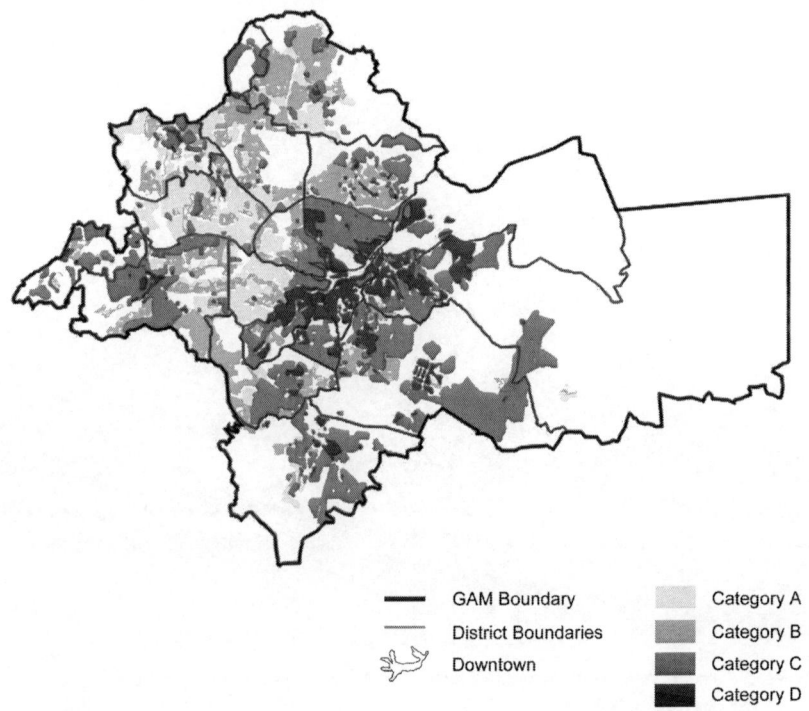

Figure 1: Categorization of residential land in the Greater Amman Municipality boundary before its expansion in 2007 (Alazazmeh 2014, based on Potter 2009)

1.2 Urban Development

The so called "two Ammans" concept stated by Ham and Greenway does exist, yet it is only a general and broad idea to describe the city. In planning, the Greater Amman Municipality categorizes residential land into four categories. The minimum plot size, the maximum allowed percentage of the plot to be built upon, the plot's boundary and the distance between buildings are all aspects defining the categories. They are given alphabetical notations: From A to D, from largest to smallest respectively. The study presented by Robert B. Potter of the old municipal boundary of Amman (before 2007) portrays the distribution of wealth within the city. The analysis of existing residential land helps to define the structure of the city and expose the fabric of its suburbs.

"Plots designated as category A have an area of at least 900 square meters. The built-up area should be no more than 39% of the plot, leaving space for 'green'

Figure 2: Category A Residential building located in Abdoun, one of the wealthy western quarters of the city (Alazazmeh 2014)

areas" (Potter 2009: 86). As illustrated in Figure 1, Category A residential land is almost merely located in the west part of the city center, the downtown area. The conditions of the existing buildings in downtown were relatively poor due to their tectonic quality. Furthermore, the topography and the high density of the area made it impossible for spacious housing to be built. Thus, the idea of investing and sprawling away from the city center became much more attractive for the financially capable, including the affluent expatriates returning from the Gulf. It follows that a north-western growth pattern resulted from the historical classification of Jabal Amman as a wealthy sector of the city. As it was on the west side of the city, a trend was formed and still continues.

"Category B residential plots are between 750 and 900 square meters. The built-up area of the plot can be up to 45%" (Potter 2009: 87). The concentration of Category B residential plots on the western part emphasizes the physical

Figure 3: Category B Residential building located in 'Wadi Al Seer' district, westwards to the city center (Alazazmeh 2014)

division and segregation within the city. Larger plot sizes, the value of the plots, more esthetic building facades and higher residential taxes are all factors allowing only the high-income Ammanis to live in this part of the city. Due to the higher residential taxes, urban services are of better quality, as a result, it becomes more attractive for potential residents.

"Category C land denotes plots of around 400 square meters, with residential buildings occupying up to 51% of the plot", and finally "category D describes smaller residential plots of up to 200 square meters, with a maximum permitted built-up area of 55%" (Potter 2009: 87f.). Both categories seem to dominate the core of the city expanding mostly eastwards from the present day downtown area.

The Circassian settlement in the late 19th century was one of the earliest signs of the rebirth of the Amman region after the Decapolis under the Roman rule. After their exodus from their homeland North Caucasus, as part of the Russian

Figure 4: Category D Residential land in the downtown of the city overlooking "Jabal Al-Qala" (Alazazmeh 2014)

conquest, the Circassians (a group of mainly Sunni Muslims) settled at the river in the valley of the seven mountains around the Roman amphitheatre which is today the downtown area. This settlement gradually expanded to the adjacent mountains, initiating a region of the city that is now categorized as residential D land.

Palestinian refugees have also greatly contributed to this category. The influx of Palestinian refugees in 1948 and later on during the Six-Day War in 1967 expanded the city's population exponentially. Due to their political situation, the majority of these refugees were of low socio-economic status. Amman, on the other hand, was not ready for such a sudden and vast demographic change. Thus the city ensued the construction of informal settlements around the city center that are now categorized as types C and D. Official refugee camps, such as that of Jabal Hussein and Wahdat, were set up to accommodate the most deprived refugees of the mid-twentieth century. The United Nations Relief and Works Agency located its aiding urban and social services in those camps. They were a major attraction for the tremendous incoming refugees of 1967 who settled in the neighborhoods of those camps in the form of large informal settlements (Ababsa & Daher, 2011). Such settlements posed a number of challenges to the city's structure such as high birth rates, urban pollution and the reduction of agricultural land through construction.

One can easily notice from the analysis of Robert B. Potter not only the geographies of inequality between the west and east sides of Amman, but also that as the residential category increases, the type seems to sprawl further away from the city center. As a result, it can be stated that in the second half of the 20th century when the city was rapidly growing, the suburbs to the downtown were mostly category A and B residential buildings that housed the high social class. It was only this social group that could afford isolation from the city center and its services.

2. Suburbanization in Amman

Over the past decade, capital accumulation has been the major concern of cities throughout the Middle East. It was thought to bring an increase in the economic status of the acting cities by attracting international investments and developments. This trend became more desirable after the success of the Dubai model, introducing real estate development as the new "religion" (Daher 2010) contradicting the more sensitive approach of the region in the mid-twentieth century when a more human scale was used.

The recent crises in countries such as Iraq, Syria and Lebanon have made Jordan more appealing for international investors due to its security and political stability resulting in a real estate boom in the last couple of years. King Abdullah responded to this rapid growth by suggesting the Greater Amman Municipality in May 2006 to create a master plan for Amman.

> "It is crucial that we all do our utmost to ensure that our beloved city will continue to be a magnet for pioneering development projects and a fertile ground in which innovative ideas can take root and blossom",

the King's words clearly describe the state's intentions (Abdullah bin al-Hussein 2006 in Parker 2009: 116). In 2008 the Greater Amman Municipality finally published a plan for Amman. "The Amman Plan presents a somewhat unorthodox approach to metropolitan, urban, and community planning" (Municipality 2008). On the surface, this plan is intended to introduce some order and planning into the ever-growing city (Potter 2009), but the King's words better describe its genuine objective.

Through adopting a neoliberal economic position, the city helped strengthen this extant real estate boom.

> "Neoliberalism is in the first instance a theory of political economic practices that proposes that human well-being can best be advanced by liberating individual entrepreneurial freedoms and skills within an institutional framework characterized by strong private property rights, free market and free trade." (Harvey 2005: 2)

In Jordan,

> "the state finds itself gradually pulling out of its responsibilities from fragile sectors such as education, healthcare, social security and social housing, and instead becomes more involved in real estate development as a facilitator, regulator and provider of indirect subsidies for multinational corporations." (Daher 2013: 101)

Numerous developments led by partnerships of multinational corporations and the state drastically contributed to the urban transformation of Amman. So far, the Al-Abdali "Regeneration" Project, which is still in progress, has had the most influence, being Amman's masterpiece model of gentrification.

2.1 Suburbanization within the city

Mawared, the corporation responsible of Al-Abdali Regeneration Project, is a financially and administratively independent state-owned corporation. According to the website, its aim is "generating considerable investment opportunities for the private sector creating job opportunities and stimulating economic growth" (Mawared 2010). In other words, it tends to privatize public property. It became involved with several inner-city military plots (including Al-Abdali) with the objective of relocating the military on the expense of introducing land capable of investment. Only five years after its inception in the year 2000, "MAWARED had become Jordan's leading urban regeneration entity and its largest real estate developer" (Daher 2013: 110). But it is the 5 billion dollar Abdali project that shines as the "jewel in Mawared's crown" (Parker 2009: 115). Mawared made the investment in the 350,000 square meters in the heart of Amman very appealing by offering the land well below market price (Parker 2009). The state also had its share of subsidies to the development such

Figure 5: Ongoing construction of towers and large scale buildings in a human scale context (Alazazmeh 2014)

as tax exemptions and the loosening of building regulations and zoning ordinances (Summer 2005).

"New Downtown of Amman", the development's first slogan, greatly describes the risk and effects it will have on the structure of the city. With the original downtown being less than two kilometers away, the new development will compete and possibly attract more users through its shiny architecture and interesting "helicopter scale", a term introduced by Jan Gehl to describe site plans designed with no consideration to the "5 kilometers per hour" or human scale (2013).[1] When taking into consideration the proposed functions such as an information technology park, a medical tourism center, higher education facilities and high-end commercial residential space, the development will

---

[1] Jan Gehl, a Danish architect, urban design consultant, and a scholar on public space sarcastically defines top-bottom developed masterplans that are site insensitive, possibly legit in any other empty piece of land, as "helicopter scale" masterplans. As if the planner/architect was designing while looking down on the site from a helicopter.

Figure 6: Modern and shiny architecture contrasting the traditional and old neighborhood (Alazazmeh 2014)

surely marginalize the users of the old downtown who cannot afford to benefit from these services and are subject to a very real threat of alienation. Merriam Webster's dictionary defines a suburb as "an outlying part of a city or town". If the definition is only considered physically, then the term does not apply due to the fact that the development is situated in the very heart of the city. However, if the term is deconstructed by highlighting qualities such as being far from the center, with the center being the local users, and the unease of accessibility, not due to distance (in this case) but to social segregation, then it seems to follow that the term can be applied here. The Al-Abdali Regeneration Project can be considered as a suburb to the city, within the city.

The project has also affected public transportation in the city. Before assigning the area as the new downtown, Abdali was the major hub of public transport to the north. This hub was relocated to Tabarbour on the northern outskirts of the city. In addition, the public transportation station at Raghadan in the very downtown of Amman has been relocated eastwards to Mahatta (Parker 2009). These changes have greatly affected public transportation users and forced them away from the city center. Commuters dependent on public transportation in Amman are mainly of the lowest social class due to the fact that car ownership is common and preferable. As a result, the changes have mostly affected this specific group. The case of the Raghadan hub still remains controversial where officials state that it was only a temporary relocation, while critiques argue that it was planned from the start.

2.2 The Suburb's Destiny

Regardless of the truth behind the relocation of the public transportation hubs, there seems to be a clear intention to gentrify the downtown area of the city and push its low-income users further away creating a more socially segregated Amman. Furthermore, in 2008, the Greater Amman Municipality has initiated a plan to regenerate the downtown strip of the city. This so-called Wadi Amman project involves the revitalization of a long strip of land of four kilometers in Amman's historic downtown. The aim of this project is to flourish the downtown socially and economically by attracting a diverse group of users, as the current users are mostly of a relatively low social status.

This interest of the city in the center of Amman resulted in a sort of interchange between the classical typology of the urban and the suburban spaces. The centralized developments alongside the government's initiatives are causing the so called untouchables to flee away. As a result, it became more popular to find low category residential buildings in the suburbs, in contrast to the A and B category buildings during the 20th century. The case studies below help to support this theory.

In 2008 the Housing and Urban Development Corporation in Amman, under the royal initiative, launched the project "Decent Housing for Decent Living" which planned to build 100,000 homes over a five year period to shelter the most impoverished families in the city (Ababsa & Daher, 2011). The project introduced low-income social housing in the districts Marka, Al-Jiza, Abu-Alanda and Sahab, which are all located on the urban periphery in the eastern edge of the city. Several of these housing projects are developed by Taameer Jordan Holdings (Daher 2013), a private firm that is "set out to be one of the largest companies to operate in the real-estate development on a regional level" (Taameer 2014). Two case studies of different districts (Marka and Al-Jiza) will be further analyzed and discussed in order to better understand the initiative's context and objectives.

Figure 7: Panoramic view of the Category D Residential complex within its vacant surrounding (Alazazmeh 2014)

2.2.1 Marka

Marka is located north-east of the downtown. Based on the Greater Amman Municipality boundary towards Al-Zarqa, the area has a strategic location linking both cities. According to GAM (2009), it is considered one of the oldest industrial zones in Jordan with the first factory being initiated more than half a century ago. It contains around 1,000 factories providing more than 30,000 jobs for the local people.

Marka has a number of very important landmarks. It has a highly rated college, a vocational center and an airport. Marka's airport is not the major one in Amman, however, it bears a certain importance. The Polytechnic college and the vocational school invite many students to the district. One can easily apply the concept of a satellite city to Marka. It is a district that offers educational facilities, job opportunities, a large retail area and even an airport, yet it is considered to be of low social and economic status. The site of the project is an isolated residential complex. Although the complex may seem unattractive due to its isolation and architecture it is fully occupied. Adjoining a major urban expressway (Al-Hizam road) that connects Amman with Al-Zarqa, the complex is surrounded by empty land. It is barely possible to find residential homes of higher socio-economic status in the region (as can also be derived from Robert B Potter's study on the categorization of existing residential land in Amman).

Not all residents of the complex possess automobiles. Therefore group rides and shared taxis are being planned in order to commute and access services that are concentrated on the other side of Al-Hizam road. The residents developed a sort of community allowing them to share benefits (this observation is based on an ethnographic study by the author on this specific complex in the year 2010). Walking is infrequent in this extremely pedestrian unfriendly zone due to the absence of sidewalks, insufficient lighting and limited pedestrian crossings.

Figure 8: Transformation of the adjoining streets and spaces to playgrounds shows how isolated and infrequently accessed the area is (Alazazmeh 2014).

The project's site, as most of the surrounding land, is classified as Residential D type, which is considered to be the least esthetic of all. The demand and supply of Residential D housing help to interpret the economic context of the district and its inhabitants. The buildings are of simple design and materials. The interchange of the pale yellow and red colors on the plaster-finished square buildings attempts to break the homogeneity of the complex and create some sort of familiarity. As the goal of the design is only functional extremely simple facades were constructed.

2.2.2 Al-Jiza

The second case study under the same mother project is called Ahl Al-Azm residential city in Al-Jiza. The area of Al-Jiza, located near Queen Alia International Airport (the major airport of the country) towards the south- eastern edge of the city, has only recently been added to the Greater Amman Municipality.

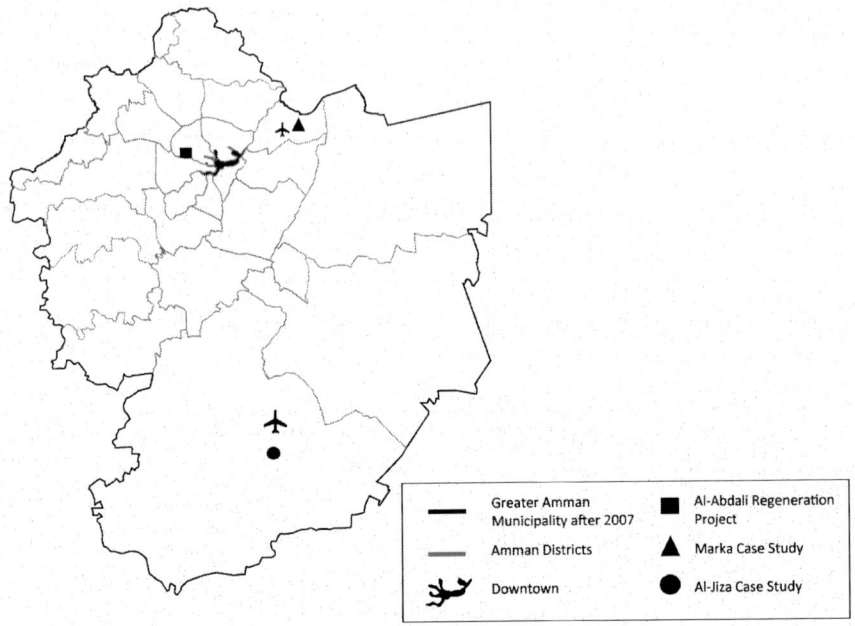

Figure 9: Location of all sites (Al-Abdali Regeneration Project, Marka and Al-Jiza case studies) in relation to the Downtown (Alazazmeh 2014)

The project will, as stated by the developer's website, cater "the need of all society segments in the Kingdom, especially middle to low-income families, going in line with the increasing demand on residential units" (Taameer 2014).
The development will provide not only good infrastructure and services, but also reasonable and flexible measures for ownership. Taameer Jordan explains the site's location that "It steps away from the crowded cities to bring life and activity to a more secluded area [...]" (Taameer 2014). This secluded area is on the very outskirts of the city and therefore disconnected from public transportation networks and social services. But the promising campaigns and rhetoric of the project organizers tend to successfully persuade potential residents who are mostly belonging to the low social sector (Daher 2013). Many real estate factors play a role in the choice of location, so the act might not be intentional, but the overall effect on the social structure of the city seems clear. Critics argue that these marginalized projects are targeting the poor to encourage them

to move out of inner-city neighborhoods allowing the center to be subjected to developers.

3. Conclusion

After years of urban renewal, social polarization between the west and east still defines contemporary Amman. The wealthier tend to settle westwards from the downtown, whereas the relatively poor are more concentrated in the east. This segregation is a result of a natural and dynamic division of social class that started in a scale no larger than the downtown and its surrounding Jabals. Unfortunately, this division is being emphasized through the rising elitary developments that seem to have no interest in the east. "Build to the East?! We cannot do that, because then people would have to pass through East Amman and Wihdat", declared a GAM official referring to the low social class of the east and its existing refugee camps (Ali bin al-Hussein 2007 in: Parker 2009: 118). So,

> "property developments underway only focus on limited areas within the city: Abdali and the Eastern development belt, leaving large overpopulated areas underequipped, lacking in social housing and centers of employment[...]" (Ababsa & Daher, 2011).

Even those inner city projects seem to accumulate the existing social segregation in the city, such as the Al-Abdali project. They are aiming to support the underprivileged. However, instead of renovating their existing spaces they are offered accommodation on the outskirts of the city on remote lands in the desert denying their right to the city (near industrial hubs such as the case of Marka, or even airports as in the case of Al-Jiza). This in turn contributes to a more socially polarized Amman. This seems to be the common result of the case studies. Whether targeting the elite or the relatively poor, both types of neoliberal projects lead to "geographies of inequality" in the city (Daher 2013).

To avoid another so called Al-Abdali effect on the city, the Urban strip Project should be carefully dealt with. The uses and functions proposed are very sensitive as they are capable of uniting the two parts of the city or further segregate them. They must be inclusive and satisfy all social groups without any preference. The approach in dealing with the inhabitants and the existing buildings is also crucial; gentrification is an effect that should be avoided in such a context. The downtown is culturally and historically significant with beautiful architectural proportions and dynamism. These aspects, alongside its relation to the Al-Abdali project, must be taken into consideration when planning so as to preserve the intrinsic character of the heart of the city.

Suburbanism in Amman has undergone numerous changes over time. It has shifted from the hands of Bedouins to the high-income class and back to the relatively poor. The suburbs have been and continue to be a major aspect of the urban policies of the city. Their significance on the environment and the region is underestimated. "Architects must search for their role of forecasting and planning the future whatever the future is, by finding alternative solutions to defend this small arable land" (Ghul 2007). Ghul argues that the rapid growth of Amman has had a negative effect on the environment, the city is expanding through its suburban settlements at expense of the limitedly arable land. Amman is majorly extending towards the northeast approaching the second major city of the country Al-Zarqa. Urban and regional planning must determine the fate of Jordan's major cities and their relation to one another in order to avoid unaccounted problematic results in the future.

References

Ababsa, Myriam/ Daher, Rami (2011), *Cities, Urban Practices and Nation Building in Jordan*, Beyrouth: Presses de l'Ifpo.

Daher, Rami (1999), *Gentrification and the Politics of Power, Capital and Culture in an Emerging Jordanian Heritage Industry*, 2: Bd.X, Amman.

— (2010), *Urban Landscapes Of Neoliberalism: Cranes, Craters And An Exclusive Urbanity*, Amman: Jordan Business.

— (2013), "Neoliberal Urban Transformations in the Arab City", *Urban Environment*, Volume 7, 99 -115.

Gehl, Jan (2013), "Cities for people", *A lecture by Jan Gehl*, Melbourne, http://www.youtube.com/watch?v=KL_RYm8zs28 (Accessed April 2013).

Ghul, Ali F. (2007), *Urban Growth and Regional Planning in the Arab World*, Amman: University of Jordan.

Harvey, David (2005), *A Brief History of Neoliberalism*, Oxford: Oxford University Press.

Innab, Saba (2008), "City of Events: a Close Look at Al Abdali Bus Terminal and Beyond", in: Niemann, Rayelle/ Dettwiler, Erik (eds.), *CITYSHARING*, May 2008, http://www.citysharing.ch/invited-projects~68.html (Accessed March 2014).

Makhamreha, Zeyad/ Almanasyeha, Nazeeh (2011), "Analyzing the State and Pattern of Urban Growth and City Planning in Amman", *European Journal of Social Sciences*, 2 Vol. 24.

Mawared (2010), *Mawared Building communities*, http://www.mawared.jo/our_company2.shtm (Accessed 2013).

Municipality Greater Amman (2003), *Urban Strip Charette*, Amman: Greater Amman Municipality.

— 2008), *The Amman Plan: Metropolitan Growth*, Amman: Greater Amman Municipality, www.ammancity.gov.jo.

— (2009), *The Story of Amman, Amman City 100*, http://www.ammancity100.jo/en/content/story-amman/ancient-history (Accessed May 1, 2014).

— (2011), *Laws and Regulations, ammancity*, http://www.ammancity.gov.jo/ar/gam/laws.asp (Accessed 2014).

Parker, Christopher (2009), *Tunnel-bypasses and minarets of capitalism: Amman as neoliberal assemblage*, Ghent: Political Geography, 28.

Potter, Robert B./ Darmame, Khadija/ Barham, Nasim/ Nortcliff, Stephen (2009), *Ever-growing Amman, Jordan: Urban expansion, social polarisation and contemporary urban planning issues*, Habitat International 33, 81-92.

Saleh, Bassam/ Rawashdeh, Samih (2007), "Study of Urban Expansion in Jordanian Cities", *International Journal of Applied Science and Engineering*, Vol. 1.

Summer, Doris (2005), *Neo-Liberalizing the City: Transitional Investment Networks and the Circulation of Urban Images in Beirut and Amman*, Master Thesis in Urban Planning, Beirut: American University of Beirut.

Taameer Al Jiza (2014), *Taameer Jordan Holdings*, http://www.taameer.jo/index.php?option=com_content&task=view&id=19&Itemid=48 (Accessed January 2014).

Changing Face of Suburbia: A Narrative of Indian Cities

Priyambada Das and Vaishali Anavatti Satyamurthy

Introduction

A Greek philosopher Heraclitus once said, "The only thing that is constant is Change" which is very apposite for a country like India in the present day. India is the second most populous country in the world and privileges to be the largest democracy with 1.24 billion inhabitants. India, originally with an agriculture based rural population, seems to be shifting faces in the present day. 30.1% of this colossal population lives in cities and studies have projected that India will face an unprecedented scale of urbanization as 350 million people will move to the cities by 2030 increasing the urban population to 40.7%. It is even expected to double by 2050. India currently has 54 urban agglomerations, each with a population of one million or more (Chadchan/Shankar 2012: 37). With cities facing expansion at an alarming rate, suburbanization is the palpable consequence. Although suburban development is not a new concept in the country's growth, the suburban landscape has undergone insensitive and unyielding changes in the last few decades. According to the World Bank, suburbs of large Indian metropolises support 9% of the country's population while providing 18% of employment. Besides, a third of India's new towns are coming up within 50 kilometers of existing one million cities. Undoubtedly, Indian suburbs are the places where major opportunities as well as challenges are located. To quote the World Bank's report (2013: 1):

> "Rapid growth of metropolitan suburbs is the most striking feature of India's spatial transformation."

The process of suburbanization started or became a highlighted feature in North America, mainly the United States of America, although it has been a worldwide phenomenon for almost a century. In India, the phenomenon saw the day of light at different periods in the last century but became more evident in the last few decades. Suburban growth of large Indian metropolises has drawn attention of quite a few scholars and researchers. Sridhar in her paper[1]

---

[1] Cities with Suburbs: Evidence from India.

(2004) shows how the availability of labor's skills plays an important role in suburbanization of manufacturing, transport, communications and commerce jobs in India. In another research[2] (2007) she argues that strong land use regulation in core cities, such as floor area ratio or urban land ceiling, is pushing new developments and people towards suburbs. Dupont's article[3] (2006) sheds light upon the issue of conflicting stakes and governance of metropolitan peripheries while examining selected case studies from India. The World Bank's recent report[4] (2013) reviews India's urbanization beyond municipal boundaries and its challenges in terms of land policy distortion and infrastructure shortfalls. Gururani's essay[5] (2013) on Gurgaon[6] also shows similar concerns. Kose's research[7] (2014) discusses state and national level policy initiatives and unfolds dimensions of peri-urban governance in India.

Our current research is based on the hypothesis that the character of suburban development in India has changed considerably in recent years. It takes the example of two big metropolises in India, Kolkata and Bengaluru. Both are administrative capitals and important financial hubs of their respective states and they are experiencing rapid peripheral growth. This article tries to explain how suburbs have changed over time in these two cities, by defining significant stages of suburban development. It not only inquires social, economic or political reasons behind such changes but also describes the recent development through case studies.

1. Development in Kolkata, India

Kolkata, formerly known as Calcutta, in Roy's word is a "stark manifestation of the stereotype of the Third World megacity" (2011: 93). It is not only the administrative capital of West Bengal state; it is also the main commercial and financial hub of east and north eastern part of India. Kolkata Metropolitan Area

---

[2] Impact of Landuse Regulations: Evidence from India's cities.
[3] Conflicting stakes and governance in the peripheries of large Indian metropolises - An introduction.
[4] Urbanization beyond Municipal Boundaries: Nurturing Metropolitan Economies and Connecting Peri-Urban Areas in India.
[5] On Capital's Edge: Gurgaon, India's Millennial City.
[6] A satellite town located 32 kilometers south west of New Delhi.
[7] Urban Peri-urban Governance.

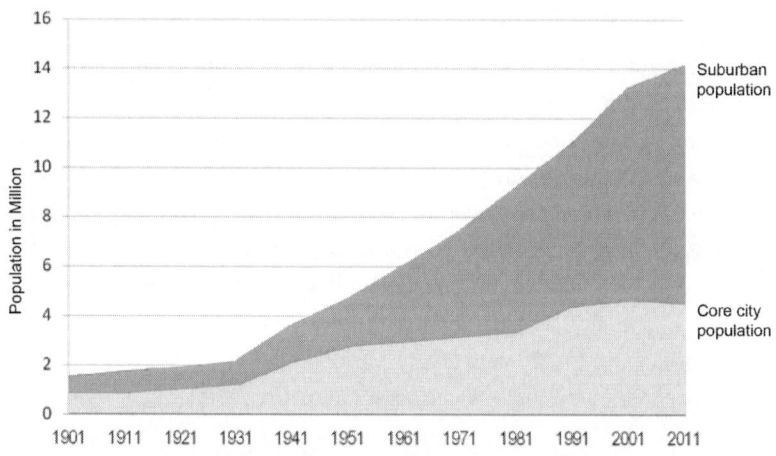

Figure 1: Population Change in Kolkata Metropolitan Area (Cox 2012)

(KMA) is the third largest urban agglomeration in India followed by Mumbai and Delhi. It covers 1851 square kilometers of land and according to 2001 census holds a population of 14.1 million. Compared to other metropolises in India KMA is characterized by highest residential density with 8,000 persons per square kilometer (KMDA 2008: 1). The core city of Kolkata has a population density of 24,760 persons per square kilometer, which is much higher than the World Health Organization's recommendation of 2,500 persons per square kilometer (Bardhan, Kiyo, and Hanaki 2011: 1). However, a recent study shows, that the core city has experienced minimal population growth over the last two decades, whereas suburban population of Kolkata is growing at a high rate (Cox 2012). Obviously it seems evident that one needs to look closer to the characteristics and challenges posed by this development.

1.1 Significant Stages of Suburban Development

To explain important stages of Kolkata's suburban development, this article follows the three stage model as dismissed by Chakravorty - "colonial economy during the first global period", "post colonial economy during the nationalist period" and "reform economy during the second global period" (2000: 57).

1.1.1 Suburbs during Colonial Economy

The city of Kolkata owes its origin to Colonial rule. In contrary to the city core which emerged as the seat of British administration Kolkata's suburbs started to develop for industrial purpose. In 1835, the first jute industry of this region was established at Rishra, approximately 23 kilometers away from the main city (Chakravorty 2000: 59). More jute mills started to develop along the west bank of Hooghly River, mainly towards the north of the city. The city's first dock in Khidirpore (1854) and railway station in Howrah (1880) also were established at the outskirts of the city. The use of suburbs for locating industries continued even in the beginning of 20th century, as various medium scale metal and iron work industry came up during this period. (Chakravorty 2000: 59).

1.1.2 Suburbs during Post Colonial Economy

A shift of the country's capital from Kolkata to New Delhi in 1912 caused adverse impact on the city's economy. Additionally, following the Partition[8] of India, a significant portion of Kolkata's hinterland became part of Bangladesh[9]. Religious conflict and political uproar in the newly formed neighboring country resulted in huge migration to Kolkata. To reiterate the words of Chaudhuri (cited in: Downton 2004: 312), during this period Kolkata has absorbed the biggest mass migration in human history "with incredibly meagre resources, little attention, and less sympathy" which forced the city to expand outward. Undoubtedly, immense pressure on the core city, resulted in a rapid development of suburbs in the post colonial period.

To combat with this urban crisis, Calcutta Metropolitan Development Authority (CMDA) came up with a "bi-nodal" urban planning strategy (1966) that resulted in the planning and building of two satellite towns (Kalyani and Saltlake City) respectively at the northern and eastern periphery of the metropolitan area. Apart from relieving the population pressure of the city core these new towns were also envisaged as administrative and educational centers. Afterwards, the planning authority formulated a "multi-nodal" development strategy (1976) for Kolkata, in which throughout the metropolitan region many more suburban

---

[8] In 1947, the British Indian Empire was divided into the sovereign Dominion of Pakistan (which later split into Pakistan and Bangladesh) and the Union of India (present Republic of India).
[9] East Pakistan at that time.

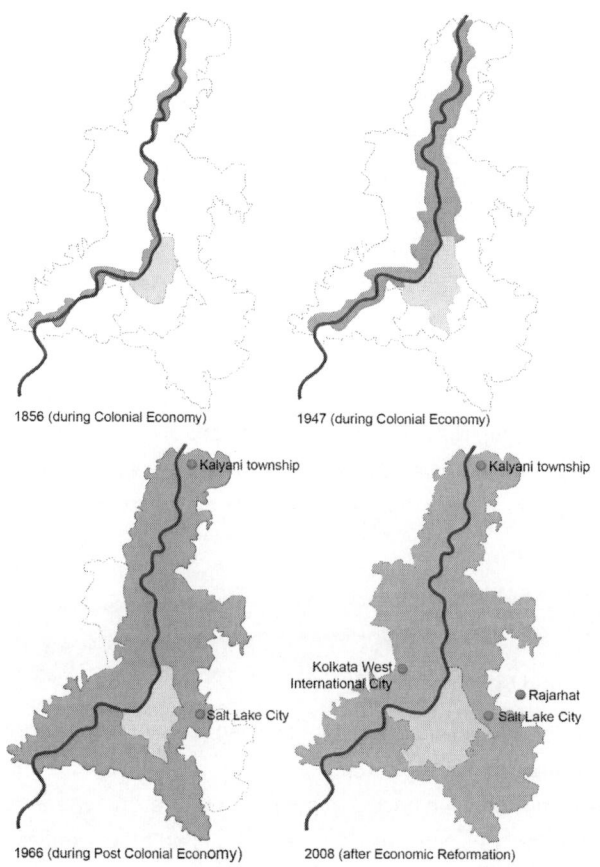

Figure 2: Suburban Growth of Kolkata (Das 2014)

nodes were proposed (ETH Studio Basel 2008a: 75-77). Considering such planned dispersal of people and industry to metropolitan towns was an essential feature of the UK's new town building program[10]. One could argue that Kolkata's development has been influenced by the British idea of "new towns".

1.1.3 Suburbs after Economic Reformation or Liberalization

After India's economic reformation in 1991, as an inevitable result of a liberal economy, foreign investments were directed to the city. The 7th national five

---

[10] Took place after World War II, mostly between 1947 and 1970.

year plan (1985 - 1990) opened up avenues for private sector participation in urban development and entrusted housing construction responsibility mainly in the hand of the private sector (Batra 2009: 16). As real estate, service sector and manufacturing industry have become lucrative destinations for new investors, several gated residential communities, IT enclaves, theme parks, office complexes, Special Economic Zones (SEZs)[11], transportation and logistics hubs have started to dominate the suburban landscape of Kolkata.

MHUPA's[12] report on urban housing shortage shows that West Bengal has 1.33 million housing deficiency, of which the majority is concentrated in Kolkata. In the last two decades, the demand of new housing stock, availability of private investment and emergence of IT, ITES sectors have resulted in a development of new towns in the suburbs. Rajarhat New Town, developed by the state with the help of private investment; Kolkata West International City (KWIC), developed entirely by foreign direct investment, are few examples of such new development.

1.2 Changes in Suburban Development

1.2.1 Urban Morphology and Building Types

This section explains how suburban morphology has changed over time by selecting three areas from three different time periods. The study area from Chitpur (figure 3a) shows a scenario of the northern periphery of the city where development started in the late 19th century. The larger building blocks indicate industrial developments along the river, whereas randomly laid smaller blocks show the unplanned development of one or two story high residential buildings which are common in this area.

The study area from Salt Lake City (figure 3b) illustrates a very different scenario on the eastern periphery of the city which came into existence in the later part of the 20th century. Similar buildings and plot sizes and the grid iron road network indicate that it is a part of a planned township. Large blocks indicate buildings for administrative use. Four story high apartment housing and one or two story high owner occupied houses are quite common in this area.

---

[11] According to India's SEZs Policy (2000), SEZs are an engine for economic growth supported by quality infrastructure complemented by an attractive fiscal package and with minimum possible regulations.

[12] Ministry of Housing and Urban Poverty Alleviation.

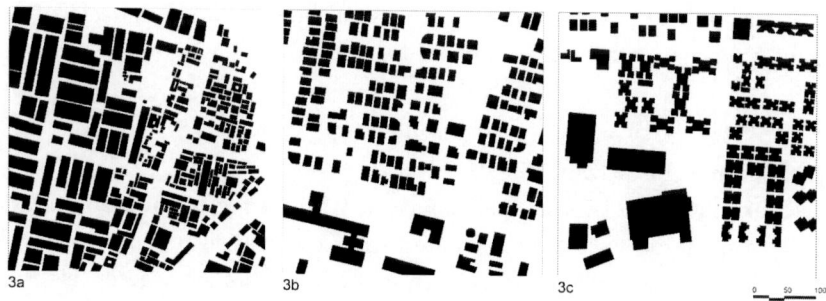

Figure 3: Change in Suburban Morphology, Kolkata (Das 2014)

Figure 4: New Building Type - High-rise in Rajarhat, Kolkata (Sukanta Halder 2014)

The study area from Rajarhat (figure 3c) represents a scenario at the extreme eastern edge of the metropolitan region which is a very recent development. On the right, building blocks with the same size and profile represent high rise and gated residential complexes which are common nowadays. The building heights of these enclaves vary from ten to thirty stories. And the big blocks on the left side are offices for IT and other multinational companies.

1.3 Case Studies

While discussing the changing face of Kolkata's suburbs, it is worth to mention two major planning interventions namely Salt Lake City and Rajarhat New Town. Salt Lake was planned in 1960s whereas Rajarhat started developing since the late 1990s. One being envisioned before and the other after economic liberalization, these examples explicitly show how suburban characters have transformed in the last few decades.

1.3.1 Salt Lake City

Location and Connectivity

Salt Lake City, also known as Bidhannagar, is a satellite town located in the eastern fringe of Kolkata. It is situated approximately eight kilometers away from the city core and it has three entry points which are easily accessible from the city. A metropolitan highway and a railway connection located on the west side of this township connect it with rest of the metropolitan area. A clear hierarchy of street typology can be found within the township. Salt Lake City is often referred as "Commuter town" as most inhabitants travel out to work with their private cars and outsiders come here for administrative and IT sector job (ETH Studio Basel 2008c: 137). The absence of a metro link, the lack of public transportation and the high dependency on private car certainly creates difficulty for commuters.

Cluster and land-use

The township is characterized by a slow pace of development. It was originally meant to prevent an overcrowding of the core city by accommodating 328,000 inhabitants (Tošković 2008: 100). In the 1970's it became an important destination for government offices and institutes. During 1980 to 1990 large scale public infrastructure projects such as a stadium or an entertainment park started to come up here. From 1995 onwards the city witnessed a boom in the IT sector resulting in the rapid development of new office complexes and shopping centers. From the beginning of the 21st century many luxurious hotels came up in this area as it started attracting the international hotel industry (ETH Studio Basel 2008c: 71–72.). In Salt Lake City, almost 50% of the land is under residential use, followed by 23% of land which is being used for transportation purpose. A significant amount of land, approximately 12%, has also been assigned for open spaces. Among other uses, commercial, governmental and educational uses can be found. (Tošković 2008: 100)

Social milieu

To achieve a high population density, 70% of apartment housing and 30% of individual housing were initially proposed in this township. Unfortunately, in reality 30% of apartment housing and 70% of individual housing have been built resulting in a much lower population density. At its inception, the town was envisaged mainly for middle income people; However, presently it contains a mixed social character as it is inhabited by a significant number of high income people, a moderate amount of middle income people and a very small number of people from an economically weaker section. (ETH Studio Basel 2008c: 83f.)

Urban Governance

Salt Lake City is administrated by its own elected body known as Bidhannagar Municipality. The municipality is responsible for sanctioning building plans, providing essential basic services to citizens, maintaining civic infrastructure of the township. However, all land in Salt Lake is owned by the Urban Development Department of State Government and individuals can possess the land only on leasehold[13] basis.

1.3.2 Rajarhat New Town

Rajarhat New Town is one of the ten expansion zones outside Kolkata's metropolitan boundary. It has been envisaged as a future destination for 750,000 people, large industries, technology hubs and central business districts. The construction of this township began in 1999 and it was built in six phases. According to Sengupta & Sharma (2007: 1):

> "Set within the context of economic liberalization, the New Town development aims to rejuvenate the Kolkata's stagnant economy by triggering land and housing development and to improve its image as an investment friendly destination. This new town is often portrayed as the symbolic revival of Kolkata a global economic player."

Location and transportation network

Rajarhat New Town is located on the eastern periphery of Kolkata. It is situated ten kilometers away from the core city and only one kilometer away from the airport. Rajarhat is primarily a car oriented development. At present, busses are the only available public transport mode, although bus terminals are not ade-

---

[13] Leasehold is a form of property tenure where one party buys the right to occupy land or a building for a given length of time.

quately spread over the township. In the near future, a metro line will provide a better connection to the airport, Howrah station[14] and the core city of Kolkata.

Cluster and land-use

Initially, half of Rajarhat's total land area was reserved only for residential development, while commercial and office areas together with industries were allotted around 11%. However, in 2006, the share of residential use was reduced and quite a significant amount of IT industry (5%), cultural and health facilities (9%) were integrated into the area (Sengupta and Sharma 2007: 15–16.). Presently, the most common form of dwelling found in Rajarhat are gated high rise buildings whose height varies from 10 to 30 storeys. Provisions of 4-5 storey residential apartments for the low to middle income groups and single family houses for upper middle and high income groups are also there. But compared to individual or co-operative housing, high-rise buildings are being developed at a much faster rate by single developers or joint venture companies. This results in an unforeseen suburban landscape of disconnected enclaves or scattered islands in the middle of nowhere. After residential use, the commercial area is the second largest component of Rajarhat which comprises one main and three sub central business districts (CBD). IT hubs, public institutions, especially significant cultural facilities like MoMA (Museum of Modern Art), are integral part of this suburb. In terms of type of open space, the New Town shows a shift from individual block parks of Salt Lake to a more continuous space of public green.

Social milieu

According to Mitra, Rajarhat has an ambitious goal of eradicating 15% of total land and housing deficit of the core city (cited in: Sengupta and Sharma 2007: 29). But its methods of land procurement, absence of small and medium developers in the development process, profit seeking attitude of involved public agency, exclusion of urban poor can be questioned. Where almost 70% of total households in the Kolkata metropolitan area come under the low income group (LIG) and economically weaker section (EWS), Rajarhat's projected population includes only 17% LIG and 4% EWS (ETH Studio Basel 2008b: 23, 101). The study shows that the cost of developed land in Rajarhat is nine times higher than the

---

[14] Most important railway station of Kolkata.

Figure 5: Island of developed areas in Rajarhat, Kolkata (Sukanta Halder 2014)

cost of raw land. Besides, land price to income ratio is quite high in this new town, which means that common people cannot afford the land (Sengupta and Sharma 2007: 19, 25). To summarize, these factors indicate how development in Rajarhat has gone beyond the reach of a major part of the society.

Urban Governance

The Housing Infrastructure Development Corporation (HIDCO), set up by Government of West Bengal in 1999, played a major role in the location selection and land acquisition of this township. Apart from preparing the Landuse and Development Control Plan (LUDCP), this organization is responsible for developing the civic infrastructure of Rajarhat. Until now, this township does not come under any urban local body[15] but in 2007 the New Town Development Authority (NKDA) was formed as a transitional arrangement. NKDA sanctions new development plans and renders various civic services of Rajarhat New Town.

To conclude, both Salt Lake City and Rajarhat New Town are examples of state initiated suburban development in Kolkata. However, the role of private inves-

---

[15] Municipal corporation or municipality or city council.

tors and the numbers of public private partnership (PPP) projects are much higher in Rajarhat. Aspiration to provide world class infrastructure for the IT sector and multinational companies, the construction of exclusive residential enclaves for the high income group, and widening the gap between the urban poor and the elite class characterize the development of Rajarhat New Town. Undoubtedly, such development is quite distinct from former suburbs of Kolkata.

2. Suburban Development in Bengaluru, India

Bengaluru is the capital city of the southern federal state of Karnataka in the Republic of India. The official language of Bengaluru is Kannada and the spoken languages include Kannada, Hindi and English. The city of Bengaluru emerged in the year 1537 as "Benda Kalooru" when Magadi Kempegowda the first built a mud fort and shifted with a little less than 200 people from his kingdom "Magadi" and to use it as a summer home owing to its pleasant climate all-round the year.[16] The fort was around the settlement and a "Pētē" (market) area was created outside the fort with an extensive and exclusive shopping area. The settlement developed as a "Pētē Ooru" (market settlement) for a very long time. The "Benda Kalooru" fort was lost to the British during the Second Anglo Mysore war in 1779 after which they leased the entire area to the Wodeyars, the Kings of Mysore in 1791. In 1809, the British cantonment was formed mostly for the British elite. The city now started developing as two separate entities: one being the "Pētē Ooru" - "Benda Kalooru" and the other being the British cantonment now anglicized as "Bangalore". The city was united to form "Bangalore" in 1929 (Kamath 2012: 47) until it was renamed as Bengaluru in 2013. It witnessed two main development periods between 1930 to 1950 and in the early 1980's owing to the industrialization in the first period and the real estate boom in the second. It now started losing its character as the "Garden City" and started becoming a personification of sophistication and gentrification. Even though the city saw a lot of real estate development, there was quite a minimal suburban development. The city came to a limelight globally and was called "Silicon Valley of India" (Vandrevala 2001) after the major Information Technology explosion from 1990 until early 2000.

---

[16] Magadi is a town in the Indian state of Karnataka located about 60 kilometers from present day Bengaluru city.

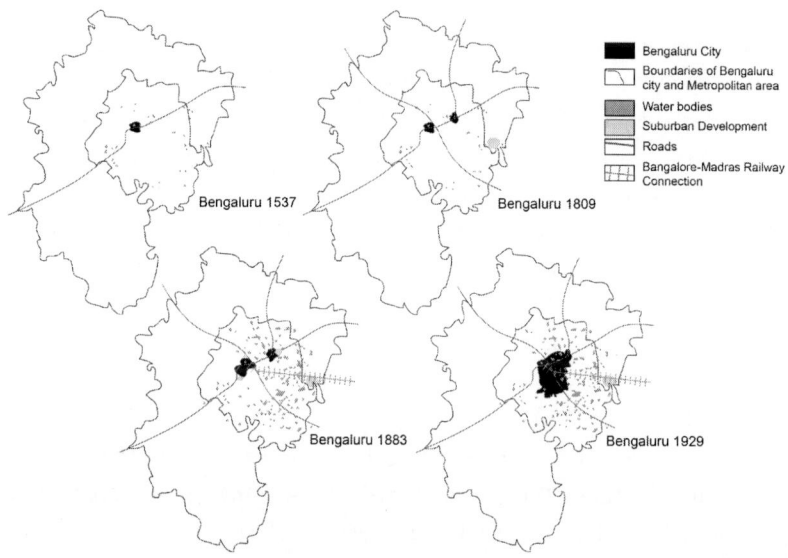

Figure 6: Development of Bengaluru, India (Satyamurthy 2014)

The city of Bengaluru is the third most populous city and the fifth most populous urban agglomeration in India with a population of 9,621,551 (Census Commission of India 2011) in the year 2011. The city occupies an area of 1,276 square kilometers and the metropolitan Bengaluru covers an area of 2,196 square kilometers with a population density of 19,435 inhabitants per square kilometers and 7,500 inhabitants per square kilometers respectively (Bangalore Development Authority 2011). 90.6% of the inhabitants live in urban Bengaluru and the remaining 9.4% constitute the rural population. 30% of the urban population lives in slums and 27% in suburban Bengaluru (Champa 2011: 7).

Bengaluru has a very well connected public transport system consisting of buses, metro and auto-rickshaws for local commuting and trains and airplanes for national and international commuting. There is a common airport, Kempegowda International Airport, for both national and international connections. 52% of Bangaloreans use public transport for commuting while the remaining use private transport (Champa 2011: 7) owing to the highest traffic density in India (Bangalore City Traffic Police 2013).

2.1 Significant Stages of Suburban Development

The city of Bengaluru is not unaware of the process of suburban development. In fact, it saw traces of suburban development from pre-independence time[17] with the earliest phase of suburbanization being as early as 1881. But with the arrival of the software industry during the post-liberal economic time, it faced an unprecedented surge of suburban development when many saw the face of light around Bengaluru city (Sridhar 2013). Historically, however, one can identify three significant periods of suburban development; from 1880 to the early 1950's, from the early 1980's to the next decade and from the late 1990's to the present, similar to most parts of the country.

2.1.1 Colonial Era

Owing to the British intervention, the city started seeing industrialization and new transport systems. There was sudden intense immigration of people looking for work due to the enhanced connectivity. In 1881, three urban extensions, Richmond Town, Benson Town and Frazer Town, were developed as suburban localities around the "Bangalore" cantonment. Frazer Town was mainly a residential area while Richmond Town and Benson Town were mixed land use of residential and commercial areas (Kamath 2012: 54). In 1882, the Wodeyars gifted 3,900 acres (15.79 square kilometers) of land to the Eurasian and Anglo-Indian Association for the establishment of agricultural settlements, such as "Whitefield", which also started developing as a suburban area to "Bangalore" (Peck 2007).

In 1906, two extensions were designed and developed in the north and south of the "Pētē" known as Malleshwaram and Basavangudi respectively. These extensions were developed as residential suburbs of "Benda Kalooru" (Kamath, 2012: 55). These localities form a part of central Bengaluru today.

2.1.2 Post Independence

From 1981, for the next decade, the city saw a monstrous real estate growth. Many parks and lakes in the city were encroached for the construction of residences and offices. Colonial bungalows were demolished to create many elite and sophisticated neighborhoods in the form of gated apartment complexes

---

[17] India was a British colony until August 14, 1947. India was declared an independent country on August 15, 1947.

(Kamath 2012: 62). Almost no suburban development happened during this period but there was a significant change in the identity and the façade of the city. Most people preferred buying properties within the city and developing gated communities, which was deemed prestigious. This period also saw many immigrants of which very few preferred the suburb increasing the population density within the city rapidly.

2.1.3 Post Economic Liberalization

The main era of suburban development started with the arrival of the software industry in the post-economic liberalization period since the late 1990's when many suburban developments saw the face of light around Bengaluru city. Many new neighborhoods like the Electronic City, settlements around Manyata Technological Park and Marathalli were formed. These neighborhoods mainly developed around the IT industry and most of the residents are employees in the offices in the neighborhood. The central area of these neighborhoods have a huge concentration of software offices and social infrastructure like fine dining restaurants and shopping malls and these are surrounded by residential apartment towers and gated row housing colonies. Many already existing neighborhoods like Whitefield, settlements around Kalyani Magnum Technological Park saw intensive immigration and development after this intervention by the Information Technology industry.

2.2 Changes in Suburban Development

When the Information Technology industry just arrived, most of these neighborhoods were isolated and probably even neglected. The once historically important Whitefield gained a renewed importance after the establishment of Information Technology Park Limited (ITPL) and underwent a drastic transformation from agriculture to the software industry. Whitefield forms a very rare neighborhood to study and observe as it has maintained its unique identity since historical times. Unlike many historical suburban neighborhoods like Basavangudi and Malleshwaram that were encroached as the city grew and became a part of the city, Whitefield still maintained its identity as a suburban development.

Whitefield was an Anglo-Indian and a Eurasian settlement in the outskirts of Bengaluru. In 1882, Chamaraja Wodeyar, the Maharaja of Mysore, gifted 3,900 acres (15.79 square kilometers) of land to the Eurasian and Anglo-Indian Association for the establishment of agricultural settlements, which also started developing as a suburban area to "Bangalore". David Emmanuel Starkenburgh White, President of the Association by that time, enthusiastically helped in its advancement (Peck 2007). The area was later called "Whitefield" as a respect and commemoration to Mister White (Nagesh 2008).

Whitefield, which was once a quintessential village known for its tranquility, cultural heritage, farmlands and Eurasian architecture is today known for its IT parks, five-star hotels, gated residential communities and shopping malls. In 2010, there were 172,357 residents in Whitefield out of which approximately 67% worked in the offices in the neighborhood while the remaining travelled to other parts of Bengaluru everyday (Falling Rain Genomics 2010). The population has been rising steadily since and the trend does not seem to be changing anytime soon. The residents of Whitefield mostly classify into upper middle class and middle class making it an expensive neighborhood.

2.2.1 Urban Morphology

The settlement was established with 45 houses of which some were on the village site and the remaining were on farms scattered throughout, which was not less than 4.83 kilometers in length and about 3.22 kilometers wide, and contained about 2000 acres (8.09 square kilometers) of land fit for cultivation. The main crops cultivated were mangoes, timber and casuarina. The village site formed a large outer circle of 0.46 kilometers in diameter with about 25 houses on the circumference and the school, post office, playground, and lawn Tennis courts in the center forming a smaller inner circle. The Protestant and Roman Catholic Churches were near as well as the Whitefield Stores, Waverly Inn and The Refreshment Room. Outside the circle, there was a football field, a cricket ground and other entertainment facilities. The village was to the right of the public road, which formed a tangent to the circular village, at a point 2.41 kilometers from the railway station. The appearance of the village was very striking as its approach was through a road with "Hamilton Hill" on the left and the "Kaolin Hill" on the right. The outer and inner circle formed the main feature of this settlement. Today, this has become an Archeological Survey of India's (ASI) Heritage Site (Peck 2007).

Figure 7: IT Offices, Information Technology Park Limited, Whitefield (Satyamurthy 2014)

2.2.2 Building Typology

After the inception of Whitefield, many colonial bungalows were constructed in the outer circle. Many of these old cottages and bungalows were demolished for the construction of offices and apartments until the ASI intervened and declared it as a heritage site (Peck 2007). So architecturally, a mix of colonial bungalows, Eurasian cottages, high-rise glass buildings and apartment blocks can all be seen in the same horizon. The feeling of a confused architectural style and building typologies is evident. As opposed to the low-rise central city with a maximum of five storeys, the neighborhood saw a high-rise development of a minimum of 15 to 20 storeys post 1990.

2.2.3 Cluster and Land Use

The main land use was agricultural with mixed land use within the circles when the settlement was established. Like most of the other Indian cities, there was a strong conflict between the post liberal suburban development and rural land uses in Bengaluru (Sridhar 2013) and Whitefield was no exception to this. Presently, the development in Whitefield is mostly demarcated as IT parks and office buildings, a mix of residences and commercial buildings and a few open spaces.

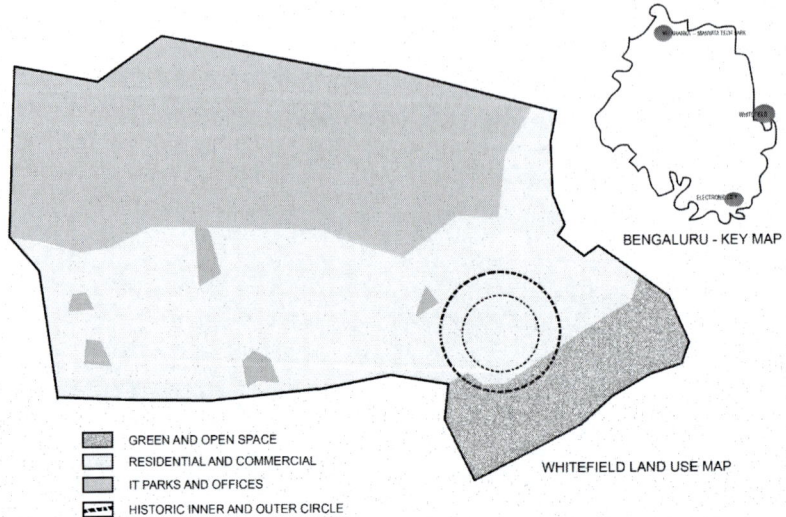

Figure 8: Whitefield Land Use (Satyamurthy 2014)

2.2.4 Social Milieu

A circulating book club was in existence in early 1900's. Sports field and churches formed the main gathering spaces for most of the people and some enjoyed the occasional drink at Waverly Inn and The Refreshment Room (Peck 2007).

In June 1960, the Sathya Sai Baba Ashram "Brindavan" was established which temporarily gave Whitefield the much deserved attention. It was strategically located next to the Whitefield railway station to enable easy access for the visitors. A hospital was established to help the poor by providing medical help free of charge. This brought in many people to Whitefield on a regular basis (Sai Baba for Beginners Trust 2012).

Today, it is known as a food center owing to its innumerable multi-cuisine restaurants and breweries and a shopper's paradise owing to the number of shopping malls. A large number of the residents of this neighborhood belong to the upper middle class, which has had a direct influence on the cost of living resulting in expensive fine dining and expensive branded shopping.

Figure 9: Phoenix Market City, Shopping Mall in Whitefield (Satyamurthy 2014)

2.2.5 Urban Governance and Connectivity

The Whitefield Railway Station was on the Madras-Bangalore line. The settlement itself was to the south of the Railway. The first house in the settlement in its northern boundary was 0.81 kilometers from the station and the last house on its southern boundary was about 4.83 kilometers further on. A fine road with a good avenue of trees ran through the settlement, from the North to the South, dividing it into two parts (Peck 2007).

With a heightened attention being given to these neighborhoods after the software industry intervention, the city authorities took a special interest and improvised infrastructure facilities like road network and public transport. The Bangalore Metropolitan Transport Corporation launched an extensive bus service connecting the suburbs to the central city. A Bangalore Commuter Rail service was proposed and is hoping to receive its approval in 2015 from the Railway Board (Aiyappa 2013).

The suburban development is very well connected across the city with an extensive public transport system of busses. It also has an extensive road network connecting it to the central city of Bengaluru and even the neighboring cities. There are two major four-lane roads connecting Bengaluru city and Whitefield, which intersects with the Karnataka State Highway 35 running in the North-South direction (Champa 2011: 77).

The major problem of this suburb is that few of the infrastructure facilities are not able to cope up with the intense and sudden expansion. For example, the entire suburban development faces a major water shortage problem for most part of the year and the inhabitants have extra water scarcity troubles during summer (TNN 2012). The Bruhat Bengaluru Mahanagara Palike [(BMP - Municipal Government) governing Whitefield is making continued efforts to cope up with the increasing population and costs but has a long distance to catch up with.

2.2.6 Urban Policies

The settlement always faced issues with the water supply. Owing to the inexperience of the early settlers at the time of inception of Whitefield, wells were dug and sunk in unsuitable places and many of them failed. The Mysore Government constructed a few good wells but could not complete their mission of constructing a well for a never-failing supply of excellent water.

From 1990 onwards, for more than a decade, the city saw massive expansion with regard to the number of software companies and amount of software export. From 1992 to 2003, the number of IT sector offices increased from thirteen to 1,154 which is 8776.9% and sales of software export recorded an increase from 1.19 million USD to 2627,7 million USD which was a remarkable growth of 220,435.7% (Sastry 2008). Due to this, the neighborhood saw a colossal number of immigrants. Even today, during the hot months of the year, especially between March to May, a scarcity of water is felt (Peck 2007). Recently, the Bangalore Water Supply and Sewerage Board granted ten billion to improvise the water supply situation in nine suburbs of Bengaluru with Whitefield being one of them (TNN 2012). In January 2014, Whitefield got its own Traffic and Transit Management Centre (TTMC), which now provides facilities of public transport and parking spaces in an effort to facilitate the residents and commuters.

Conclusion

The main finding of this research which substantiates our hypothesis is that India's economic liberalization and consequent boom in IT industry and real estate have severely influenced the character of suburbia. Such phenomenon is not only limited to Bangalore or Kolkata, but it has become common in all large metropolises of the country. The new suburban landscape, characterized by IT Parks, high rise gated communities, Special Economic Zone (SEZ) in different parts of India, can be defined as the "changing face" of Indian suburbia.

Few inferences can be drawn from the examples discussed in the previous two sections. First of all, the scale of new suburban developments is much bigger than what it used to be. For example, looking at Kolkata, Rajarhat New Town is six times bigger than Salt Lake in its physical extent. The pace of such development is also unprecedented. Secondly, locationwise these new developments show some biasness. Apart from the fact, that they are generally located in close proximity to the city core (e.g. Rajarhat ten kilometers away from the city center, Whitefield 20 kilometers from the main city), most of them are flourishing near airports or along a major connecting corridor (figure 10). After economic liberalization, the cities authorities' pro market orientation and openness to private investment could also be identified as a major shift. An increasing number of public private partnerships for urban development and the dominance of profit seeking developers in this field validate this fact.

It should be noted that in recent years the notion of a monofunctional suburbia has been replaced by diversely programmed developments. Several factors such as a liberalized economic environment, the housing shortage and the restriction of building density in the inner cities are pushing people as well as jobs towards the periphery. As a result, the combination of residential complexes, central business districts, transportation hubs, offices and IT parks creates a new suburban landscape. Unfortunately, at the same time one can observe the development of "enclaves" or disconnected islands of wealth and deprivation in suburbia. Most of the new residential and commercial developments are focusing on high income groups while ignoring the housing need of the economically weak population. Pugh's 1989 study shows for example that Kolkata Metropolitan Development Authority used to spend 25% of its budget on slum improvement and 14% on new housing development previously. But under the Mega City Program, which was implemented from 1994 to 2007, only 1.7% was assigned for slum improvement and 46% for housing, new area development and commercial facilities (in: Chakravorty 2000: 75). Though few government policies, such as the Basic Services for Urban Poor (BSUP)[18] have been proposed to

---

[18] Submission of Jawaharlal Nehru National Urban Renewal Mission (JNNURM), came into action from 2005-2006.

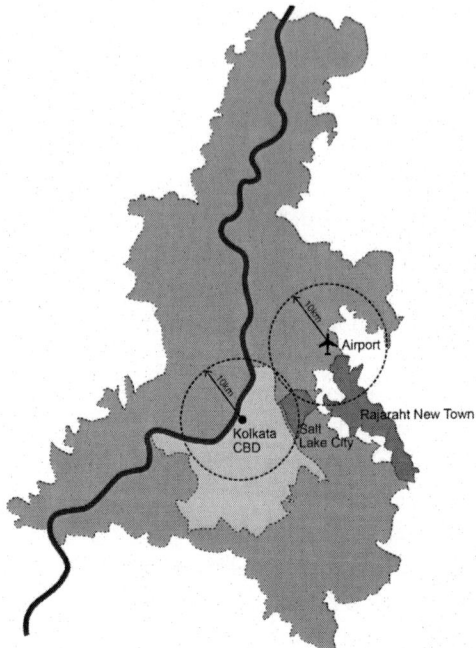

Figure 10: Proximity of suburbs, Kolkata (Das 2014)

improve the situation, the co-existence of high end condominiums, shopping malls, gated high rises on one hand and slums on the other hand still reflects the economic polarization of suburban society.

In conclusion, the data from the Ministry of Statistics and Program Implementation shows that employment in high-tech and export oriented manufacturing as well as in real estate and transport sector have increased tremendously between 1998 and 2005 in suburban areas (The World Bank Report 2013: 3). It confirms the fact that suburbs of large metropolises are leading the country's production of goods and services that India trades with the global market. It can be said, these newly developed suburban areas are not only showcasing India's economic resurgence, but also becoming more and more visible in the global network. Therefore, much more attention should be given in both research and planning of upcoming suburbs to ensure a sustainable and viable urban development in India.

References

Aiyappa, Manu (2013), "Commuters trains in Bangalore get closer to becoming a reality", The Times of India, http://articles.timesofindia.indiatimes.com/20131210/bangalore/45033530_1_railway-board-railway-budget-commuter-rail (Accessed December 15, 2013).

Bangalore City Traffic Police (2013), *Bangalore Traffic Police*, http://www.bangaloretrafficpolice.gov.in/index.php (Accessed November 30, 2013).

Bardhan, Ronita/ Kiyo, H. Kurisu/ Hanaki, Keisuke (2011), "Linking Urban Form & Quality of Life in Kolkata, India", in: *47th ISOCARP Congress*, http://www.isocarp.net/data/case_studies/1923.pdf (Accessed September 12, 2014).

Batra, Lalit (2009), "*A Review of Urbanisation and Urban Policy in Post-Independent India*", New Delhi, http://www.jnu.ac.in/cslg/workingPaper/12-A Review of Urban (Lalit Batra).pdf (Accessed September 3, 2014).

Biswas, Arindam (2010), "The Spatial Evaluation of Sustainability in Urban Growth: Measurement, Analysis and Approach for South - east Region of Kolkata, India", in: *9th Conference of Asian City Planning*, http://rdarc.itakura.toyo.ac.jp/webdav/ask/public/ACP2010/2.pdf (Accessed September 3, 2014).

Census Commissioner India (2011), *Regional Census Karnataka,* Government of India - Ministry of Home Affairs, Bangalore.

Chadchan J; Shankar R (2012), "An Analysis of Urban Growth Trends in the Post-Economic Reforms Period in India", in: Gulf Organization for Research and Development (ed.), *International Journal of Sustainable Built Environment Vol 1*, 36-49.

Chakravorty, Sanjay (2000), "From Colonial City to Globalizing City?", in: Marcuse, Peter/ van Kempen, Rohnald (eds.), *Globalizing Cities, A New Spatial Order?*, Oxford: Blackwell Publishing, 56-77.

Champa, Bharat, (2011), *Hosayugada Vastavagalu: Tadeyalagada Upanagareekarana*, Bangalore: Manasa Lightage Foundation.

Cox, Wendell (2012), *The Evolving Urban Form: Kolkata: 50 Mile City*, in: New Geography, August 10, 2014, http://www.newgeography.com/content/002620-the-evolving-urban-form-kolkata-50-mile-city (Accessed August 10, 2014).

Downton, Paul F. (2004), "Compact City Environmental Strategies: Calcutta's Urban Ecosystem", in: Jenks, Mike/ Burgess, Rod (eds.), *Compact Cities: Sustainable Urban Forms for Developing Countries*, London/New York: Routledge, 311-320.

ETH Studio Basel (2008a), "A Plan for 15 Million", http://www.studio-basel.com/assets/files/files/01_City Dimensions_web.pdf (Accessed August 11, 2014).

— (2008b), "Kolkata East Side Story", http://www.studio-basel.com/assets/files/files/04_Rajarhat_web.pdf (Accessed August 11, 2014).

— (2008c), "Salt Lake City: An Ideal City Just Completed", http://www.studio-basel.com/assets/files/files/03_Salt Lake City_web.pdf (Accessed September 3, 2014).

Falling Rain Genomics (2010), "Whitefield India Page", http://www.fallingrain.com /world/IN/19/Whitefield.html (Accessed November 6, 2014).

Kamath, S (2012), "Aitihasika Mysooru Nadu. Bengaluru Huttidaga", *Kannada Sahitya Parishat*, Bangalore.

KMDA (2008), *Annual Report 2008*, Kolkata, http://www.kmdaonline.org/pdf/aar08/1-5.pdf (Accessed August 10, 2014).

Peck, William (2007), "Whitefield Diaries", http://www.children-of-bangalore.com/whitefld.html (Accessed December 5, 2013).

Roy, Ananya (2011), "Reforming the Megacity: Calcutta and the Rural-Urban Interface", in: Sorensen, André/ Okakta, Junichiro (eds.), *Megacities: Urban Form, Governance, and Sustainability*, Vol. 10, Tokyo: Springer Japan, 93-110.

Sai Baba for Beginners Trust (2012), *The World of Sai Baba at Prashanti Nilayam*, http://www.saibabaforbeginners.com/white.html (Accessed November 10, 2013).

Sengupta, Urmi/ Sharma, Sujeet (2007), "Government Intervention and Land Development in New Town, Kolkata: Emerging Lessons for the Policymakers?", *Fourth Urban Research Symposium*, http://siteresources.worldbank.org/INTURBANDEVELOPMENT/Resources/336387-1269364687916/6892589-1269394475210/sharma.pdf (Accessed September 6, 2014).

Sastry, Gundappa Sathyanarayana (2008), "Emerging Development Issues of Greater Bangalore", *Institute for Social and Economic Change*, Bangalore.

Sridhar, Kala Seetharam (2013), "Cities with Suburbs: Suburbanization of India's Cities" *Indian Institute of Human Settlements*, Bangalore.

The World Bank (2013), *Urbanization beyond Municipal Boundaries: Nurturing Metropolitan Economies and Connecting Peri-Urban Areas in India*, Washinton DC.

TNN (2012), "Taps will flow in the Outskirts", *The Times of India*, http://articles.timesofindia.indiatimes.com/2012-03-22/bangalore/31224806_1_cauvery-water-bwssb-unaccounted-for-water (Accessed January 7, 2014).

Tošković, Dobrivoje (2008), "A Review on Salt Lake City, Kolkata, India: Master Planning and Realization", *Spatium*, 98-105 http://www.doiserbia.nb.rs/img/doi/1450-569X/2008/1450-569X0818098T.pdf (Accessed September 3, 2014).

Vandrevala, P (2001), "India's Silicon Valley", *Business Week*, http://www.businessweek.com/adsections/indian/infotech/2001/silicon.html (Accessed November 18, 2013).

Authors

Mazen Alazazmeh

Mazen Alazazmeh is an architect with a Master of Urban Studies from Bauhaus-Universität Weimar. Experiences in Exterior Architecture, Landscape Architecture, and Urban Planning in Jordan, Germany and Belgium respectively, allowed the author to develop a wider perspective on his home city Amman, Jordan.

Stefanie Bremer

Dr. Stefanie Bremer is an urban and traffic planer- spatial designer. She worked for several years as an assistant professor at Universität Duisburg-Essen as well as at Technische Universität Dortmund. 2008 she joined the urban planning office "orange edge" in Hamburg. The planning office works in the field of integrated infrastructure planning and design, new urban mobility and participation. The office works for German cities, the Federal Ministry of Transport, Building and Urban Development, different urban planning and culture institutions and private companies, for example the Volkswagen AG. The office already gained some awards for their work: Deutscher Städtebaupreis 2012 (Sonderpreis), ADC-Award 2010, Deutscher Ingenieurspreis Straße und Verkehr.

Priyambada Das

Priyambada Das is pursuing a master degree in European Urban Studies at Bauhaus-Universität Weimar. She practiced as a Landscape Architect for two years in AECOM Pvt. Ltd., India after finishing her study in Architecture and Landscape Architecture. In 2014, she has also worked as an intern at Space Syntax, London.

Holger Gladys

M.Arch Holger Gladys is an Amsterdam-based architect und urbanist. After graduating from the Amsterdam Berlage Institute, he worked for various architectural and urban design offices. Since 2003 he is teaching architecture and urban design at the Amsterdam Academy of Architecture and the Bauhaus-Universität Weimar. He is a member of the Weimar Institute for European Urban Studies. In 2013 he has been guest professor at the Virginia Tech State University, Washington Alexandria Architecture Center.

Carlos Andrés Romero Grezzi
Carlos Andrés Romero Grezzi is an architect and postgraduate in Environmental Urban Development (Universidad Nacional de Córdoba). He is also a PhD Candidate (Geman-Argentinian Program: Urban and Territorial Studies – Bauhaus-Universität Weimar and Universidad Nacional de Córdoba). His major interests include public space, environmental development and territorial organization.

Iana Korolova
Iana Korolova studied environmental design at Kyiv State Institute of Decorative and Applied Art and Design, named after Mykhaylo Boychuk. After graduation, she has worked as an interior designer for two years. She has taken part in the international architectural festival "Canactions" in Kyiv. Currently, she is enrolled in the 'European Urban Studies' master programme of the Bauhaus University in Weimar. Lately, she has worked as a landscape architect at TOPOTEK1, where she has been involved in several competitions.

Arvid Krüger
Dipl.-Ing. Arvid Krüger has a diploma in city and regional planning / spatial planning (KTH Stockholm and TU Berlin). From 2009 to 2013 he was working as a local renewal manager in Berlin Lichtenberg. Before he worked at a freelancer for planning consultancies, research institutes and the Deutsche Bundestag. Since 2012 he is working at the Bauhaus-Universität Weimar, chair "Urban Planning", teaching in the study program "Urbanistik".

Sigrun Langner
Jun.-Prof. Dr.-Ing. Sigrun Langner is assistant professor for landscape architecture and landscape planning at Bauhaus-University Weimar.
In 2012 she gained a PhD. from Leibniz University Hannover. Her research interest is the potential of a design-oriented cartography for understanding and designing large-scale urban landscapes. Her current research focuses on „(r)urban landscapes" as a result of the urbanisation of the rural space and the ruralisation of the urban space.

Between 2005 and 2012 she was teaching at the Faculty of Architecture and Landscape at the University Hannover. She is a member of „Studio Urbane Landschaften" – a transdiciplinary network for research, teaching and practical work.
She is registered Landscape Architect and Co-owner of Station C23 – architecture landscape urbanism in Leipzig. Station C23 is a multidisciplinary office with a focus on landscape architecture in larger urban contexts.

Jan Polívka
Jan Polívka is Associate Professor of Urban Design and Land Use Planning at the TU Dortmund University. Research and practice in the fields of urban design, urban quality assurance and regulations, urban regeneration and urban development concepts, urban redevelopment and suburban transformation.

Monica Jimena Ramé
Monica Jimena Ramé is an architect and postgraduate in Cultural Management (Universidad Nacional de Córdoba). She is also a PhD Candidate (Geman-Argentinian Program: Urban and Territorial Studies – Bauhaus-Universität Weimar and Universidad Nacional de Córdoba). Her research interests include Latin America´s urbanism and heritage and urban and regional governance and development.

Ion Alexandru Retegan
Ion Alexandru Retegan is a Romanian architect. He has studied architecture at the 'Ion Mincu' University of Architecture and Urbanism in Bucharest, and Ecole d'Architecture Marseille-Luminy in Marseille. He is currently enrolled in the 'European Urban Studies' master programme of the Bauhaus University in Weimar. He has worked as a graphic designer and architect in Bucharest. He has also written for the Romanian architecture magazine Zeppelin. Recently, he has worked as a researcher for the international architecture magazine Volume, studying the topic of self-building.

Iana Samakaeva
Iana Samakaeva studied architecture at Kazan State University of Architecture and Engineering. During her studies, she was an intern at "Barcelona Regional" urban planning bureau and worked as a teacher in a design school. After graduating in 2011, she has worked as an architect for two years in Kazan, and has

been responsible for the large scale urban design project IT city Innopolis. As part of that project, she was the architect of the Innopolis IT University, the first of its kind in Russia, which is currently under construction. She is now studying for her Masters degree at Bauhaus University in Weimar and working as an architect and urban planner at KCAP Architects&Planners.

Vaishali Anavatti Satyamurthy

Vaishali Anavatti Satyamurthy is an architect from Bengaluru, India pursuing a dual degree master M.Sc Advanced Urbanism at Bauhaus University, Weimar – Tongji University, Shanghai. She worked as an architect for two years in Bengaluru, India before starting her master in Urban Planning. Lately, she has worked as an urban planner at Orange Edge, Hamburg.

Johanna Schlaack

Prof. Dr.-Ing. Johanna Schlaack is guest professor at the Center for Metropolitan Studies at TU Berlin and co-founder of the urban think tank "Think Berl!n". Her areas of research include airports and (sub)urban development, Smart Cities, sustainable regional development strategies, infrastructures and integrated urban design.

Barbara Schönig

Prof. Dr.-Ing. M.A., is professor for Urban Planning at Bauhaus-Universität Weimar since 2012 and Director of the university's Institute for European Urban Studies since 2013. She holds an M.A. in German Literature and History of Art and a Diploma in Urban and Regional Planning. She received her PhD at TU Berlin. She taught at the Chairs for Sociology of Architecture and Planning at TU Berlin (2002-2009) and Spatial and Infrastructural Planning at TU Darmstadt (2009-2011). Her research interests include suburbanization, metropolitan planning and governance, affordable housing, and comparative urban research.

Cristian Gabriel Terreno

Cristian Gabriel Terreno is an architect and M.Sc in Environmental Urban Development (Universidad Nacional de Córdoba). His also a PhD Candidate (Geman-Argentinian Program: Urban and Territorial Studies – Bauhaus-Universität Weimar and Universidad Nacional de Córdoba). He is an assitant professor for

Architecture and Urban Theory. His major interests include urban theory, environmental development and GIS.

Regina Vidosa
Posgrado Magister Regina Vidosa is a sociologist (Universidad Nacional de Buenos Aires). She is also a PhD Candidate (Geman-Argentinian Program: Urban and Territorial Studies – Bauhaus-Universität Weimar and Universidad Nacional de Córdoba). Her major interests include economic geography, territorial organization and regional development.

Elodie Vittu
Dipl.-Ing. Elodie Vittu has a French and German diploma in urban and regional planning. Since 2008 she is working at the Bauhaus-Universität Weimar, chair "spatial planning, spatial research", teaching in the study program "Urbanistik" and writing a PhD on "right to the city movements in Europa and Latinamerica".

Sie haben die Wahl:

Bestellen Sie die Schriftenreihe
Städtebau – Architektur – Gesellschaft
einzeln oder im **Abonnement**

per E-Mail: vertrieb@ibidem-verlag.de | per Fax (0511/262 2201)
als Brief (*ibidem*-Verlag | Leuschnerstr. 40 | 30457 Hannover)

Bestellformular

☐ Ich abonniere die Schriftenreihe *Städtebau – Architektur – Gesellschaft* ab Band # ____

☐ Ich bestelle die folgenden Bände der Schriftenreihe *Städtebau – Architektur – Gesellschaft*

____; ____; ____; ____; ____; ____; ____; ____; ____; ____

Lieferanschrift:

Vorname, Name ....

Anschrift ....

E-Mail .... | Tel.: ....

Datum .... | Unterschrift ....

Ihre Abonnement-Vorteile im Überblick:

- Sie erhalten jedes Buch der Schriftenreihe pünktlich zum Erscheinungstermin – immer aktuell, ohne weitere Bestellung durch Sie.
- Das Abonnement ist jederzeit kündbar.
- Die Lieferung ist innerhalb Deutschlands versandkostenfrei.
- Bei Nichtgefallen können Sie jedes Buch innerhalb von 14 Tagen an uns zurücksenden.

ibidem-Verlag
Melchiorstr. 15
D-70439 Stuttgart
info@ibidem-verlag.de

www.ibidem-verlag.de
www.ibidem.eu
www.edition-noema.de
www.autorenbetreuung.de